EMPTY REVELATIONS

Empty Revelations

An Essay on Talk about, and Attitudes toward, Fiction

PETER ALWARD

McGill-Queen's University Press
Montreal & Kingston · London · Ithaca

© McGill-Queen's University Press 2012

ISBN 978-0-7735-4038-5

Legal deposit third quarter 2012
Bibliothèque nationale du Québec

Printed in Canada on acid-free paper that is 100% ancient forest free
(100% post-consumer recycled), processed chlorine free

This book has been published with the help of a grant from the Canadian
Federation for the Humanities and Social Sciences, through the Aid
to Scholarly Publications Program, using funds provided by the Social
Sciences and Humanities Research Council of Canada.

McGill-Queen's University Press acknowledges the support of the Canada
Council for the Arts for our publishing program. We also acknowledge
the financial support of the Government of Canada through the Canada
Book Fund for our publishing activities.

Library and Archives Canada Cataloguing in Publication

Alward, Peter Wallace, 1964–

Empty revelations: an essay on talk about, and attitudes toward fiction /
Peter Alward.

Includes bibliographical references and index.
ISBN 978-0-7735-4038-5

1. Discourse analysis, Narrative. 2. Discourse analysis, Literary. 3. Fiction –
Technique. 4. Fiction – History and criticism. I. Title.

P302.7.A43 2012   808.301'41   C2012-901407-9

This book was typeset by Interscript in 10.5/13 Minion.

For Jennifer and Theo

Contents

Preface   ix

Introduction   3

PART ONE   AUTHORS AND READERS – NEGATIVE

1 Compositional Speech Acts   15

2 Reader Engagement   34

PART TWO   AUTHORS AND READERS – POSITIVE

3 Word-Sculpture   63

4 Narrative Informants   83

PART THREE   FICTIONAL NAMES AND FICTIONAL TALK

5 Empty Revelations   115

6 Fictional Discourse   140

Conclusion   170

Notes   173
Bibliography   195
Index   203

Preface

This project has its origins in my early work in the philosophy of language and, in particular, on the contents of referring expressions in propositional attitude contexts. The guiding idea underlying my original account of reference within such contexts was that failures of substitutivity of coextensional expressions occurred therein because believing subjects put together the spatio-temporal parts of the various objects with which they were familiar in the wrong way. A subject who, for example, believes that Bob Dylan wrote *Blonde on Blonde* while refraining from believing that Robert Zimmerman wrote *Blonde on Blonde* has, roughly, simply failed to realize that the spatio-temporal parts of Dylan and Zimmerman she has respectively encountered are parts of the same enduring person. A lingering problem for this view, however, concerns how to incorporate beliefs about non-existents which, after all, lack any spatio-temporal parts to put together correctly or incorrectly. And I thought a solution to this problem might be found in an account of the contents of fictional names.

But what started out as a project narrowly focused on issues in the philosophy of language evolved into a much broader discussion of fiction and literature. Although an account of referring expressions did emerge (chapter 5) which avoids the difficulties which beset its predecessor, what also emerged were accounts of fictional composition (chapter 3), fictionality (chapter 3), fictional truth (chapter 4), psychological engagement with fiction (chapter 4), and fictional storytelling (chapter 6). And even though much of the discussion throughout is informed by my background in the philosophy of language, one happy upshot of the project is that I am now primarily a philosopher of art and literature rather than a philosopher of language.

There are numerous people whose help with this project I wish to acknowledge. My colleagues at both the University of Lethbridge and the University of Saskatchewan have patiently listened to preliminary versions of much of the material contained here and have always offered very useful feedback, as have audiences at the Canadian Philosophical Association Annual Congress and the Pacific Division Meetings of the American Society for Aesthetics. Particular thanks go to John Woods. His invitation to co-author a piece he had been commissioned to write on the logic of fiction got me started on a project I had been talking about for several years. Particular thanks as well to Dom Lopes who offered me advice and encouragement along the way. Finally, I thank the Faculty of Arts and Science at the University of Lethbridge for providing me with a study leave during the 2006–07 academic year at which time a significant portion of this manuscript was completed.

Parts of this book are drawn from previous published works: "Word-Sculpture, Speech Acts, and Fictionality," *Journal of Aesthetics and Art Criticism* 68, no. 4 (2010); "That's the Fictional Truth, Ruth," *Acta Analytica* 25, no. 3 (2010); and "Onstage Illocution," *Journal of Aesthetics and Art Criticism* 67, no. 3 (2009). I thank the editors and publishers involved for their permission to use material from these publications.

EMPTY REVELATIONS

Introduction

Fiction is ubiquitous. Its scope ranges from books, movies, and television shows to daydreams, games of make-believe, and impromptu improvisational performances parodying co-workers. For many of us, hardly a day goes by when we do not encounter or participate in fiction. Moreover, even when we are not caught up in fictional stories, they often remain the subject matter of our thought and talk. We wonder what will happen next in our favourite television shows and inform friends who failed to watch about what they missed; we feel sympathy for the characters who suffer in the novels we read and hope things will turn out better for them; and we argue with one another about what really happened in the movies we have seen and what lessons we can draw from them.

But despite the important role it plays in our lives, fiction remains deeply puzzling. This is primarily due to the fact that, as a result of our encounters with fiction, we think and talk about people, places, and events that do not exist. To agree that Cosmo Kramer is a hipster doofus, to hope that the Rohirrim will win the Battle of Helms Deep, or to argue that Rick's Café Américain will continue to thrive under Signor Ferrari's ownership is to agree, hope, or argue about non-existents. And the most prominent accounts of thought and talk seem to entail that thought and talk about non-existents are, in an important sense, empty.

1 FICTION

The central focus of this essay is what might be called literary fiction. Works of literary fiction consist primarily of written and spoken texts: paradigmatic examples include novels, novellas, and short stories. Given that there are many other kinds of fictional works which consist only in part of texts, however, the boundaries of this subcategory of fiction cannot be precisely drawn; penumbral cases include such things as plays, songs, and even movies and television shows. Nevertheless, the intended target of this discussion is, I hope, at least tolerably clear.

It is important to emphasize from the start that the category of literary fiction is to be distinguished from that of literature. Literature includes works of fiction and non-fiction: Truman Capote's *In Cold Blood*, for example, falls into the latter category.[1] And literary fiction includes works that do not, by any measure, count as literature; drugstore romance novels come to mind as a rather obvious example.

Moreover, literary fiction includes both written and spoken texts. Tales told around the campfire and bedtime stories told to children, as well as published (and unpublished) novels and short stores, fall into this category. It is worth noting, however, that categorizing texts in this way risks blurring what will prove to be an important distinction between the composition of fictional works and storytelling performances of them. The products of both composition and storytelling are fictional texts[2] – paradigmatically written in the former case and spoken in the latter[3] – but the activities that yield these texts are substantially different. Failure to properly appreciate this distinction has led to erroneous accounts of both authorial activity and fictionality itself.[4] This distinction will be developed more fully in chapter 1.

Although this essay's focus is literary fiction, it is worth pausing for a moment to see how this subcategory fits into a broader theory of fictionality. In my view, the various forms of fiction, and the relations among them, can be fruitfully understood in terms of a theatrical model.[5] At the core of this model is the distinction between being onstage – where the actions of actors and the props with which they interact jointly generate fictional truths – and being offstage – from where the audience observes these events and thereby discerns fictional truths. As I shall argue, storytellers are best understood to be actors onstage engaging in performances in which they portray characters who reveal what is going on "behind the scenes." And reading and listening to fiction can be understood as appreciating from offstage a play in which the fictional work is a prop and the storyteller, if there is one, an actor. Works of photographic and cinematic fiction can be incorporated into the theatrical model by treating them as theatrical performances to which the audience's perceptual access is manipulated and controlled in various ways. And works of sculptural and painted fiction can be viewed as props in plays without actors.[6] This is, of course, just the barest of sketches of the theatrical model, but one which I hope suffices to show its promise.

2 FICTIONAL DISCOURSE

The central goal of this essay is to provide an account of fictional discourse. There are three primary kinds of fictional discourse that will be investigated: fictive, metafictive, and trans-fictive.[7] Fictive discourse consists of the sentences which actually constitute works and texts of literary fiction.[8] Examples include

> And they were also eyes without expression, without soul, eyes that could watch lions tear a man to pieces and never change, that could watch a man impaled and screaming in the hot sun with his eyelids cut off[9]

and

> Wherever people are obtuse and absurd … and wherever they have, by even the most generous standards, the attention span of a small chicken in a hurricane and the investigative ability of a one-legged cockroach … and wherever people are inanely credulous, pathetically attached to the certainties of the nursery and, in general, have as much grasp of the realities of the physical universe as an oyster has of mountaineering … *yes*, Twyla: there *is* a Hogfather.[10]

Metafictive and trans-fictive discourse, in contrast, consist not of the sentences which constitute works of literary fiction but rather sentences used by readers and critics to make claims about the characters and events described in fictional stories. In metafictive discourse, the claims concern the goings on in particular fictional stories, whereas in trans-fictive discourse, the claims concern relations between characters and events from distinct fictional stories, or relations between fictions and non-fictional entities, or the fictional status of such entities. Examples of metafictive claims include

> Goriot was reduced to poverty supporting the extravagant lifestyles of his daughters[11]

and

> Jack Aubrey and Stephen Maturin's musical forays were sometimes poorly received.[12]

And examples of trans-fictive claims include

Woodrow Call is not a historical figure[13]

and

Gandalf the Grey is a more powerful wizard than Albus Dumbledore.[14]

The features of the various kinds of fictional discourse that are of interest here include the types of speech acts performed, the contents of sentential utterances, and the contributions of fictional names to such contents. I consider each feature in turn. Concerning speech acts, the central issue is what sorts of illocutionary acts are performed by speakers who engage in the various kinds of fictional discourse. As should be fairly clear, metafictive and trans-fictive discourse pose no particular difficulties in this regard; speakers who engage in it normally perform familiar kinds of illocutionary acts, especially acts of assertion.[15] Fictive discourse is a more complicated matter, in part because it includes both the utterances of storytellers and the products of authorial compositional activity. Since storytellers paradigmatically lack the requisite mental states to perform familiar kinds of illocutionary acts,[16] the question is whether they engage in illocutionary pretense[17] or perform *sui generis* fictive illocutionary acts.[18] But it is far from clear that composition involves the performance of substantial speech acts at all.

By the contents of utterances of fictional discourse I mean what might be called their illocutionary contents: what is asked or asserted or requested. If, as Cappelen and Lepore would have it, illocutionary content is distinct from semantic content, it is the former which is of concern here.[19] Now whether or not the illocutionary content of an assertion ought to be identified with its truth conditions, the illocutionary content nevertheless determines its truth conditions. As a result, an account of the illocutionary contents of utterances of fictional discourse needs to be beholden to an adequate account of fictional truth. Please note: the relevant sense of truth here is truth *in* fiction as opposed to truth *through* fiction. Our concern is whether or not claims of various kinds accurately represent the events in some fictional story or other, rather than whether a fictional story can accurately (or uniquely) represent certain actual events.

The final feature of fictional discourse to be investigated here is the phenomenon of fictional names. Fictional names are a subclass of character names – names of fictional people, places, etc. – that occur in fictional stories. In particular, they are names of those characters that are *not* immigrants to fiction – actual entities that play roles in fictional stories, such as the London of the Holmes stories. The challenge is to find an account of fictional names that reconciles the fact that they are empty – lacking actual referents – with the substantial contributions they make to contents of the utterances in which they occur.

3 THE ACT/ATTITUDE ANALYSIS

Of central importance in this essay is what might be called act/attitude analyses of fiction. An act/attitude analysis is one which illuminates some aspect of fiction in terms of the speech acts or propositional attitudes of a figure of some kind. Currie, for example, defines fiction in terms of the *sui generis* fictional illocutionary acts performed by authors,[20] and Lewis analyses fictional truth in terms of the assertions of fictional tellers.[21] Although such analyses share a common form, they are often intended to serve distinct purposes. These purposes include such things as drawing the boundary between fiction and non-fiction, providing an account of truth in fiction, characterizing authorial compositional or storytelling activity, and capturing the psychological states of engaged reader/listeners. In some cases, a single act/attitude analysis is intended to serve multiple purposes. Searle, for example, attempts to both define fiction and characterize authorial activity by appeal to the notion of illocutionary pretense.[22] Moreover, there is a certain amount of disagreement over exactly which purposes a given act/attitude analysis can serve. For example, while Currie defines fiction, as above, in terms of the *sui generis* fictional illocutionary acts of authors, he analyses fictional truth in terms of the beliefs of a figure he calls the "fictional author."[23] Byrne, in contrast, argues that fictional truth can be analysed in terms of authorial *sui generis* fictional illocutionary acts as well.[24]

A central motivation for act/attitude analyses of at least some aspects of fictionality is to reconcile the emptiness of fictional names with the substantiveness of various claims made using them. If, for example, the fictional names which occur in a metafictive utterance, such as

Michael Henchard loved Elizabeth-Jane as his own daughter[25]

are understood to fall outside the scope of an intensional operator of some kind, then either the names, and the utterance in which they occur, will have to be taken to be contentless[26] or they will have to be understood to be disguised descriptions or to refer to abstract or non-actual entities.[27]

For those reluctant to embrace any of these options,[28] the alternative is to take such expressions to fall within the scope of a perhaps tacit fictionality operator, as in

> It is *The Mayor of Casterbridge* fictional that Michael Henchard loved Elizabeth-Jane as his own daughter.

In order to serve the purposes for which it is invoked, however, this operator will have to have two features. First, it will have to be possible for the truth-value of a sentence containing a fictionality operator to differ from the truth-value of the complement sentence on which it operates, when both are uttered in a single context. So, for example, the truth of

> It is *I am a Barbarian* fictional that Caligula was assassinated by one of his slaves[29]

needs to be compatible with the falsity of

> Caligula was murdered by one of his slaves.

And second, referring expressions will have to be capable of undergoing a meaning or content shift when they occur within the scope of this operator. Even if "Goriot" is contentless when it occurs in

> Goriot was reduced to poverty supporting the extravagant lifestyles of his daughters,

as I would argue it is, the expression needs to be contentful when it occurs in

> It is *Old Goriot* fictional that Goriot was reduced to poverty supporting the extravagant lifestyles of his daughters.

The appeal of the act/attitude analysis of the fictionality operator is that speech act and propositional attitude operators, arguably at least, have both these features. First, it is commonplace to note, for example, that the truth-value of what someone might be judged to say or believe is independent of the truth-value of the judgment that she said or believes it. And second, although it remains controversial, a Fregean approach to speech act and propositional attitude attributions, according to which referring expressions undergo a content shift when they occur in such attributions, is both plausible and defensible.[30]

Distinctions among act/attitude analyses can be drawn not only in terms of what aspect of fictionality they are designed to analyse or what sort of speech act or propositional attitude is invoked in the analysis. They can also be drawn in terms of the subject to whom the act or attitude is attributed by the analysis. One fundamental distinction is between those analyses that proceed in terms of attributions to tellers of various kinds and those that invoke readers or listeners. I will briefly consider each in turn.

Tellers can be categorized in terms of a pair of distinctions, one ontological and the other linguistic. The first distinction is between tellers whose speech acts occur in the actual world and those whose speech acts occur in non-actual worlds. The non-actual worlds at issue are paradigmatically fictional worlds, but the possibility of tellers whose speech acts occur in neither actual nor fictional worlds will prove important in what follows. The second distinction is between tellers who engage in serious discourse, or fact-telling, and those who engage in non-serious discourse, or storytelling.[31] This pair of distinctions yields four categories of tellers: actual fact-tellers, actual fiction-tellers, non-actual fact-tellers, and non-actual fiction-tellers. Actual fact-tellers include both authors of non-fiction and ordinary speakers who make assertions and perform familiar sorts of illocutionary actions. Actual fiction-tellers include authors of fiction and actors who speak onstage, among others. Non-actual fact-tellers most prominently include fictional narrators, such as Dr Watson, but, as will be argued below, they also include non-actual tellers who describe the goings on in fictional worlds they do not inhabit. Finally, non-actual fiction-tellers include storytelling narrators – fictional narrators who clearly indicate that the stories they tell are fictional – and idealized author figures of the sort invoked for various theoretical purposes by hypothetical intentionalists.[32]

Although similar distinctions might be made among readers of, and listeners to, fiction, for the purposes of this essay the important distinction is between engaged and disengaged readers/listeners. An engaged reader/listener of fiction is one who is "caught up in the story"; disengagement can involve mere inattention, or an academic interest in plot elements, style, and the like. This distinction is important, first, because an account of engagement with fiction is needed to explain emotional reactions and other sorts of reader/listener responses to it. A second reason – and one of more central concern in this essay – is that speakers who make metafictive and trans-fictive utterances can be either engaged or disengaged, and this affects the proper analysis of their speech acts. This will be one of the primary themes addressed in chapter 6.

4 FICTIONAL ANTI-REALISM

Despite the current prominence of various forms of fictional realism,[33] it should be emphasized that the view on offer here is unabashedly anti-realist: any appeal to an ontology of fictional entities in either the account of fictional discourse or of fictional names (or elsewhere) is eschewed. Moreover, no systematic critique of the fictional realist approach is presented (although particular worries about realism are raised at various points in the text). Rather than offering a systematic critique of alternative views, this manuscript develops a novel Fregean anti-realist theory and explores the extent to which it can solve the problems that arise for various kinds of fictional talk. And, in my view, this project is interesting in its own right.

Nevertheless, given the aforementioned prominence of fictional realism, it is worth saying a few words by way of motivating the anti-realist stance taken here. Fictional realism normally takes one of two forms: the *concrete non-existent* form[34] and the *abstract existent* form.[35] According to the former, a fictional entity, such as Sherlock Holmes, is a concrete, flesh and blood, human being who does not actually exist but nevertheless in some sense is or has being. According to the latter, although Holmes actually exists, he is an abstract entity rather than a flesh and blood human being. My objections to the concrete non-existent form of realism are primarily ontological. I find myself simply disinclined to accept an ontology which includes non-existent things. Moreover, given that some fictions are impossible, the *concrete non-existent* view seems to require an ontology which includes impossible objects, rendering it, in my eyes at least, even less palatable.[36]

I am willing to concede that the abstract existent form of realism is largely immune from such ontological worries. Nevertheless there are two other independent reasons to balk. First, as Everett has persuasively argued, fictional realism runs into serious difficulties individuating fictional characters, difficulties which simply do not arise for anti-realist views.[37] In particular, he has argued from the existence of fictional stories in which it is indeterminate whether a character a is numerically identical to a character b, together with the fictional-character platitude

> if a story concerns a and b, and if a and b are not real things, then $a=b$ in the world of the story if and only if the character of a = the character of b (or $Ca=Cb$),

to the conclusion that fictional realists are committed to untenable indeterminate identities. And second, since abstract entities lack many or most of the features possessed by the people, etc., described by fictional stories, no straightforward account of metafictive discourse is forthcoming on the abstract existent view. Instead, any such view will have to invoke an intensional fictionality operator of the kind deployed in the Fregean anti-realist view on offer here in any event. Of course, none of the worries raised here are decisive; but, I hope, they are at least sufficient to motivate the anti-realist approach adopted here.

5 CONTENTS

This essay consists of three parts, each of which includes two chapters. The first part consists of a primarily negative investigation of various act/attitude analyses that have been defended in the literature. The first chapter takes a critical look at various analyses of authorial compositional activity and at attempts to deploy them in accounts of fictional truth and the definition of fiction. A central theme of this chapter is that the failure to properly accommodate the distinction between fictional composition and storytelling performances seriously undermines many of the analyses on offer. The second chapter takes a critical look at a number of analyses of reader engagement with fiction and at attempts to deploy them in accounts of emotional reactions to fiction and fictional truth. A central theme of this chapter is that appreciative phenomena can be explained by the supposition that engagement with fiction requires only *de re* (and *de dicto*) imaginative activity on the part of reader/listeners and not any kind of *de se* imagining.

The second part of this essay consists of a defence of positive views of authorial composition and reader engagement. In chapter 3, a "word-sculpture" model of authorial compositional activity is developed according to which authors need not perform speech acts any more substantial than that of mere inscription or utterance production. And a weak institutional theory of fictionality, which invokes the fiction-centred word-sculpture practice, is defended. In chapter 4, an account of reader/listener engagement is developed according to which fictional works are imagined to be reports of narrative informants – non-actual fact-tellers – whom storytellers pretend to be. In addition, an analysis of fictional truth in terms of the revelations of narrative informants is defended.

Finally, in the third part of this essay, problems having to do with fictional names and fictional discourse are addressed. In chapter 5, a broadly

Fregean theory of fictional names is developed and defended. According to this view, the contents of fictional names are intersubjective collections of cognitive states and relations of readers/listeners. And in chapter 6, accounts of the various kinds of fictional discourse are developed which draw on the conclusions regarding reader engagement, fictional truth, and fictional names which will, by that point, have already been defended.

PART ONE

Authors and Readers – Negative

1

Compositional Speech Acts

The focus of this chapter is the nature of compositional speech acts – the speech acts authors perform in the process of composing works of fiction. This is, of course, an interesting issue in its own right, but it is also important because analyses of authorial speech acts are frequently deployed in accounts of fictional truth[1] and talk about fiction,[2] as well as in accounts of the boundary between fiction and non-fiction.[3] Roughly, the class of fictional works is identified with the class of texts that are the product of compositional speech acts, and fictional truth is defined in terms of the contents of these speech acts.

A central theme of this chapter, however, is that much of the literature on authorial speech acts has proven to be insufficiently attentive to the distinction between composition and storytelling. Composition is the process by which authors produce works of fiction; storytelling, in contrast, consists of a kind of performance wherein fictional stories are told, by their authors or others, to a listening audience.[4] Failure to adequately attend to this distinction has yielded analyses of authorial speech acts which are, arguably, well suited to elucidate storytelling but extremely ill-suited to illuminate composition. Moreover, insofar as such analyses apply to storytelling but not to composition, they cannot yield adequate accounts of the fiction/non-fiction boundary or of fictional truth. After all, if it is required of works of fiction that they be the products of storytelling acts, then unperformed compositions will not count as fiction. And if fictional truths are taken to be the contents of storytelling acts, then there will be no truths in unperformed compositions.

Since this chapter's focus is compositional speech acts, it may prove fruitful to say a few things about speech act theory more generally. Following Searle, I distinguish between four basic types of speech acts:

utterance acts, propositional acts, illocutionary acts, and perlocutionary acts.[5] Utterance acts are acts wherein subjects produce token expressions of a language. For present purposes, it will be assumed that the expressions in question are sentences. It is worth noting that utterance acts can yield either spoken or written sentences. (In cases where written language is specifically at issue, subjects will be characterized as having performed "inscriptional" acts.) Insofar as a speaker (or writer) successfully produces a grammatical sentence,[6] the product of her utterance is meaningful. Of course, meaningfulness in this sense[7] does not suffice to ensure that the utterance uniquely determines or expresses a proposition. After all, the sentence produced may contain ambiguous elements which fail to be disambiguated by features of the context in which it is uttered. Consider, for example, an utterance of

Math teachers want their students to multiply,

whose purpose is to provide an example of an ambiguous sentence.

Propositional acts are performed by means of performing utterance acts. A speaker who performs an utterance act thereby performs a propositional act when features of the context of utterance suffice to ensure that the uttered sentence uniquely picks out a proposition. Such features include the speaker's psychological states, conversational purposes, the spatio-temporal location of her utterance, and the like. Successful performance of a propositional act, however, does not by itself suffice for the performance of an illocutionary act of any kind. Consider, for example, an utterance of

The toilet seat is up,

whose purpose is to identify a proposition which could serve as the content of a number of distinct illocutionary acts.[8]

Just as propositional acts are performed by means of performing utterance acts, illocutionary acts are performed by means of performing propositional acts. They can be thought of as propositional acts performed with illocutionary force, roughly the combination of a basic purpose of some sort – to assert something, or get someone to do something, etc. – and a number of presuppositions regarding such things as the psychological state of the speaker, the existence of the requisite sort of conventional procedures, etc. Of particular importance in chapter 6 are the sincerity obligations – to believe what one asserts, to desire what one requests, etc. – that apply to speakers who perform illocutionary acts.

Moreover, illocutionary actions are typically distinguished from other sorts of purposeful actions by the intention on the part of the speaker that her purpose be achieved by means of the recognition of the purpose by her listeners.[9] So, for example, someone who asserts,

> Jones is the murderer,

and someone else who plants evidence pointing in the direction of Jones may share the purpose of instilling in others the belief that Jones committed the murder; but only the former intends to instill this belief by means of her audience's recognition of her intention that they believe it.

Finally, perlocutionary acts are acts of producing effects in listeners by means of performing illocutionary acts. When a speaker's illocutionary action causes some (normally intended) effect in her audience, she thereby performs the perlocutionary act of affecting the audience in that way. So, for example, a speaker who asserts that the end is near and whose assertion instills in a listener the belief that the end is near, thereby performs the perlocutionary act of instilling this belief in the listener. It is worth emphasizing that even if the illocutionary purpose and the perlocutionary effect coincide, as in the example at hand, the illocutionary act and the perlocutionary act are nevertheless distinct. After all, a speaker can successfully assert that the end is near even if her illocutionary purpose – that her audience come to believe that the end is near – is frustrated.

In what follows, I investigate a number of prominent attempts to analyse compositional activity in terms of speech acts of various kinds. It should be noted that given that authors of fiction rarely intend readers to believe the contents of the (declarative) sentences they produce, nor are they under any (sincerity) obligations to believe them themselves, the suggestion that composition involves the performance of assertions and other familiar sorts of illocutionary acts is hardly plausible.[10] Nevertheless, the notion of illocutionary action lies at the core of the most widely accepted accounts of compositional activity. Searle and Lewis, for example, have argued that although authors do not actually perform familiar sorts of illocutionary acts, they pretend to do so.[11] And Currie and Byrne have argued that while authors do genuinely perform illocutionary acts, they perform *sui generis* fictive illocutionary acts rather than making assertions, requests, and the like.[12] Less familiar are the views of Hoffman and others according to which composition involves the performance of distinctively fictive perlocutionary acts and, in particular, doing so by means of making specifically fictional kinds of invitations or requests.[13] Finally, Beardsley and others have defended the view that authors do not perform illocutionary acts at all.[14] Rather, they represent illocutionary actions by making the kinds of utterances that could be used in illocutionary action while refraining from illocutionary commitment. As will become apparent, my own view is that Beardsley is on the right track. What is required, however, is an adequate account of what fictional composition involves over and above the performance of such minimal speech acts.

It is worth (re-)emphasizing that this chapter focuses on compositional speech acts as opposed to acts of storytelling. As a result, the central concern is whether the process of fictional composition is properly understood to consist in illocutionary pretense or *sui generis* fictional illocutionary action or what have you. And even if none of these explanations is adequate, the option still remains to analyse storytelling along one or another of these lines. The proper analysis of storytelling will be taken up in chapter 6.

1.1 ILLOCUTIONARY PRETENSE

At the core of what is perhaps the most prominent account of fiction is the idea that authorial compositional activity is, at bottom, a kind of pretense. And in particular, what authors are supposed to pretend to do is to perform illocutionary acts. Searle, for example, says, "the author of a work of fiction pretends to perform a series of illocutionary acts, normally of the representative type."[15] And Lewis says, "Storytelling is fiction. The storyteller purports to be telling the truth about matters whereof he has knowledge. He purports to be talking about characters who are known to him, and whom he refers to, typically, by means of their ordinary names. But if his story is fiction, he is not really doing these things."[16] For simplicity I am going to focus here on assertive pretense. But given the wide variety of kinds of sentences that occur in fictional texts, authors must presumably be thought to pretend to perform other sorts of illocutionary acts as well.

On Searle's view, engaging in pretense involves actually performing an action which is a constituent part of the act which one pretends to perform: "It is a general feature of the concept of pretending that one can pretend to perform a higher order or complex action by actually performing lower order or less complex actions which are constitutive parts of the higher order or complex action."[17] In the case of illocutionary pretense, this would typically involve performing an utterance act by means of which one could, in other circumstances, actually perform the illocutionary act one is pretending to perform. So, for example, one might pretend to assert that George W. Bush has hidden the true extent of his intelligence by means of performing the act of uttering the sentence

George W. Bush has hidden the true extent of his intelligence.

Two related questions might be raised at this point: the first concerns how it is that a speaker is able to avoid making an assertion by means of her utterance; and the second concerns what a speaker needs positively to do in order to successfully pretend to do so. Searle answers both questions by appeal to conventions of fiction that function to "suspend the normal illocutionary commitments" of the utterances a speaker might make.[18] A speaker who (intentionally) invokes these conventions when she utters the above sentence about Bush's intelligence both avoids making the corresponding assertion and succeeds in pretending she has done so.

It is unclear, however, that Searle's answer here is adequate. It seems to presuppose that unless a speaker actively does something to block or prevent it, she will automatically perform an illocutionary act whenever she utters a grammatical sentence. But a more natural suggestion would be to suppose that the performance of an illocutionary action by means of an utterance requires an appropriate illocutionary intention on the part of the speaker (among other things), and that refraining from illocutionary action requires only that the speaker make her utterance without this intention. Moreover, if what Searle's conventions do is simply prevent the performance of illocutionary action, invoking them when making an utterance will not suffice to enable the speaker to thereby engage in illocutionary pretense. After all, a speaker who refrains from making an assertion by means of an utterance might in so doing be simply presenting an example of a sentence of a certain kind rather than pretending to make an assertion. My own view is that in order to pretend to make an assertion by means of her utterance, a speaker need only (intentionally) invoke certain fairly general pretense conventions – conventions which allow us to pretend to perform acts of one kind by means of performing acts of another kind – while at the same time lacking any illocutionary intentions. This will be developed more fully in the discussion of storytelling in chapter 6. Please note: Searle also characterizes the kind of illocutionary pretense in which he takes authors of fiction to engage as non-deceptive.[19] Presumably this requires that the author indicate to her audience in some way that she is invoking the relevant conventions.

Before considering difficulties that arise for the view that fictional composition consists in authorial illocutionary pretense, it is worth noting a number of variations of this view. As above, Searle's view is that the act of pretense is performed in the very act of composition. As she composes, the author pretends to perform illocutionary acts of various kinds. Lewis, in contrast, seems to suggest that illocutionary pretense may also be performed by means of what is done with the product of the act of composition: an author "may type a manuscript and send it to his publisher, but … there is an act of storytelling."[20] A distinct view is defended by Brown and Steinmann.[21] They hold that authors of fiction engage in illocutionary pretense during the process of composition, but what they pretend to do is make second-order reports of the speech acts of a fictional narrator, rather than pretending to perform the first-order speech acts themselves. So, for example, an author who composed the sentence

It was a dark and stormy night

does not thereby pretend to assert that it was a dark and stormy night, but rather pretends to report that the fictional narrator made that assertion.

The critical response to the illocutionary pretense view has primarily focused on the question of whether it yields an adequate account of the boundary between fiction and non-fiction rather than on whether it provides a defensible account of compositional or storytelling activity per se.[22] Currie, for example, has argued that the appeal to illocutionary pretense draws the boundary of the class of fictions too broadly. One can, after all, engage in non-deceptive pretense without thereby producing a work of fiction – for example, by imitating the conversational manner of a friend.[23] And Walton has argued that the appeal to illocutionary pretense draws the boundary too narrowly, by excluding non-literary fictions. After all, there is little reason to suppose that the process of making non-literary works of fiction necessarily involves illocutionary pretense on the part of artists: "Pierre-August Renoir's painting *Bathers* and Jacques Lipchitz's sculpture *Guitar Player* surely belong in the fiction category. But I very much doubt that in creating them Renoir and Lipchitz were pretending to make assertions."[24]

But insofar as the focus is on the nature of compositional speech acts, as it is in this chapter, these criticisms gain little purchase. The fact that one can engage in illocutionary pretense without thereby producing fiction does not establish that fictional composition fails to consist in such pretense. After all, the kinds of speech acts in which authors of fiction engage need not be unique to fiction. And the fact that the creators of painted and sculptural fictions do not engage in assertive pretense does not show that composers of literary fictions fail to do so. After all, given that the former are visual and tactile fictions rather than linguistic fictions, it would be surprising to discover that their production necessarily involved the performance of speech acts at all. One might rejoin, however, that if the composition of literary fiction involves illocutionary pretense, we should expect the creation of painted and sculptural fictions to involve some kind of pretense, perhaps the pretense of producing works of painted or sculptural non-fiction. And this is exactly what we do not find. In my view, the reason there is no temptation to understand painted and sculptural fictions in terms of any kind of pretense is that, unlike the literary case, there is no distinction between the creation and the performance of such fictions. In the literary case, however, there is a distinction between composition and storytelling performance. And the plausibility of an illocutionary pretense account of storytelling, together with the failure to pay proper attention to this distinction, leads to the temptation to understand compositional speech acts along similar lines. But, as we shall see, no such account of fictional composition is defensible.

There are two points in the compositional process during which an author might be thought to engage in illocutionary pretense: during the process of producing the text which constitutes the fictional work, and by means of something that is done with the completed work. Consider, first, the process of text production. This activity is directed toward the production of a sequence of written or spoken sentences which are typically recorded in some way – in a word-processed computer, by means of some audio device or, more traditionally, on sheets of paper or in memory. Now, as part of the process of selecting which sentences to include in this sequence, an author might pretend to perform various illocutionary actions by means of uttering candidate sentences, perhaps in order to discern if they are the sort of thing one of her characters, or her narrator, might say. This might be especially appropriate if she was soliciting input to this effect from a collaborator. But few authors would select every sentence they include in their works by means of some such procedure and there is simply no reason to believe that authors of fiction must do so. Moreover, there is even less reason to suppose that in recording the sentences they have selected, by whatever procedure, for inclusion in their works, authors must or even frequently do engage in any kind of pretense: in most cases, doing so would simply have little point.[25] Although it is presumably true that an author of fiction could pretend to assert the sentences she recorded, given the normal goals served by recording fictional works, her behaviour in so doing would simply be odd.

A more promising suggestion would be to suppose that authors engage in illocutionary pretense not during the production of their texts but by means of something they do with their completed works. Of course, authors might do any number of different things with their completed and recorded fictional works. For present purposes, we can distinguish between three broad categories of such activities: first, authors sometimes disseminate their works – showing them to friends, or sending them to publishers; second, they may perform them – engaging in public readings in various forums; and third, they may do nothing at all with them – simply ignoring the computer files they have produced, or leaving a written manuscript at the bottom of a box in an attic. Authors who refrain from performing or otherwise disseminating their works are very unlikely to engage in illocutionary pretense by means of what they actually do with them. An author might pretend to do something or other by means of putting her manuscript in a box or moving a computer file to a storage device of some kind – she might pretend to thereby submit it to a publisher, for example – although even this would presumably be relatively rare. But pretending to thereby engage in illocutionary pretense – and, in particular, to pretend to perform a series of illocutionary acts corresponding to each sentence in the completed work – is almost unheard of.[26] And an author who ignores or forgets about her completed work simply cannot be thought to have engaged in any kind of pretense at all.[27]

The suggestion that authors engage in illocutionary pretense by means of disseminating their works fares little better. This idea is most naturally cast as follows: when an author of a work of non-fiction gives a copy of her manuscript to a friend to read, or sends it to a potential publisher, she thereby performs illocutionary acts corresponding to each sentence contained therein; hence, when an author gives a copy of her work of fiction to a friend or publisher, she pretends to provide him with a work of non-fiction, and thereby pretends to perform illocutionary acts corresponding to each sentence contained therein. But it is far from clear that authors of non-fiction do, or even can, perform illocutionary acts corresponding to each sentence when they disseminate their works; after all, doing so seems to require that extremely complex illocutionary intentions underlie what are, at first glance, more or less simple acts of dissemination. More to the point, there is little reason to suppose that authors of fiction typically pretend to be disseminating works of non-fiction when they provide copies of their works to friends or publishers, let alone that they must do so. And although such pretense presumably does occur on occasion,[28] it would nevertheless be extremely rare for an author to thereby pretend to assert each (declarative) sentence contained in her work.

Finally, illocutionary pretense seems most at home as part of an account of storytelling performances. It is quite plausible to suppose that by means of each sentence she utters, a storyteller pretends to perform an illocutionary action of some kind. In fact, in chapter 6 I will argue that this is the correct account of storytelling. For present purposes however, it is worth recalling that composition and storytelling are distinct kinds of activities.[29] And not only do many authors refrain from ever performing their works, unless their works are very short, those who do, rarely perform them from start to finish. Moreover, when fictional works are performed, the storyteller is frequently someone other than the author; consider, for example, parents reading bedtime stories to their children. In light of such worries, one might retreat to Searle's account of playwriting: "the author of the play is not in general pretending to make assertions; he is giving directions as to how to enact a pretense which the actors then follow."[30] But whatever its virtues as an account of the activity of playwrights, taking the compositional activity of authors of novels, short stories, and the like to be generally directed toward producing instructions for storytelling performances is not tenable. Many authors do not intend their works to be performed at all, and so cannot be thought of, in any non-trivial sense, as providing directions for such performances. No account of compositional speech acts which includes the activities of such authors can take storytelling to be a required or universal goal of composition.

1.2 PRETENSE AND FICTIONAL NAMES

In addition to analysing both compositional activity and fictionality in terms of illocutionary pretense, Searle deploys the same notion in his accounts of metafictive discourse and fictional names. First, Searle distinguishes the speech acts performed by readers and critics when they talk about fiction from both the ordinary illocutionary action of non-fictional speech and the illocutionary pretense in which he takes authors to engage: "we need to distinguish not only between serious discourse and fictional discourse, as I have been doing, but also to distinguish both of these from serious discourse about fiction."[31] Instead, he takes such speakers to be performing assertions and other familiar sorts of illocutionary acts while "sharing in the pretense" of the authors who created the fictions under discussion. Second, Searle claims that, by means of their pretended acts of referring, which in part constitute their acts of assertive pretense, authors create fictional characters, characters they pretend (or imagine or make-believe) exist: "by pretending to refer she pretends there is an object she refers to."[32] And a reader or critic who shares in an author's pretense can refer to these authorial creations and make assertions or perform other illocutionary actions concerning them: "I did not *pretend* to refer to a real Sherlock Holmes; I *really referred* to a fictional Sherlock Holmes."[33]

Searle's account of fictional names and the metafictive use of them is, however, quite puzzling. The difficulties that arise for it can be made clear by recasting Searle's account in terms of the following five theses:

(1) Fictional characters do not (actually) exist.[34]
(2) A speaker can refer only to what exists.[35]
(3) Readers and critics can really refer to fictional characters when they share in an author's pretense.[36]
(4) Fictional characters exist in fiction.[37]
(5) Authors create fictional characters by pretending to refer to them.[38]

The most serious worry is that the first three theses are prima facie inconsistent.[39] If speakers can refer only to what exists and fictional characters do not exist, then any kind of reference to fictions seems to be ruled out, whatever "shared pretense" amounts to. Moreover, the last two theses are more or less mysterious: it is unclear what it means for something to "exist in fiction" and, as a result, it is unclear how authors, by means of their acts of pretense, can cause something to come to exist in fiction.

Neo-Searleans, such as Miller and Martinich, have responded to the first worry by rejecting one or another of (1) to (3). Miller, for example, rejects thesis (3). He argues that fictional characters are hypothetical objects – objects that would have existed had the relevant author's pretended assertions been genuine and true. But, he claims, "in discourse about fictional entities qua hypothetical entities these entities are not strictly speaking referred to. For in fact hypothetical entities do not exist."[40] Martinich, in contrast, rejects thesis (2). He argues that fictional characters are intentional objects, to which critics can refer but which do not exist: "Because referring is an intentional activity, only an intentional object is needed. Sometimes the intentional object is also an existing object, and sometimes not."[41] Miller's view seems to be that the expressions we call fictional names are not genuine proper names, but function more like definite descriptions; as such, his view is similar in important ways to Lewis's theory.[42] According to Martinich, in contrast, fictional names are genuine proper names; what distinguishes them from non-fictional names is that their referents are frequently non-existent objects.[43] Views of these kinds, and the difficulties that arise for them, will be discussed in chapters 2 and 5.

In my view, contra Miller, Martinich, et al., there is a plausible and consistent interpretation of Searle's position that takes authors and readers to be participants in games of make-believe. A central component of paradigmatic games of make-believe are props – objects which participants in such games imagine or make-believe have different properties than they in fact do. So, for example, the participants of a sword-fighting game might make-believe that a stick is a sword. Moreover, the participants themselves can also be props in the very same sense. There could, for example, be a game in which the participants make-believe that one of their members is a monster (and in which she, in turn, pretends to be and, perhaps, imagines being, one). Now one way to make sense of claim (5) is to suppose that by engaging in their illocutionary pretense, authors generate games of make-believe. And, as long as we take *pretending to refer* to involve the indication of some actual object or person, an author can be viewed as having created a fictional character in the following sense: she has conferred upon some object the status of being a prop in the game, which participants are to make-believe is the character. On this interpretation of Searle, the following sense can be made of theses (3) and (4): for those playing the game of make-believe the prop is the character, and since the prop exists in fact, the character exists in the game, or in fiction, if you prefer. Moreover, as long as a critic is a participant in the game, or "shares in the pretense," she can really refer to the character by means of referring to the prop. But since in fact – that is, outside the game – the prop is not the character, the character does not exist, as thesis (1) would have it. Finally, the reason the author only pretends to refer to the character by means of indicating (what will become) the prop, rather than really doing so, is because the object she indicates does not become a prop in the game until she indicates it.

Although this suggestion makes sense of Searle's view, it has little to recommend it as a general account of fictional names. As above, there is no reason to believe that authorial composition involves much if any illocutionary pretense at all, let alone behaviour which could plausibly be construed as conferring upon various people and objects the status of props in games of make-believe. On certain occasions, of course, storytellers might do so; consider, for example, a parent who, while reading a story to her child, indicates he is to make-believe that his stuffed animal is a character in the story. But not only do storytellers fail to do this on every occasion of storytelling, even when a storyteller does create props corresponding to some of the characters in the story she tells, it would still be extremely rare for her to do so for each character in the story. There might simply be too many characters and too few potential props at hand. As a result, there just will not, in general, be enough fictional existents for even listeners attending such performances to refer to in order that they might say what they want to say about the characters and events in the story.[44]

1.3 FICTIVE ILLOCUTIONS

Perhaps the most prominent alternative to the illocutionary pretense account of compositional speech acts is the fictive illocution approach. On this view, contra the illocutionary pretense account, when authors compose, they perform genuine illocutionary actions. But rather than performing familiar sorts of illocutionary acts – assertions, requests, and the like – they perform *sui generis* fictive illocutionary acts. So, for example, an author who utters

> It was a dark and stormy night

neither asserts that it was a dark and stormy night nor pretends to do so. Rather she thereby performs a fictive illocution. And what distinguish fictive illocutions from their more familiar cousins are the illocutionary intentions of the speakers who perform them. Whereas the intended effect of assertion is listener belief in the asserted proposition, the goal of fictive illocutionary action is that the listener imagine or make-believe[45] the proposition expressed by the utterance. And so, according to the fictive illocution approach, an author who utters

> It was a dark and stormy night

intends that her audience imagine or make-believe that it was a dark and stormy night by means of the recognition that she intends them to do so.[46]

In addition to being deployed in analyses of compositional activity, fictive illocutions have been appealed to in accounts of fictionality[47] and accounts of fictional truth.[48] The primary line of critical reaction to all such appeals, however, has concerned whether the notion of a *sui generis* fictive illocutionary action is even defensible. Searle, most prominently, has criticized this idea by arguing that (i) "[in] general, the illocutionary act (or acts) performed in the utterance of the sentence is a function of the meaning of the sentence"[49] and (ii) the very same sentences are used both in fictive and non-fictional discourse. As a result, if there were a uniquely fictive speech act, the sentences of our language would have to be ambiguous – differing in meaning as between their use in fiction and their use in serious discourse. Searle seems to be presupposing that the linguistic meaning of a sentence does not simply determine the proposition it expresses relative to various contextual parameters; it also determines the illocutionary action performed in its normal or, perhaps, literal use.

Currie, unsurprisingly, rejects this presupposition, which he refers to variously as the "determination principle"[50] and the "functionality principle."[51] He correctly notes that a given sentence can be used to perform different types of illocutionary actions on different occasions of use. So, for example, "You will open the window" can be used to make an assertion or issue a command, among other things. And he argues that our ability to perform different illocutionary actions with a given sentence does not stem from any ambiguity in meaning; instead it results from differences in "what the speaker means by the sentence."[52] This is, of course, compatible with the claim that when, but only when, a sentence is used *literally* the illocutionary act performed is a function of its meaning. After all, one might argue that when, for example, a speaker uses "You will open the window" to issue a command, she is using it non-literally. Currie goes on, however, to argue that an author of fiction will often use a declarative sentence he utters literally "in the sense that the proposition he intends to convey to his audience is exactly the proposition expressed by the sentence he utters."[53] And since authors of fiction do not assert the declaratives they use, this gives us an example of a single sentence used literally (and with the same meaning) to perform distinct illocutionary actions on different occasions. The trouble with Currie's manoeuvre here is that it simply presupposes that what authors of fiction do is perform illocutionary actions. But this is exactly what is at issue.

But even if Searle's functionality principle is ultimately unsatisfactory, a similar argument against *sui generis* fictive illocutions can be generated using only Hoffman's weaker (and less contentious) Expressibility Principle: for any illocutionary act, there is a possible linguistic expression whose literal meaning is such that its utterance in the right circumstances is the performance of that act.[54] Assuming, as above, that the sentences of English are not systematically ambiguous, this principle and the fact that speakers use the very same sentences in fiction and non-fiction together suggest that the sentences authors produce when composing fictional works do not *literally* express fictive illocutions.[55] Rather, there must be distinct (possible) sentences which literally express the fictive illocutions which the sentences authors of fiction utter figuratively express. Moreover, the most promising candidates for literally expressing fictional illocutions are sentences such as

Make-believe that it is a dark and stormy night![56]
Let us imagine that it is a dark and stormy night[57]

and

I invite you, whoever you are, to imagine that it was a dark and stormy night.[58]

But these sentences actually express commands, suggestions, or invitations rather than *sui generis* fictional illocutions. As a result, they are distinguished from other commands, suggestions, and invitations in terms of their intended effects on listeners – what listeners are commanded or invited to do, or what it is suggested they do – rather than in terms of their illocutionary force. The upshot, according to Hoffman, is that fiction-making is marked off from other sorts of activities in virtue of being a unique kind of perlocutionary action rather than in virtue of being a unique kind of illocutionary action.[59]

Rather than adjudicate the issue between Hoffman and Currie, in what follows I will consider both the hypothesis that fictional composition involves the performance of a *sui generis* fictive illocutionary act and the hypothesis that it involves making a specifically fictional kind of command, request, or invitation. But before doing so, it is worth considering whether either hypothesis yields an adequate account of fictionality. Consider again painted and sculptural fictions. Just as there is no reason to suppose that the artists who produce such works engage in illocutionary (and any kind of) pretense, there is also no reason to suppose they perform *sui generis* fictive illocutionary acts, or command, suggest, or invite appreciators to imagine various things. Currie attempts to incorporate such fictions under his definition of fictionality by claiming that the artist's intention regarding how her work be appreciated is what determines its status as fiction: "What is it that makes a painting, sculpture, or photograph fictional? I say it is this: that the artist intended the audience to make believe the content of what is represented."[60] But it is worth noting that this revised account of fictionality invokes the artist's attitude toward the completed work and not any (speech) acts performed during its production.

It is also worth noting the poverty of Currie's approach when it comes to adjudicating the status of even literary works, as opposed to individual utterances, as fiction or non-fiction: "For in some perhaps irremediably vague way, the fictionality of works is going to depend on the fictionality of statements."[61] In effect, Currie has left us with no informative theory of the fictionality of works. This, together with the revisions needed to count (certain) painted and sculptural works as fictions, suggests a rather Waltonian moral: "the basic concept of a *story* and the basic concept of *fiction* attach most perspicuously to objects rather than actions."[62] An account of fictionality which is focused on the work as a whole, as opposed to the speech acts performed in choosing and recording the sentences which make it up, will be developed in chapter 3.

Our main concern, of course, is whether or not authorial compositional speech acts are best understood as *sui generis* fictive illocutionary acts or as certain kinds of commands, suggestions, or invitations. As above, there are two points at which authors might be thought to perform speech acts of one or another of these kinds: during the writing process itself, or by means of something that is done with the completed text. And, also as above, there is little reason to suppose that authors must, or even frequently do, perform such acts. Doing so might have some point in the process of selecting sentences for inclusion in a fictional work: the feedback of a collaborator who accepts an invitation to imagine the content of a candidate sentence, or complies with a command or request to do so, might be relevant to an author's decision to include it. But again, it would be the rare author who tries out all her candidate sentences in this way. Moreover, even if a given author were to perform illocutionary acts as part of the process of selecting (some of) the sentences to be included in her work, she could not be supposed to be performing the same kind of illocutionary act on each occasion. An author who uttered

It was a dark and stormy night

might thereby invite a listener to imagine that it was a dark and stormy night, but an author who uttered

Was it a dark and stormy night?

could not be supposed to be doing the same thing. If authors perform illocutionary acts during the sentence-selection process, they would minimally have to perform a wide variety of different kinds of speech acts – fictional analogues of each of the acts we perform in ordinary speech.[63] Finally, as above, there would simply be little point in performing illocutionary acts of any kind during the process of recording the sentences that had been selected for inclusion in a fictional work.

The alternative, again, is to suppose that illocutionary acts are performed by means of something that is done with completed works of fiction. As above, authors who do nothing with their completed works simply cannot be thought to thereby perform any speech acts at all. And although the fictive illocution view and its perlocutionary cousins offer a prima facie plausible account of storytelling performance, I will argue in chapter 6 that the illocutionary pretense analysis is preferable. The question that remains, therefore, is whether by disseminating their completed works – sending them to publishers or giving them to friends to read – authors of fiction perform illocutionary acts whose intended effect is that the recipients of their works imagine the propositions expressed by the sentences contained therein. And there are two separate issues that need to be addressed by way of answering this question: whether authors intend recipients of their works to imagine or make-believe these propositions; and whether authors invite, suggest, or command that recipients do so, or perform *sui generis* illocutionary acts to that effect.

Regarding the first issue, I am willing to concede that authors of fiction intend that the recipients of their works imagine or make-believe the propositions expressed by the sentences contained within, but with the following caveat. Authors who give their works of fiction to friends typically intend that their friends read their works as fiction. And authors who send their works to publishers typically want their works to be evaluated as fiction, which presumably requires that someone working at the publishing house read their works as fiction. Now, arguably, reading a work as fiction requires imagining or making-believe the propositions expressed by the sentences contained therein; and so in this sense authors who disseminate their works typically intend that the recipients of them engage in such imaginative activity. But it is worth emphasizing that many authors may not realize that this is what reading as fiction requires. Hence, the sense in which they intend recipients to imagine the propositions expressed by their works is the same sense in which, for example, Lois Lane can be said to believe that Clark Kent can fly simply in virtue of believing that Superman can. And insofar as we are concerned to individuate intentions in terms of how subjects conceive of their intended goals, we cannot attribute this intention to authors on this basis.

The remaining issue is whether by her act of disseminating her work, an author thereby commands, invites, or suggests that the recipient read her work as fiction – that is, imagine the propositions expressed by the sentences contained therein – or performs a *sui generis* fictive illocutionary act to that effect. What is important to note, however, is that normally accompanying some such act of dissemination is an illocutionary act on the part of the author – a suggestion that her friend read the work, or a cover letter requesting that it be considered for publication, or the like.[64] And it is this accompanying illocutionary act – and not the act of dissemination itself – which (arguably) counts as a command, suggestion, or invitation that the recipient read the work as fiction, or as a *sui generis* fictive illocutionary act to that effect. But this robs the fictive illocution analysis – and its perlocutionary cousins – of all interest, at least insofar as it is intended to serve as an analysis of compositional speech acts. After all, anyone – author or non-author – could make the same request, command, etc., regarding any literary work – fiction or non-fiction. The ability to perform the illocutionary act in question is entirely independent of the compositional process at issue.

1.4 REPRESENTATION

One final view worth considering here is Beardsley's account of composition as the representation of illocutionary action.[65] Beardsley distinguishes between two senses in which a speaker or writer might be described as saying something. In one sense, to say something is to perform an illocutionary action of some kind. This occurs when an utterance is made "under certain conditions, according to certain language conventions."[66] These conditions typically include, among other things, the adoption of requisite illocutionary commitments by the speaker. So, for example, a speaker who utters

It was a dark and stormy night

thereby asserts that it was a dark and stormy night only if she commits herself to the corresponding belief.[67] In another sense, to say something is to represent rather than perform an illocutionary action. A speaker says something in this sense when she "[refrains] from illocutionary commitment in order to produce a fiction."[68] The idea seems to be that a speaker who utters the above sentence fails to assert that it was a dark and stormy night but instead represents an assertion to that effect just in case she refrains from adopting a commitment to the belief it was a dark and stormy night, and her purpose in so refraining is to produce fiction.

Beardsley models the representation of illocutionary acts by utterances of this latter kind on quoted dialogue. An utterance of

It was a dark and stormy night

(made without illocutionary commitment) represents an assertion to that effect in the same sense as does the quoted sentence in

Mary said, "It was a dark and stormy night."[69]

And, according to Beardsley, this kind of representation is best understood in terms of selective similarity between the words used to represent an illocutionary action and the illocutionary act represented: "by selecting words that could be used, under appropriate imaginable conditions, to perform an illocutionary action, [a poet] can represent an action of that sort."[70] It is worth noting that, on Beardsley's view, an author performs the speech act of representing an illocutionary action by means of producing a text which represents an illocutionary action. Moreover, what illocutionary act the author thereby represents is independent of any representational intentions she might have; it depends instead on what representational practices are in place.[71] Indeed, according to Beardsley, a text need not have been produced with representational intentions, or even with any intentions at all, in order to represent an illocutionary act: "And I see no objection to regarding even the verbal output of a myna bird as crude verbal depiction of illocutionary action: the bird does not actually greet you or curse you but gives a pretty good imitation of it."[72]

Now while I take it that Beardsley is on the right track here, the account he gives of compositional speech acts is not ultimately adequate.[73] Authors of fiction surely do refrain from illocutionary commitment when they are selecting and recording the sentences which constitute their fictional works.[74] The trouble is that one can make an utterance while refraining from illocutionary commitment without thereby engaging in fictional composition. One might, for example, utter

It was a bright and calm morning

as an example of a sentence consisting of seven words while refraining from committing oneself to the belief that the morning in question was bright and calm. Nevertheless, one's act in so doing would not count as fiction making.[75] As Walton puts it, "[fiction] is not just language stripped of some of its normal functions; it is something positive, something special."[76] Beardsley does, of course, suggest that in order to engage in fictional composition, a speaker needs to refrain from illocutionary commitment for the purpose of producing fiction. But in lieu of an account of the nature of fiction, or an account of this fiction-making purpose which does not presuppose an account of fictionality, Beardsley's account of composition is ultimately empty.

1.5 CONCLUSION

The upshot of this discussion is that composition is neither illocutionary action nor illocutionary pretense: compositional speech acts lack illocutionary force and the authors who make them refrain from illocutionary commitment. But, of course, simply making an utterance without performing an illocutionary act does not suffice for fiction-making; a distinguishing mark of compositional speech acts still remains to be found. In my view, however, the distinction is not to be found by treating composition as a kind of communication; instead it should be viewed as a kind of art-making. Fictional composition is the process of creating an artifact of a certain kind – a novel, or a novella, or a short story. Now, of course, the constituents out of which these artifacts are made – words and sentences – are primarily used for communication, and authors certainly do communicate by means of the dissemination of their fictional works. Nevertheless, composition per se is best understood as a process of constructing fictional artifacts out of their basic constituents, as a kind of word-sculpture. This idea will be developed more fully in chapter 3.

2

Reader Engagement

The focus of this chapter is on the nature of appreciator – reader and listener – engagement with fiction: the psychological states of reader/listeners who are "caught up in the story." An appreciator's encounter with a fictional work can be either engaged or disengaged: as a first gloss, an engaged reader/listener can be thought of as one who is attending to or focused on the fictional story, and characters and events which occur therein, as such; a disengaged appreciator, in contrast, although aware of the fictional story, is one who is focused on other features of the fictional work, such as the style in which it is written, or similarities and differences between it and other works, or who is simply distracted.[1] Consider, by way of analogy, the distinction between a theatre-goer whose concern is with features of the actors and the set and one concerned with features of the characters they portray.

Engaged reading/listening involves standing in a presumably complex psychological relationship to fictional works and the fictional events and characters described or generated by them. As such, it can be viewed as a species of propositional attitude. The primary task of this chapter is to elucidate the nature of this attitude. Much of the recent literature has focused on the affective states of engaged appreciators. Of central concern has been the so-called "paradox of fiction," which can be formulated as a set of four incompatible claims:

(1) Engaged reader/listeners sometimes have genuine emotional reactions to the fictional works they read (or to which they listen).
(2) The objects of these emotions are fictional characters and events.
(3) Genuine emotions logically presuppose belief in the existence of their objects.

(4) Engaged reader/listeners (normally) do not believe in the existence of fictional characters and events.[2]

As is common practice, I will take the principal desideratum of an account
of appreciator engagement to be that it provides a satisfactory solution to
the paradox. As formulated, this requires the rejection of at least one of
the claims which make up the paradox, as well as a rationale for so doing.

In what follows, it will prove fruitful to distinguish between the actual
world and the fictional world generated by a given work of fiction. The
actual world is this one; its inhabitants include the author of the work and
any readers there might be, as well as the work itself. The fictional world
generated by the work, in contrast, is a world in which the events described
in the fictional work occur and whose inhabitants include the fictional
characters who participate in these events. Please note: as I use it, talk of
worlds is a useful bookkeeping idiom without ontological import.

The natural, and perhaps naive, view is that engagement with fiction is
a trans-world relationship that holds between readers inhabiting the
actual world and characters and events occurring in fictional worlds. One
might worry, however, that this picture is both ontologically profligate –
invoking an ontology of non-existent objects – and mysterious – allowing
actual people to stand in cognitive relationships to these suspect objects.
There are, however, two ways of interpreting the trans-world picture. First,
one can understand it to involve psychological relations between actual
subjects and an independent realm of non-existent fictional entities. And
second, one can understand it to involve what might be called "fictionalizing attitudes" toward actual entities which, in effect, transform them
into fictions. Consider theatre, once again, by way of analogy. The audience at a stage production can be thought of as inhabitants of our shared
actual world directly observing characters and events occurring in the fictional world of the play. But at the same time, what they observe is nothing
more than the actors and props on stage. Their attitudes toward these
items transform them into characters and other fictional entities. Insofar
as the second interpretation is adopted, the above worries about the trans-
world picture are easily dispelled.

Nevertheless, the paradox of fiction, among other things, has driven
many theorists to abandon the naive trans-world picture in favour of
accounts of engagement as an intra-world relation. There are two basic
variants. Some theorists take engagement to be a relation between (actual)
appreciators and other actual entities, rather than between reader/listeners
and fictional entities.[3] Others take it to be a relation between fictional

entities and appreciators who have imaginatively entered into fictional worlds.[4] Please note: strictly speaking, views of the former kind take the objects of the suspect emotions to be actual, rather than fictional, entities; an advocate of such an approach could take engagement to involve a relation to fictional entities (even if so doing would come at the cost of a certain theoretical inelegance).

Two broad categories of attitudes have been taken to lie at the core of engagement with fiction: doxastic attitudes and imaginative attitudes. Included in the former category is, of course, belief, but also such attitudes as the suspension of disbelief, half-belief, and "predicational" belief.[5] And included among the latter category are various kinds of imagination and make-believe.[6] The upshot is a pair of distinctions in terms of which accounts of reader engagement can be fruitfully categorized: whether engagement is a trans-world or intra-world relation; and whether it is a doxastic or imaginative attitude. These distinctions yield four basic accounts of engagement: trans-world doxastic, intra-world doxastic, intra-world imaginative, and trans-world imaginative. In chapter 4, an account of the latter sort will be developed and defended. In this chapter, each of the alternative approaches will be critically evaluated in turn. Please note: as above, intra-world accounts include both actual world and fictional world accounts, and so one might expect doxastic and imaginative variants of each. In the literature, however, one finds only doxastic variants of the actual world approach and imaginative variants of the fictional world approach.[7]

Currently most prominent – and the primary stalking horse of this chapter – is the intra-world imaginative approach. As a result, it will prove fruitful to more fully develop the differences between it and the trans-world imaginative approach I favour. There are three basic types of imaginative activity in which readers might be thought to engage: *de dicto*, *de re*, and *de se* imagining. *De dicto* involves imagining propositions about fictional characters and events. For example, one might imagine *de dicto* that Gandalf the Grey fought a balrog[8] or that Moist von Lipwig was placed in charge of the Ankh-Morpork Royal Mint.[9] *De re* imagining involves imagining of an actual object that it is thus and so. So, for example, one might imagine *de re* of *Making Money* that it is a report of actual events or of Ian McKellen that he is Gandalf the Grey. Finally, *de se* imagining is imagining experiencing or otherwise doing something. For example, one might imagine *de se* seeing Gandalf fight a balrog or reading a report about von Lipwig's tenure at the Ankh-Morpork Mint.

Now according to both the intra-world and trans-world imaginative approaches, engagement with fiction involves *de dicto* imagining on the part of reader/listeners. Moreover, according to the latter and most versions of the former,[10] engagement involves *de re* imagining as well – in particular, imagining *de re* of the fictional work that it is a report of actual events.[11] The difference is that according to the intra-world imaginative account, but not its trans-world cousin, engagement involves *de se* imagining as well, imagining experiencing or reading a report of the fictional events in question. At bottom, imagining *de se* doing such things is what imaginatively entering into a fictional world consists in, and hence in effect defines the intra-world imaginative approach to engagement. It is, of course, true that engagement in certain sorts of fictions – adult role playing games, children's games of make-believe, and the like – involves *de se* imagining. The trans-world imaginative approach defended here, however, is designed to provide an account of engagement only with literary fiction (although I would argue that it applies to a broad range of fictional genres, including theatrical and cinematic fiction among others). It is also true that appreciators of literary fiction in fact sometimes do imagine *de se* experiencing and doing various things vis-à-vis the fictions with which they are engaged. The approach defended here does not deny that this can occur; it merely claims that reader/listeners need not undertake any *de se* imaginative activity in order to properly appreciate the fictional works with which they are engaged.[12]

2.1 TRANS-WORLD DOXASTIC RELATIONS

This section focuses on accounts of engagement which take it to be a matter of appreciators having appropriate beliefs, or belief-like states, regarding fictional characters and events. One central motivation for a view of this kind is a perhaps naive commitment to the view that affective responses to fictional works are genuine emotional reactions whose objects are fictions. After all, insofar as readers' reactions count as genuine emotions, engagement has to be a doxastic relation, at least if one accepts standard analyses of emotions. And insofar as the objects of these emotions are fictions, engagement has to be a trans-world relation.

In what follows, three versions of the trans-world doxastic approach to engagement will be considered: Radford's inconsistency view,[13] views which invoke the suspension of disbelief, and Schaper's two-tiered account.[14] A recurring theme in this discussion is the significance of the distinction between what might be called "predicational" and "existential" beliefs regarding fictions.[15] Predicational beliefs are beliefs about the goings on *within* fictional worlds – beliefs about the properties fictional characters and events have in the stories in which they occur. The belief that, for example, Bilbo Baggins engaged in a riddle competition with Gollum would count as predicational in this sense.[16] Existential beliefs, in contrast, are beliefs about the existence or non-existence of the objects of predicational beliefs. The belief that Bilbo Baggins exists – that is, is an inhabitant of the actual world – or that Gollum does not, would count as existential in this sense. Please note: predicational beliefs about fictions are to be distinguished from explicitly fictional beliefs: whereas the belief that *Bilbo outsmarted Gollum* counts as predicational, the belief that *in* The Hobbit, *Bilbo outsmarted Gollum* does not.

According to Radford, engaged reader/listeners have contradictory existential beliefs about the fictional characters they encounter: they both believe and disbelieve that these characters exist.[17] As a result, emotional reactions to fiction in particular, and engaged appreciation in general, "involve us in inconsistency and so incoherence."[18] Radford's charge of inconsistency relies on the following quite plausible assumption regarding the relation between predicational and existential beliefs about fiction: "in order to feel concern for someone in a certain situation or to be moved by someone's plight, one has to believe that he is, or is more or less likely to be, in some parlous situation or desperate plight, and so, *a fortiori* that there is such a person."[19] A predicational belief regarding the plight of a character is required in order to have a genuine emotional attitude toward him, and this requires an existential belief to the effect that said character (actually) exists. The inconsistency arises because as long as a reader/listener realizes that the work with which she is engaged is fictional she will believe that the character in question does not exist. And so when an appreciator reacts emotionally to a work of fiction, she both believes and disbelieves in the existence of a character (at the same time and in the same sense of "exists").[20]

There are, of course, a number of reasons to be dissatisfied with Radford's position (as with any analysis of reader attitudes that invokes inconsistent belief sets). First, although it is true that most of us do find ourselves with inconsistent beliefs from time to time, this is typically the product of epistemic difficulties of various kinds: inattention or confusion or simply a lack of information. Moreover, it is an inherently unstable state: when we discover an inconsistency in our beliefs we are normally moved to correct it. But engaged reader/listeners need not and typically do not suffer from such epistemic ailments. They know perfectly well that the stories they read/listen to are incompatible with actuality, nor are they moved by this fact to become disengaged or to stop reading/listening altogether. Second, Radford's view seems to imply that engagement with fiction is more difficult than it in fact is. It may be reasonably easy to accidentally lapse into inconsistency as a result of epistemic difficulties of the kind noted above; and it is more or less unproblematic to replace a previously held belief with one inconsistent with it. But it is extremely difficult, if not impossible, to voluntarily and knowingly adopt a belief that is inconsistent with a belief one already holds and intends to retain. And this seems to be what Radford requires of engaged appreciators.[21] Finally, the attribution to engaged reader/listeners – a rather large collection of people – of a heretofore unnoticed inconsistency in their beliefs is a strategy of last resort and, as such, should be endorsed only if all else fails.

The problem of inconsistency can be avoided if one adopts a view which combines Radford's solution to the paradox of fiction with the familiar notion of the "suspension of disbelief." The idea is that when not engaged with fiction, readers and listeners (typically) have existential beliefs to the effect that the characters they encounter in works of fiction do not exist. When caught up in fictional stories, however, they suspend their beliefs in the non-existence of such figures, rendering them, for a time, inoperative.[22] So, an appreciator who is engaged with *The Hobbit* does not disbelieve in the existence of Bilbo Baggins – or, perhaps better, her belief in his non-existence is inoperative – despite being in this doxastic state both before and after her encounter with the novel. As a result, she can have a predicational belief to the effect that Bilbo is in danger if he loses the riddle game sufficient to ground her genuine fear for Bilbo's safety – as well as the belief in Bilbo's existence this seems to presuppose – without falling prey to inconsistency. Please note: to say a belief is inoperative is to say it does not currently play a role in cognition and behaviour.

Schaper argues, however, that the suspension of disbelief account of appreciator engagement falls prey to insuperable difficulties.[23] In particular, it runs afoul of the problem of the naive backwoodsman, a figure (of fun?) "who jumps onto the stage trying to stop the characters in some Jacobean drama … from perpetrating their evil designs."[24] Engaged reader/listeners are not a species of naive backwoodsman, moved to act, in whatever way they believe is available to them, to rescue the characters about whom they read or hear from whatever unfortunate circumstances these characters find themselves in. And what keeps engaged appreciators from performing acts of this kind are exactly their (operative) beliefs that the characters in question do not exist. The suspension of belief account, by denying engaged appreciators their negative existential beliefs about fictional characters, erroneously turns them into naive backwoodsmen.

Schaper offers her own trans-world doxastic account of engagement which she claims avoids Radford's attribution of inconsistent beliefs to engaged reader/listeners without turning them into naive backwoodsmen. Schaper's strategy is to sever the entailment relation between predicational and existential beliefs; according to Schaper, the belief that Bilbo Baggins engaged in a riddle competition with Gollum does not entail the belief that Bilbo exists. As a result, Schaper is able to explain appreciators' emotional reactions to fiction by appeal to their predicational beliefs about the plights of fictional characters. And she is able to avoid attributing inconsistency to engaged reader/listeners – without turning them into naive backwoodsmen – by denying that such beliefs entail existential beliefs to the effect that the fictional characters exist.[25] More strongly, she argues that being moved by fiction requires the belief that one is engaged with a work of fiction, and, hence, the belief that the character in question does *not* exist.[26] Schaper's point here is most clearly illustrated by appeal to theatre: unless the audience believes it is a play they are observing, and not real life, they will be moved only by the plights of the actors onstage and not by the plights of the characters they portray.

The difficulty with Schaper's view is that it is not clear that an account of predicational beliefs is forthcoming according to which they both (i) fail to entail the corresponding existential beliefs and (ii) provide adequate underpinnings for emotional reactions to fiction. The first thing to note is that, strictly speaking, the issue is not entailment relations between predicational and existential beliefs, but between the corresponding believed propositions. That is, the issue is whether

(i) Joe Fiction is in such-and-such plight

entails

(ii) Joe Fiction exists,

and not whether

(iii) Mary Reader believes that Joe Fiction is in such-and-such plight

entails

(iv) Mary Reader believes that Joe Fiction exists.

Moreover, according to the standard account of entailment, a proposition *P* entails a proposition *Q* just in case there are no possible worlds in which *P* is true and *Q* is false.[27] And according to this account of entailment, (i) clearly does entail (ii). After all, any world in which Joe Fiction has any properties at all – including that of being in a plight of a certain kind – is a world in which Joe Fiction exists.

There are, of course, a number of strategies that Schaper might deploy in order to avoid this conclusion. One strategy would be to acknowledge that predicational propositions do entail the corresponding existential propositions but insist that engaged readers, in effect, fail to recognize these entailments and, hence, believe the former propositions without believing the latter. This strategy, however, runs afoul of the same sort of difficulties that undermined Radford's view. If engaged readers believe predicational propositions about the plights of fictional characters and, as Schaper claims, believe negative existential propositions about fictional characters – propositions to the effect that fictional characters do not exist – then the fact that the former entail positive existential propositions about the same characters again leaves readers with inconsistent belief sets.

A more promising strategy involves embedding the contents of predicational beliefs in an intensional fictionality operator of some sort. After all, even if

(i) Joe Fiction is in such-and-such plight

entails

(ii) Joe Fiction exists,

it is not the case that

(v) In the Story, Joe Fiction is in such-and-such plight

entails

(ii) Joe Fiction exists,

(at least as long as the "in the Story" operator is appropriately construed). The trouble with this manoeuvre, however, is that it undermines Schaper's solution to the paradox of fiction. The belief that a fictional character is undergoing some difficulty or other might very well explain an engaged reader's emotional reaction; but a reader's emotional reaction to the belief that *in a fictional story* a character is undergoing some such difficulties is exactly what needed explaining in the first place.

Schaper, however, rejects an analysis of predicational belief contents in terms of a fictionality operator: "[we] can understand what happens to Anna [Karenina] without assuming either that Anna exists or that our beliefs about her are beliefs about a text."[28] Instead, she endorses an analysis in terms of intentional objects: "it is the fact that our beliefs about fictional characters and events concern [intentional] objects which underlies … the reasonableness of such beliefs and the associated emotions."[29] The idea seems to be that the class of intentional objects – the potential objects of belief and other attitudes – is larger than the class of actual objects; and included among the subclass of non-actual intentional objects are fictional characters. Moreover, a distinction can be drawn between (ordinary) existential propositions and actual-existential propositions. Whether or not a proposition of the former kind is true at a given world depends on whether or not the intentional object it concerns exists at that world; and whether or not the corresponding actual-existential proposition is true at a world depends on whether or not the intentional object in question inhabits the actual world. And although predicational propositions entail ordinary positive existentials, they do not entail positive actual-existentials. Suppose, for example, Joe Fiction is in such-and-such a plight in non-actual world w. The ordinary positive existential – that Joe exists – will, of course, be true at w. Whether or not the positive actual-existential – that Joe actually exists – is true at w, however, depends instead on whether or not Joe inhabits the actual world: if Joe does inhabit the actual world, it is true at w (and, in fact, all possible worlds); if Joe does not inhabit the actual world, it is false at w. As a result, on Schaper's view, engaged readers can consistently have predicational beliefs about fictional characters without believing the corresponding positive actual-existentials.

There are a number of reasons one might balk at Schaper's proposal, not the least of which is the ontology of non-existent objects she seems to endorse. But even if one accepts this ontology, two central questions remain. First, it is far from clear that such entities are the objects of belief and other propositional attitudes or, equivalently, are constituents of the propositions such attitudes are attitudes toward. And second, even if they are, it is far from clear that beliefs about such entities suffice to explain our emotional reactions to fictions; just as one might wonder why someone who believes that *in a story* some character is in unfortunate circumstances responds emotionally as she does, one might also wonder why someone who believes that a non-existent character is in unfortunate (non-existent) circumstances responds emotionally. Schaper attempts to address such worries by modeling the intentional objects of fictional belief on the intentional objects of dreams. Because we can dream about both real and imaginary entities, descriptions of events occurring in dreams do not entail claims about the existence of the participants in such dream-events. Moreover, whether what we dream of is real or imaginary "does not affect our description of what goes on in the dream, nor presumably our involvement in the dream."[30]

Schaper's dream analogy, however, fails on both counts. First, it is simply not obvious that the contents of dream experiences, when what we dream of is not real, are non-existent intentional objects. Rosebury, for example, argues that the contents of such dreams are not "extra-existent objects" over and above dream experiences, but rather attributes of the dream experiences themselves.[31] And second, normally we react emotionally to dreams only when we falsely believe them to be real; once we realize that they are imaginary – either upon awaking or even while still dreaming – our emotional responses by and large subside. As a result, dream experience offers no support for Schaper's contention that engaged appreciators can have genuine emotional reactions to the plights of entities they believe do not exist.[32]

2.2 ACTUAL-WORLD RELATIONS

One possible diagnosis of the difficulties that arise for this naive approach to engagement involves attributing them to the trans-world aspect of this view. Advocates of a diagnosis of this kind retain the idea that engagement is some sort of doxastic relation while rejecting the idea that it is a relation between actual reader/listeners and fictional entities, taking it instead to be a relation between appreciators and actual entities of some kind. In particular, they typically take engagement to be a doxastic relation between actual reader/listeners and actual thoughts or thought-contents.

Lingering in the background here is an alternate account of so-called attitudes toward non-existents to the intentional object account presupposed by at least some variants of the trans-world doxastic approach to engagement. According to the intentional object approach, the constituents of thought-contents expressible by singular terms are intentional objects, some of which exist and some of which do not. When a subject has an attitude toward a non-existent, the content of her attitude includes an intentional object of the latter kind. According to what might be called the Fregean account, in contrast, the constituents of thought-contents expressible by singular terms can only be actually existing things. A subject's cognitive relations to such objects, however, are mediated by concepts or ways of conceiving of them. In effect, propositional attitudes are treated not as two-place relations between subjects and thought-contents but as three-place relations between subjects, thought-contents, and ways of conceiving of thought-contents. When a subject has an attitude toward a non-existent, she grasps (or is otherwise appropriately related to) a mediating concept but is not thereby (or otherwise) cognitively related to a corresponding object.[33]

Consider, by way of illustration, a childless grifter who, in an attempt to defraud a mark, claims that she needs to raise money in order to provide her sick child with life-saving treatment. The mark might well come to believe that the grifter has a seriously ill child and, consequently, have feelings of sympathy directed toward the putative child. Now according to the intentional object account of such attitudes, the content of the mark's belief, as well as of his emotional state, includes an intentional object which happens not to exist: the actually childless grifter's ill child. According to the Fregean account, in contrast, although the mark has a concept of the grifter's ill child, his doxastic and affective states have no objects. Nevertheless, as long as this concept is involved in the mark's cognitive states in the right way, he can be appropriately described as having genuine beliefs about, and emotional reactions to, the grifter's child (although after discovering that the grifter has no child – that is, that he has been conned – the mark's beliefs and emotions will undoubtedly change).[34]

There are a number of different ways in which this model might be invoked in an account of appreciator engagement. The simplest way to do so would be to take the characteristic reader/listener attitude to be one which involves concepts derived (in some appropriate way) from fictional works; but given that the individual concepts in question pick out no (actual) objects, the attitude in question is one which lacks an object. So, for example, just as the sympathetic mark has a belief involving a grifter's-child concept which lacks an object, the reader who fears for Bilbo's safety has a belief involving a similarly objectless lost-hobbit concept. As it stands, however, this suggestion runs afoul of the problem of the naive backwoodsman that undermined the trans-world doxastic account of engagement considered above. A reader who genuinely believes Bilbo is in danger will be moved to engage in a course of action designed to rescue him from his predicament (or if she believes no such course of action exists, she will feel a sense of frustration at her inability to do so), but engaged readers are not so moved. And if the attitude in which the empty lost-hobbit concept is involved is not belief, an explanation of why this attitude yields genuine fear for someone's safety needs to be provided. Moreover, unlike the mark who feels sympathy for the grifter's putative child, the reader's fear for Bilbo is not the product of a mistaken belief nor will it be alleviated by the realization that her lost-hobbit concept lacks an object.

A more common, and perhaps more illuminating, approach involves taking thoughts or thought-contents to be the objects of reader attitudes and emotions. McCormick, for example, claims that "what moves us in fictional works ... are not the beliefs we entertain about real objects, fictional objects, or mental objects but the contents of our own thoughts."[35] And Lamarque concurs: "Simply put, the fear and pity we feel for fiction are in fact directed at thoughts in our minds."[36] What is nice about this suggestion is that one can easily reconcile one's beliefs about a thought with the judgment that the thought – or a concept involved in it – picks out no object. The central difficulty that arises is that of explaining why a belief or other attitude toward a thought should produce any emotional responses whatsoever; prima facie they simply are not the sorts of thing one fears or pities.

At least two different sorts of response to this worry have been defended in the literature. The first approach relies on the fact that although the thoughts in question concern circumstances – paradigmatically dangerous or unfortunate circumstances – in which no person may actually find herself, they are nevertheless possible circumstances, that is, circumstances in which the subject of the thought or someone else *might* find themselves. Moreover, people are often moved in various ways by the plights of those they discover to be in circumstances of these kinds. This basic idea has been implemented in a number of different ways in accounts of reader attitudes. Novitz, for example, argues that the possible circumstances themselves, rather than thoughts of them, are the objects of readers' emotions: "Of course, it is not the *idea* that is dangerous, nor is the idea the object of one's fear. Rather, the idea is of a state of affairs that might be dangerous or otherwise fear-provoking, and it is when this is considered in the right frame of mind that a person will be frightened by the idea."[37] Weston, in contrast, takes the thoughts rather than the possible circumstances to be the objects of reader emotions, although, presumably, the thoughts can occupy this role only because the latter serve as their contents: "we can be moved, not merely by what has occurred or what is probable, but also by ideas … What I am responding to here is … a possibility of human life perceived through a certain conception of that life."[38] And Skulsky takes a related thought – that the circumstances in question are possible – to play the salient role in reader emotional reactions – "I am saddened, or I shudder empathetically or smile, *at the thought* of such and such; and the thought is a belief that such and such is logically possible"[39] – although it remains unclear whether he takes these beliefs to be the objects of readers' emotions or their causes.

The difficulty with the appeal to possible circumstances is that it is simply unclear why the belief that someone or other might find themselves in dangerous or otherwise unfortunate circumstances of a certain kind should produce any emotional response at all. Merely believing that dangerous or unfortunate circumstances are possible is normally insufficient for fear or pity. And it is worth emphasizing that the difficulty here is two-fold: on the view in question, not only do engaged reader/listeners not believe that anyone is actually in the circumstances in question, they need not believe that anyone in particular is potentially vulnerable to such circumstances. Novitz suggests that what is additionally required is that the possibility be considered "in the right frame of mind," but this merely identifies the problem rather than solving it. After all, our central question is exactly what this correct frame of mind is. Weston's suggestion – that both events and ideas can, in general, be the objects of emotions – is more promising. No specific onus would fall upon a theory of reader attitudes to explain a putatively general (albeit puzzling) phenomenon in which subjects are moved by ideas. What is required, however, are grounds for thinking that thoughts about possible circumstances of various kinds fall within the class of ideas which can serve as objects of emotions in their own right. And it is far from clear that any such grounds are forthcoming.

The second response to the worry that thoughts are not the sort of thing one fears or pities reintroduces the distinction between the object of an emotional state, or other attitude, and the concept which mediates the subject's relation to that object. The basic idea underlying this approach is that although thoughts are not (normally) proper objects of emotional states, the concepts which mediate engaged appreciators' attitudes toward their own thoughts are appropriate. They are, after all, simply descriptions of fictional characters and their plights obtained from fictional texts. As Lamarque puts it, "when we respond emotionally to fictional characters we are responding to mental representations or thought contents identifiable through descriptions derived in suitable ways from the propositional contents of fictional sentences."[40] In effect, the idea is that engaged readers (erroneously) conceive of various of their thoughts or thought contents as satisfying such descriptions. And just as there can be emotional responses that lack objects altogether, as long as the emotional attitude has appropriate concepts involved in it – remember the grifter's ill child – there can be emotions with the wrong kind of object, again as long as appropriate concepts are deployed.

There are, however, at least two difficulties that arise for this view. First, engaged reader/listeners rarely if ever *believe* of their thoughts that they are people in unfortunate or dangerous circumstances or the like. But if the characteristic reader attitude toward their own thoughts is something other than (a species of) belief, then an explanation of why this attitude generates any kind of emotional response at all is required. Second, in order to derive the correct descriptions from a fictional text one needs already to be reading it as fiction. But this undercuts a picture according to which engagement, in effect, occurs only after the relevant descriptions are derived from fictional texts and applied to thought contents. The point is easiest to see in the case of theatre. The relevant descriptions – those which correspond to the circumstances to which the audience responds – are those which characterize the plights of the characters the actors onstage portray and not the plights of the actors themselves. But in order to derive these descriptions from the activities going on onstage, the audience needs already to be caught up in the theatrical fiction. And this excludes a picture according to which engagement occurs only after a disengaged observer has applied descriptions derived from the onstage activities in some way.

Similarly, the relevant descriptions in literary fiction are to be found in the utterances or inscriptions of the narrative informant – a non-actual figure who tells the story as fact[41] – rather than those of an actual fiction-teller – the author or a storyteller. But to read/listen to a fictional text as the words of a narrative informant is, again, already to be caught up in the literary fiction. Any account which supposes that engagement occurs only after descriptions are derived from a disengaged encounter with a fictional text will not do. Please note: I am assuming here a rather tight connection between engaged reading/listening and reading/listening-as-fiction. Insofar as this assumption is erroneous – and disengaged reading/listening-as-fiction is possible – the argument here will be weakened. Even so, a view which treats reading/listening-as-fiction to be an attitude toward fictional texts and engaged reading/listening as an attitude toward reader/listeners' own thoughts is less preferable than a unified account, if one is forthcoming. And as we see shall, there are independently plausible unified alternatives to be found.

2.3 FICTIONAL-WORLD RELATIONS

Another possible diagnosis of the difficulties that arise for the naive account of appreciator engagement attributes the difficulties not only to the trans-world element of the view but also to the idea that engagement is a doxastic relation. The actual-world approach discussed above runs into similar difficulties precisely because it retains this latter feature of the naive view. Advocates of this diagnosis share with the actual-world approach the idea that engagement is an intra-world relation, but rather than taking it to be a relation between actual reader/listeners and actual entities of various kinds, they take it instead to be a relation between cognitive agents situated in fictional worlds on the one hand and fictional entities on the other. In effect, the idea is that engaged appreciators imaginatively enter into the fictional worlds generated by the works they read/listen to and thereby come to (fictionally) stand in causal and cognitive relations of various kinds to the inhabitants thereof.

At the core of this approach is the currently prominent make-believe model of reader engagement, according to which the relation between reader/listeners and fictional texts is to be understood in terms of children's games of make-believe.[42] Games of make-believe are activities governed in part by rules – sometimes ad hoc, oftentimes tacit – prescribing that the participants imagine various things and behave in certain ways. A central role is played in many games by props – objects that the rules prescribe be imagined to be thus and so. For example, the rules of a sword fighting game might prescribe imagining that a short stick is a dagger. Participation in a game minimally requires that one take oneself to be bound by the imaginative prescriptions that govern it. In many games, however, compliance with these prescriptions requires that participants take on a more active role. Participants may themselves be reflexive props in a game – prescribed by the rules to imagine being and doing various things. A participant in a sword fighting game might not only be under a prescription to imagine that a stick is a dagger but under a prescription to imagine being an assassin attempting to carry out some murderous assignment.

Engagement with fiction, according to the view on the table, is understood as participation in a game of make-believe in which the fictional work serves as a prop.[43] Engaged appreciators are under prescriptions to both imagine *de re* of the fictional texts they read/listen to that they are thus and so and to imagine *de dicto* (at least provisionally) the characters and events described in these texts. Moreover, readers are themselves reflexive props in the games they play with texts. Not only do they make-believe what is described in the text and various things of the text, they imagine *de se* being and doing various things.[44] And in so doing, they imaginatively enter into the fictional world generated by the text and thereby come to fictionally stand in causal and cognitive relations of various kinds to the characters and events described therein.

The fictional-world picture as sketched thus far is, of course, merely schematic. What is minimally needed to fill in the picture is an account of what (if anything) engaged appreciators are prescribed to imagine *de re* of fictional texts and what they are prescribed to imagine *de se* being and/or doing. And two approaches to doing just this have been defended in the literature: the "perceptual" model and the "report" model.[45] According to the perceptual model, engaged appreciators imagine experiencing the events and characters described in the fictional texts they read/listen to. This involves being in imaginative states whose contents are not propositions but rather images corresponding to the various sense-faculties – visual images and auditory images, etc., of the events described in the text. But it also involves imagining *de se* seeing and hearing, etc., these events – in effect, imagining that these images are the contents of their own experiential states.[46] Moreover, although imagining inhabiting the fictional world generated by the text she reads/listens to and imagining experiencing the events occurring therein, the engaged appreciator also imagines being invisible and impotent: neither detectable by the other inhabitants of the fictional world nor able to intervene in the events she observes. It is worth noting that, on this picture, an engaged reader/listener need not imagine anything *de re* of the fictional text; she need only use it as source material for her experiential imaginings.

According to the report model, in contrast, appreciator engagement primarily involves propositional imagining rather than experiential imagining; that is, the contents of engaged reader/listeners' imaginative states are propositions concerning the events and characters described in the fictional text rather than images of them. The engaged reader/listener imagines *de re* of the fictional text that it is a report of actual events and imagines *de dicto* that the events reported therein have occurred.[47] Moreover, although actually reading/listening to a work of fiction, in so doing she imagines *de se* reading/listening to a report of actual events. And although imagining inhabiting the fictional world in which the events described by the text occur, the engaged reader/listener does not imagine experiencing these events; rather, her access to them is mediated by the report she imagines the fictional text to be.

There are two different solutions advocates of the fictional-world account of engagement offer to the paradox of fiction. First, following Walton, we can describe someone who is undergoing the phenomenal and physiological reactions characteristic of an emotional state, without having the characteristic behavioural dispositions, as being in a quasi-emotional state.[48] So, for example, a subject who is undergoing the phenomenal and physiological reactions characteristic of fear or pity, but is not disposed to flee or provide comfort, is in a state of quasi-fear or quasi-pity. In the case of ordinary non-fictional emotions, these phenomenal and physiological reactions are prompted by emotion-appropriate beliefs about one's own or someone else's plight. For example, in the ordinary case, the phenomenal and physiological reactions characteristic of fear are caused by the belief that one is in danger; and the phenomenal and physiological reactions characteristic of pity are caused by the belief that someone else is suffering from misfortune. In the fictional case, in contrast, the quasi-emotional states are caused not by an emotion-appropriate belief about someone's plight but rather by a state of imagining or making-believe that someone finds herself in a plight of the requisite kind. An engaged reader/listener, for example, finds herself in a state she might describe as pity for a fictional character when she is in a state of quasi-pity that has been caused by imagining the character's misfortune.[49]

Recently, accounts of reader emotional reactions have been defended which invoke the simulation theory.[50] The process of simulation proceeds schematically as follows: the simulator imagines having the same mental states and being similarly situated as some object of simulation; these imagined states and circumstances are entered into a cognitive mechanism which generates further imagined mental states as outputs; and these output states are then transformed into attitudes on the part of the simulator toward the object of simulation. So, for example, someone might imagine being in a similar state of misfortune to that of an object of simulation; these imagined circumstances might then be entered into her affective mechanisms yielding off-line feelings of despair as output; and, as a result of the simulator's belief that the object of simulation is in such unfortunate circumstances, these off-line feelings of despair might be transformed into on-line feelings of pity for the object. Please note: the input and output states of simulations are not nested or second-order attitudes – states of imagining that one believes, desires, etc., such and such – but are rather truncated or "off-line" variants of the first-order attitudes themselves. That is, they share the contents and internal causal roles of ordinary (unsimulated) mental states, but lack the behavioural consequences of their unsimulated cousins.

This basic model is applied to emotional reactions to fiction in two different ways corresponding to two sorts of imagined circumstances that might prompt such reactions. In the first case, the appreciator imagines that a character in the fictional story is in danger or suffering misfortune. This reader/listener imagines being similarly situated, enters these imaginative states into her affective mechanisms which yield off-line feelings of fear or despair as output. But because she only imagines that the character exists and finds himself in the plight in question, rather than believing this to be the case, these feelings are transformed only into off-line attitudes toward him, rather than on-line attitudes. In the second case, in contrast, the reader imagines dangerous or unfortunate circumstances but in which no characters from the story find themselves.[51] In this case, the reader imagines herself being in such circumstances, enters her imagined plight into her affective mechanisms which (again) yield off-line feelings of fear or despair as output. But because there is no character she imagines to be in said plight, no transformation of these feelings along the lines sketched above need occur.

It is worth noting, however, that these accounts of reader emotional reactions do not entail a particular solution to the paradox of fiction. In particular, they do not commit one either to the rejection of reader reactions as genuine or to the rejection of the requirement of genuine emotion that involves belief in the existence of emotional objects. Walton, for example, endorses a solution of the former kind, taking readers' responses to be, in some sense, counterfeit.[52] Matravers, in contrast, endorses the latter approach, and advocates a broader account of genuine emotion.[53] And Currie simply declares himself indifferent on the issue of whether reader emotional reactions count as genuine.

There are two sorts of objections that are raised against the fictional-world (or the intra-world imaginative) approach to reader/listener engagement. The first and, perhaps, less significant worry is that it runs afoul of the phenomenology of the experience of reading/listening to fiction. Matravers, an advocate of the report model, argues that the perceptual model, at least, is incompatible with this phenomenology: "For example, if we read 'Emma groomed and dressed herself with the meticulous care of an actress about to make her debut,' the report model mandates us to imagine reading this sentence as a reported fact. What does the second model mandate us to do? Imagine seeing Emma do this? If that were the case, such an imaginative project would surely interfere with our continued reading."[54] Matravers's argument seems to be that reader phenomenology, which involves imagining reading reports of actual events, is incompatible with (simultaneously) imagining experiencing the reported events: in order to do the latter one would have to abandon doing the former.

What I want to argue, however, is that a similar problem arises for the report model: although imagining *de se* reading/listening to a report is compatible with imagining *de re* of what one reads/listens to that it is a report, engaged fiction appreciators are not typically consciously aware of doing the former. One place where this comes out nicely is in fictional works that consist of stories within stories. Consider, for example, Boulle's *La Planète des Singes.*[55] In this novel, the central story of Ulysse Mérou, the French journalist who travels to a planet on which apes are intelligent, occurs in a manuscript read by a wealthy space-travelling chimpanzee couple. On the most natural construal of the report model, readers would be mandated to imagine reading Mérou's report while imagining being a wealthy space-travelling chimpanzee. This certainly runs counter to my own experience, however, and I expect it runs counter to the typical reader's experience as well. More generally, the experience of imagining reading/listening to a report, as opposed to imagining of what one reads/listens to that it is a report, is simply unfamiliar.

The second and more serious worry is that the fictional-world approach runs afoul of a variant of the problem of the naive backwoodsman. Please recall: a central difficulty for the suspension of disbelief account of engagement is that it erroneously turns appreciators into naive backwoodsmen who falsely believe that they are reading/listening to non-fiction and, hence, are moved to intervene. Now, of course, according to the view on the table, engaged appreciators do not believe that fictional entities exist and find themselves in plights of various kinds but rather simply imagine things of this sort. The problem stems from the fact that, at the same time, they imagine inhabiting the world in which these imagined events occur, either experiencing them directly or reading/listening to reports of them. Ordinarily, when someone reacts emotionally to the plight of another, she is also moved to intervene in some way, and will attempt to do so if there is little risk or cost in so doing. Someone who fears for the safety of others typically desires to warn them of their danger; and someone who pities others typically desires to lessen their suffering. As a result, if engaged appreciators imagine cohabiting a world with fictional characters and have quasi- or off-line emotional reactions to their plights, we should expect them to have quasi- or off-line desires to intervene as well and, perhaps, to engage in imaginative attempts to do so. After all, at bottom, this is simply the expectation that a subject who imagines believing someone is suffering or in danger and imagines caring would (normally) imagine desiring to intervene. But this is exactly what we do not find.

Both the perceptual and report variants of the fictional-world approach offer explanations of the inability of reader/listeners to fictionally intervene in the plights of fictional characters despite cohabitating worlds with them, albeit very different explanations. According to the report model, they imaginatively interact only with reports of the plights of fictional characters and not with the characters themselves. A reader of fiction can no more imaginatively intervene on behalf of a suffering or endangered character than can a reader of fact intervene on behalf of a similarly situated person in real life.[56] According to the perceptual model, in contrast, it is just a brute fact about the conventions of fiction that there is nothing a reader/listener can do to make it fictionally the case that the character is rescued. As Walton puts it, when discussing Henry, who interrupts a performance by jumping onstage putatively to rescue a heroine, "it is not fictional that Henry exists, let alone that he saves anyone. There is no understanding whereby his unplugging of the sound effects, for example, makes it fictional that he saves the heroine."[57]

Matravers takes it to be an advantage of the report model that it explains why the conventions of fiction prevent physical interventions of this sort, rather than just taking this to be a brute fact about these conventions.[58] And this is right as far as it goes. But the report model does not rule out all imaginative interventions on the part of appreciators. After all, if the report is in the present tense and the described events occur proximate to the imagined location of the report, there are few impediments to imaginative intervention on the part of the reader. And even if the report is in the past tense and describes imaginatively non-proximate events, nothing prevents imaginative interventions designed to secure justice after the fact – to punish those who have harmed or endangered favoured characters, or to reward those who have rescued or benefited them.

Moreover – and this is the fundamental problem with the whole approach – neither model explains why appreciators typically lack quasi- or off-line desires to intervene and do not experience feelings of (quasi- or off-line) frustration as a result of their inability to imaginatively (or fictionally) do so. Normally someone whose desire to intervene on behalf of those she cares about is obstructed, by a lack of spatio-temporal proximity or even an inexplicable impotence, would be frustrated by this obstruction. As a result, if the fictional-world approach were correct, we would expect that engaged reader/listeners who react emotionally in these ways to the plights of fictional characters to experience (quasi- or off-line) feelings of frustration as well, at least insofar as they imagine being psychologically typical in this regard while imagining experiencing or reading a report of the (fictional) events at issue. After all, if I imagine being a psychologically typical person who believes someone is suffering and who, as a result, feels pity for him, I should imagine desiring to intervene and being frustrated at my inability to do so. But this is what we do not find: reader/listeners are simply not typically frustrated by their inability to imaginatively intervene. Of course, an advocate of this approach might insist that engaged appreciators do not imagine being psychologically typical, but rather imagine being the kind of person who cares but is unmoved to intervene.[59] This, however, renders the imaginative project required of engaged reader/listeners by the intra-world imaginative approach even more unfamiliar.

2.4 MAKE-BELIEVE AND FICTIONAL TRUTH

In addition to being offered as an account of engaged reading/listening, the notion of make-believe has been deployed in an account of fictional truth. Walton argues that a sentence of the form

In fiction F, S

should be analysed as

(W) Fiction F is such that one who engages in pretense of kind K in a game authorized for it makes it fictional of herself that she speaks truly,[60]

where authorized games are those in which it is the function of the text to serve as a prop.[61] The speaker produces an exemplar of the kind in question by means of pretending to assert "S" (while at the same time actually asserting the Waltonian paraphrase, W).[62] A given act of pretense, p, is an instance of kind K only if it is relevantly similar to this exemplar. If "S" contains no fictional names, p is relevantly similar to the exemplar just in case p is an act in which someone pretends to assert a sentence "T" which in fact expresses the same proposition as "S." But if "S" contains fictional names, then this account of the relevant of respect of similarity is unavailable because Walton insists that sentences containing fictional names do not express propositions. According to Walton, however, it can be fictionally true – i.e., the rules governing a game of make-believe can prescribe so imagining – that distinct speech acts are assertions of the same propositions, even if the utterances produced in the various acts of pretense fail to express propositions at all. In light of this, Walton claims that, when "S" contains fictional names, p is an instance of kind K just in case the rules governing authorized games involving fiction F make it fictional that the respective utterances of "S" and "T" are assertions of the same proposition.[63]

An illustration of this proposal might be timely. Suppose I were to utter

Michael Henchard was the author of his own demise.

According to Walton, in so doing I have pretended to assert this sentence, while at the same time in fact asserting its Waltonian paraphrase. Kind K, in this case, would consist of those acts of pretense of which it is fictionally true, according to the rules governing authorized *The Mayor of Casterbridge* games, that they express the same proposition as my utterance. And my assertion is true only if these very same rules prescribe imagining that each act of pretense which meets this condition is also a true assertion.

Although there are a number of reasons why one might balk at this proposal, the main difficulty, in my view, is that it bottoms out in brute facts about rules governing authorized games of make-believe. And while I have no general objection to brute facts, invoking them at this stage in an account of fictional discourse shrouds a broad and familiar phenomenon in mystery. Consider, again, the sentence

(a) In *The Mayor of Casterbridge*, Michael Henchard was the author of his own demise.

If this sentence is true (or false), then so is

(b) In *The Mayor of Casterbridge*, the Mayor of Casterbridge was the author of his own demise,

and

(c) In *The Mayor of Casterbridge*, Donald Farfrae's employer was the author of his own demise, and even,

> (d) In *The Mayor of Casterbridge*, the title character was the author of his own demise.

In fact, it is easy to find innumerable expressions are that substitutable *salva veritate* with "Michael Henchard" in (a). More generally, the same is true of any fictional name occurring in any sentence of metafictive discourse. Intuitively, the substitutable expressions are those that co-refer with "Michael Henchard." Now, of course, the intuition that there exist expressions co-referential with "'Michael Henchard" runs afoul of the equally strong intuition that "'Michael Henchard" has no referent whatsoever. Nonetheless, the ease with which we can generate expressions that are intuitively co-referential with a given fictional name, as well as the widespread and systematic nature of this phenomenon, cries out for explanation.

On Walton's view, however, the only explanation provided of this phenomenon is that the rules governing authorized games involving *The Mayor of Casterbridge* prescribe imagining that utterances of (a) and (b) are assertions of the same proposition, and that utterances of (a) and (c) are assertions of the same proposition, and that utterances of (b) and (c) are assertions of the same proposition, and so on. But there is no further explanation of this phenomenon to be found; it is just a brute fact about the rules governing authorized games involving *The Mayor of Casterbridge*. One might, of course, amend Walton's view by supposing that (i) the substitutable expressions in question (are meaningful and) stand in significant meaningful relations to one another and (ii) there is a meta-rule governing all authorized games involving works of written and spoken fiction along the following lines: distinct utterances differing only in expressions that stand in such meaning relations to one another are to be imagined to be assertions of the same proposition. But if fictional names are meaningful, then, presumably, an account of the truth conditions of metafictive sentences could be given directly in terms of these meanings. However, this would render Walton's more elaborate theory – and in particular, the detour through rules of make-believe – superfluous.[64]

2.5 TRANS-WORLD IMAGINATIVE RELATIONS

In light of the difficulties that arise for the alternatives, taking appreciator engagement to be a trans-world imaginative relation seems to be the only approach remaining on the table. An advocate of this approach might attribute the problems that undermined the naive view we first considered to be the product of taking engagement to be a doxastic relation rather than to its trans-world aspect. And she might similarly diagnose the problems that arose for the fictional-world approach as stemming from its intra-world element. Hence, to avoid the problems that arose for the alternatives, reader/listener engagement needs to be understood to involve imagining the events described in fictional stories, rather than believing them to be so, and imagining *de re* of the text that it is a report without imagining *de se* reading/listening to a report or experiencing the described events.[65]

Although a specific version of this approach will not be developed and defended until chapter 4, there are a few points worth noting about the approach in general. First, the solution to the paradox of fiction endorsed by advocates of the fictional-world approach can simply be appropriated by advocates of this latter approach. Being in a quasi- or off-line emotional state as a result of imagining finding oneself in the plight of some fictional character simply does not require imagining experiencing the reader and her plight or imagining reading a report of the same. And second, unlike a fictional-world approach, the trans-world imaginative approach does not entail that engaged appreciators should have quasi- or off-line desires to intervene in the plights of fictional characters or quasi- or off-line feelings of frustration as a result of their imaginative inability to do so. Such reactions would be expected only if appreciators imaginatively enter into fictional worlds – imagining believing fictional characters find themselves in various plights and imagining caring about them and their plights.[66] But on the view on the table, appreciators remain outsiders looking in; they care about the plights of characters they neither believe (nor imagine believing) exist and they do not imagine worldly co-habitation with them. As a result, at most they might be expected to have a genuine wish that the story turn out a certain way rather than a quasi- or off-line desire to make it so.

Currie argues, however, that the approach on offer here runs afoul of what he calls the "problem of personality." The difficulty stems from the fact that our emotional reactions to the plights of fictional people are often significantly different from our reactions to the plights of similarly situated actual people: "[we] frequently like and take the part of people in fiction whom we would not like or take in real life. The desires we seem to have concerning fictional things can be very unlike the desires we have concerning real life."[67] Currie illustrates this phenomenon by appealing to his own reaction to the plight of Paul Jago, a central character in C.P.

Snow's novel *The Masters*.[68] Jago is a candidate in an election for the mastership of a college, a position which he desperately wants and for which he is highly unsuited. He ultimately loses the election to a far more suitable candidate, Crawford, and is unsurprisingly distraught. It is worth noting that, despite Jago's lack of qualifications for the mastership, the narrator, Lewis Elliott, remains loyal to him and looks favourably on his candidacy. Currie points out that if this were a real election for a position in his own university, he would have wanted the more qualified candidate to win; "[nonetheless] I wanted Jago to win, and it was with growing dismay that I watched the decline of his fortunes."[69]

Now according to Currie, the solution to this problem presupposes the fictional-world account of engagement. On Currie's view, engaged appreciators imagine *de se* being the kind of person the fictional works they read/listen to are intended for, while imagining reading/listening to the reports they imagine these works to be. As a result, the inputs into their affective mechanisms include both (off-line variants of) the mental states of the fictional character in question and states appropriate to the kind of person the novel invites them to imagine being. *The Masters*, according to Currie, is intended for someone who is similar to the narrator, Elliott; hence, engaged appreciators imagine sharing his positive disposition toward Jago while imagining finding themselves in Jago's plight. The upshot of some such imaginative project is likely to be a more sympathetic reaction to the plight of Jago than one would have to the plight of a similarly situated actual person toward whom one lacked Elliott's positive disposition.

The trouble with Currie's argument is that it is not clear that he has provided a general solution to the problem of personality. Moreover, there is a compelling general solution which is compatible with the trans-world imaginative approach to engagement. In order to achieve full generality, Currie needs to supplement his view with a (general) account of the kind of persons fictional works invite appreciators to imagine being that tracks our differential reactions to the plights of fictions and similarly situated actual people, and it is far from clear that any non-trivial account is forthcoming.[70] Currie's positive suggestion – that reader/listeners are in general invited to imagine being similar to the narrators of fictional works – clearly will not do. The reason is that appreciators' emotional reactions to the plights of fictional characters do not systematically correspond to narrative attitudes toward those characters. Reaction to the plights of fictional characters can differ from reactions to similarly situated actual people even when the narrator is neutral and/or fades into the background. The sympathy I felt for Michael Henchard, for example, when reading *The Mayor of Casterbridge*[71] – a man who drunkenly auctioned off his wife and daughter – is far greater than I would feel for someone who actually engaged in acts of those kinds, despite the absence of a pejorative narrator. Moreover, reactions to the plights of fictional characters can be unsympathetic even when the narrator is quite favourably disposed toward them. For example, readers are typically rather unsympathetic to the plight of Barry Lyndon when reading Thackeray's "Memoirs of Barry Lyndon, Esq., Written by Himself,"[72] despite the fact that the narrator, Lyndon himself, is very well-disposed toward this character. But notwithstanding the inadequacy of this account of what kind of persons fictional works invite readers to imagine being, it is far from clear what the alternative might be.

Finally, as noted above, there is a simple and compelling solution to the problem of personality that is compatible with the trans-world imaginative model: mediation by meticulous informants. Narrators of fictional stories are normally meticulous informants, providing reader/listeners with detailed information about fictional events of the sort they rarely have about actual events. Moreover, like actual informants, not only are these meticulous fictional informants often positively or negatively biased toward the subjects of their reports, they differ in their degree of reliability vis-à-vis the events on which they report.

The reports of (actual and fictional) informants influence our emotional responses to the plights of others by influencing the inputs into our affective mechanisms, including both the circumstances we imagine being in and the mental states we imagine having. Exactly how they influence these inputs in a given case depends on (i) what the informant reports, (ii) the informant's bias for or against the subject of the report, and (iii) the informant's degree of reliability. If the informant is reliable and more or less neutral toward the subject of the report, then the influence on the recipient's (of the report) emotional response to the subject is due entirely to the contents of the informant's reports. What differentiates our responses to the subjects of reports of (neutral and reliable) meticulous informants from those toward similarly situated others is that we have a vastly greater amount of information regarding the plights of the former, including the minutiae of the deliberative process that lead them to make the decisions they do, than we do regarding the latter. And, depending on the content of this information, this can lead to very different emotional responses to the plights of such similarly situated subjects. This, I would argue, explains the atypical responses readers have to the plight of Michael Henchard.

If, however, the informant is reliable and positively or negatively biased toward the subject, the inputs to the recipient's affective mechanisms will not only reflect the detailed information she has about the subject's psychological states but will also be affected by the informant's bias; in particular, she will imagine being worthy of the informant's high (or low) regard. Again, simulations in which one imagines oneself deserving the regard – positive or negative – of a reliable informant can yield very different outputs from those in which one does not imagine oneself to be so deserving. Currie's response to the plight of Michael Henchard can be explained in this way by the fondness Elliott – a reliable meticulous informant – has for him.

Finally, if the informant is unreliable, what the recipient inputs into her affective mechanisms will depend on what, if any, inferences she draws about the subject's character and plight from the informant's unreliable reports and biases. If she judges the informant's distortions to be systematic – his denial of the possession of a property by the subject might, for example, reliably indicate that the subject has said property – then she may have a rich body of information available to input into her affective mechanisms. In my view, readers' unsympathetic reactions to the plight of Barry Lyndon stem from the fact that they are able to infer that he does not warrant the high regard he has for himself and so, when simulating him, imagine being someone unworthy of such regard.[73]

At the end of the day, the trans-world imaginative approach remains the most promising one for developing a theory of appreciator engagement. Not only does it provide a solution to the paradox of fiction without running afoul of the various problems of the naive backwoodsman, it is also compatible with a plausible and general solution to Currie's problem of personality. A worked out trans-world imaginative theory of engagement will be defended in chapter 4.

PART TWO

Authors and Readers – Positive

3

Word-Sculpture

The discussion to this point has been predominantly negative: prominent views of both authorial composition and reader engagement have been evaluated and found lacking. Henceforward the discussion will be largely positive. In this chapter, what I call the "word-sculpture model" of authorial composition will be developed. In chapter 1, views that analysed authorial activity as a species of illocutionary action were, on the one hand, rejected ultimately as a result of their insensitivity to the distinction between the composition of fictional works and storytelling performances of them: while the latter might be thought to involve some kind of illocutionary action, the former could not plausibly be understood to do so. On the other hand, the acknowledgment that, in the act of composition, authors *merely* refrain from illocutionary commitment was also rejected as inadequate: fiction-making is, after all, something positive, and not merely uttering or inscribing without asserting, etc.

The word-sculpture model provides exactly such a positive account of what composition consists in over and above mere utterance or inscription. At the core of the word-sculpture model is the idea that composition is directed toward the production of a certain kind of artifact – in particular fictional works, which are, on the view defended here, a species of word-sculpture. Characterizing fictional works in this way illuminates what I take to be two of their central features. First, fictional works are artifacts that are literally built out of words; and composition is the process whereby authors, using words as building blocks, literally construct them. And second, the relation between authors and readers is better modelled on the relation between sculptors (or, more generally, artists) and appreciators than on the relation between speakers and listeners. As with sculpture, the primary goal of the dissemination of the products of compositional activity is not the achievement of various kinds of communicative ends but that they be appreciated as fictional works.

Of course, I do not want to overstate the analogy between fictional works and other sorts of art objects, or understate the analogy between the composition and dissemination of fictional works on the one hand and communicative acts of various kinds on the other. Unlike other art objects, fictional works are constituted by words and sentences and the proper appreciation of them requires an understanding of the meanings of these linguistic items. Moreover, included among the means of deploying or disseminating fictional works are storytelling performances which consist of communicative acts.[1] And finally, given how it has been characterized so far, ordinary communicative speech seems to involve, in part, improvised word-sculpting (albeit of a kind whose products are normally short-lived.) The upshot is that, rather than being thought of as distinct from communication, the composition and dissemination of word-sculptures should be thought of as a broader category into which ordinary conversational communication – with its specific communicative goals and modes of deployment – falls as a special case. This idea will be developed in more detail below.

This chapter consists of four parts. First, the nature of the kind of artifacts authors create – word-sculptures – is elucidated. Of central importance are the nature of words, out of which word-sculptures are constructed, and the distinction between *works* and *texts*. Second, the notion of a word-sculpture practice is introduced and used in the classification of various sorts of word-sculptures. Third, the fiction-centred world-sculpture practice is developed and an account of authorial composition framed in terms of that practice is defended. And finally, a moderate institutional theory of fictionality which invokes the fiction-centred practice is proposed.

3.1 WORDS AND WORD-SCULPTURES

Word-sculptures are, as above, a kind of artifact. As such, they are created and not discovered, despite being capable of multiple occurrence or instantiation.[2] Composition is the process by which authors create such artifacts. The constituents out of which word-sculptures are made, words, are themselves artifacts, albeit not normally created by the authors who use them. In principle, a word-sculpture could consist of any finite sequence of words, but our focus here will be on those consisting, at least in large part, of (sequences of) grammatical sequences. Word-sculptures come into existence as a result of the sometimes quite complex process of selecting and recording words and sentences in which authors – or, perhaps better, word-sculptors – of various kinds engage.[3]

A key feature of words – shared by the word-sculptures of which they are constituents – is that they are capable of multiple occurrences. The word "the," for example, occurs on numerous occasions in this very manuscript. A natural approach is to take the relation between words and their occurrences to be the relation between types and tokens; and since occurrences of words are (normally) sequences of sounds or inscriptions, it is tempting to think of words as types of sound or inscription sequences.[4] There are a number of reasons to balk, however. First, being a word is a status an object acquires in virtue of playing a certain role in the intentional communicative behaviour of the members of a linguistic community. As a result, even if words are orthographic or phonographic types, not all of their tokens count as word-occurrences. In particular, accidentally formed tokens – produced by erosion patterns or the wind – do not so count because they fail to be the products of the right kind of intentional behaviour.[5] And second, not only are word-occurrences of distinct orthographic or phonographic types often occurrences of the same word – consider "color" and "colour," for example – words can survive changes in spelling and pronunciation over time.[6]

A better picture is provided by Kaplan's "common currency" account of words.[7] According to this picture, words are complex networks of appropriately causally linked events, where word-occurrences are the events that make up the networks. In effect, rather than taking words to be types and occurrences to be their tokens, Kaplan takes words to be continuants made up of stages – word-occurrences – bound together by a continuity relation. Where I differ from Kaplan is over the nature of this continuity relation. According to Kaplan, in order for a speaker's linguistic output to count as an occurrence of the same word as some prior linguistic input, the speaker need only intend to imitate (or standardize) the perceived input. Even if this intention is unsuccessful, and the input and output stand in no interesting similarity relation to one another, Kaplan claims that they are nevertheless occurrences of the same word: as long as "the source of change was … due to the filters at the psycho-physical transitions points … [and] the cognitive link that was to take place within the black box was in order, we would still say it's the same word."[8]

The trouble with this weak continuity relation is that it runs afoul of the role words play in communication. In order to understand our conversational interlocutors, we need to be able to recognize the words they produce. But if Kaplan's view is correct, we cannot do so on the basis of their observed features: the fact that an utterance/inscription looks or sounds like an occurrence of a given word, or fails to do so, does not decide the issue one way or the other.[9] The alternative is to retain Kaplan's common currency model but supplement it with a stronger continuity relation incompatible with the suggestion that every variation in spelling or pronunciation produced with the right intentions suffices for a change in sign design, allowing instead only those variations which come into sufficiently widespread use to so count. Given the relatively slow processes by which words come into and go out of widespread use, the sign designs which count as occurrences of a word will be sufficiently stable over time to accommodate the role words play in communication.[10]

Like the words out of which they are composed, word-sculptures are also capable of multiple occurrences. An occurrence of a word-sculpture consists of an appropriately unified sequence of word-occurrences.[11] There are, however, different ways to individuate word-sculptures. The primary distinction I have in mind is that between works and texts. Texts are (more or less) fixed sequences of words: two word-sculpture occurrences are occurrences of the same text just in case they consist of the occurrences of (more or less) the same sequence of words.[12] As above, this does not entail that two occurrences of a single text need to consist of sequences of word-occurrences of the same orthographic or phonographic types. Moreover, given that words can undergo changes in meaning over time, two occurrences of the same text need not even consist of word-occurrences with the same meanings.

Although every word-sculpture occurrence which is the occurrence of a work is, in the sense of identity, the occurrence of a text, works themselves cannot be identified with texts – (more or less) fixed sequences of words. As Howell has persuasively argued, fictional works such as traditional stories, fairy tales, and oral epics can have distinct occurrences – verbal performances – which consist of very different arrangements of words: "such works are not defined in terms of fixed textual sequences but rather in terms of determinate (but often still somewhat fluid) plot sequences that are verbally expressed."[13] Even if we restrict our attention to written works, any attempt to identify works with texts runs into insuperable difficulties. Not only can distinct drafts of written works differ quite radically in their word arrangements,[14] distinct editions of completed works can also differ substantially in this regard. Moreover, translations of works into different languages consist predominantly of words distinct from those found in the original, albeit largely of words sharing the meanings of those found in the original.[15]

Rather than identifying them with texts, works are better thought of on the model of Kaplan's common currency account of words as complex networks of causally linked word-sculpture occurrences. In the paradigmatic (and perhaps idealized) case, one word-sculpture occurrence counts as the first completed version of a work. It acquires this status when the author (or authors) judges it to be finished, or when the publisher decides it is ready to be sent to the printer, or the like. It is normally preceded by a sequence of word-sculpture occurrences – drafts – out of which it arose.[16] And not only will there typically be multiple copies made of it – at least if it is a written work – there will often subsequently be produced word-sculpture occurrences, consisting of (sometimes substantially) different arrangements of words, but nevertheless counting as occurrences of the same work.

Causally adjacent word-sculpture occurrences – whose causal relation is unmediated by other word-sculpture occurrences – are occurrences of the same work, on this picture, just in case they stand in a continuity relation to one another. Providing an account of the exact nature of this continuity relation is complicated by the fact that at least three different kinds of cases are subsumed by it: cases in which one occurrence is a copy of another, cases in which one occurrence is an edited version of another, and cases in which one occurrence is an oral performance of another. Nevertheless, there are three general features of this relation that can be delineated. First, it is an intentional relation. The author (or authors) of the later occurrence has to intend to produce something appropriately related to the earlier occurrence. In particular, she has to intend to produce a copy, an edited version, or a performance of the earlier occurrence.[17] Second, this intention needs to be sufficiently successful: if the author fails to successfully copy or edit or perform her intended target, then whatever she has produced is not an occurrence of the same work. Of course, what counts as success depends on whether the author is copying, editing, or performing: the requirements of a successful performance in the oral storytelling tradition, for example, are far less stringent than those for successfully producing a copy of a written work. And third, the author of the later occurrence needs to have the proper authority. Although different authors, editors, and performers can produce distinct occurrences of the same work, not every successfully produced copy, edition, or performance so counts. Consider, for example, someone who, without the permission of the still living (and copyright holding, let's say) author, produces an edited version of the latter's work. Again, what is required for such authority depends on whether the author of the latter occurrence is copying, editing, or performing the earlier one.

This continuity relation will, in general, generate complex branching networks of word-sculpture occurrences which in the ideal case will be centred around a unique first completed version. There will typically be one or more branches converging on this locus as well as a number of branches diverging from it. A work is, on the picture on the table, one of these networks. And two (adjacent or non-adjacent) occurrences are occurrences of the same work just in case they form part of the same network. There are, however, at least two deviations from ideality worth noting here. First, there may be works which lack unique causal loci and, instead, consist of multiple, perhaps even largely causally disjoint, causal networks centred around distinct word-sculpture occurrences. Works in the oral storytelling tradition often have this kind of structure. And second, there may be intuitively distinct works which share word-sculpture occurrences. I have in mind here cases in which an author of a work comes back perhaps years later and reworks an early draft in a significantly different direction. The upshot is that unless we are content to depart from the intuitive conception of a work, the account of work identity on offer here will have to be supplemented with something in addition to the continuity relation sketched above. For present purposes, however, this account will suffice.

Unlike works and texts, some word-sculptures consist, or are capable of, only a single occurrence. This category includes what might be called "word-art": artworks consisting of painted or carved (or what have you) sentences. Such artworks are, of course, constituted by word-sculpture occurrences. But if they are, in Goodman's sense, autographic,[18] then no other word-sculpture occurrence counts as an occurrence of the same art object. A more interesting (for our purposes) category consists of what might be called "illocutionary word-sculptures," which consist of sentences used in the performance of illocutionary acts. Like all word-sculptures, they are constituted by word-sculpture occurrences. But like autographic word-art, and unlike works, no other word-sculpture occurrence counts as an occurrence of the same illocutionary act. Please note: although illocutionary word-sculptures are not works, by producing an occurrence which stands in the continuity relation to an illocutionary word-sculpture, an author could create a work of which it is a part.

Finally, it is worth noting that naturally occurring phenomena – erosion patterns, sounds produced by the wind, and the like – do not count as word-sculptures, no matter how orthographically or phonographically similar they are to them: they are neither artifacts nor are they constituted by words. As a result, they cannot count as works – fictional or otherwise.

One might, of course, worry that this involves ruling out the possibility of naturally occurring fictions by fiat rather than honest toil. This worry can be alleviated, however, by noting that fictionality can, at least in principle, apply to a broader class of entities than works. This will be addressed in more detail in section IV below.

3.2 WORD-SCULPTURE PRACTICES

Again, the primary goal of this chapter is to provide an account of fictional composition. In particular, what is required is an account of what authors positively do when they perform their acts of fiction-making over and above refraining from illocutionary commitment. As it stands, however, no such account has been provided: to characterize composition merely as word-sculpting – creating word-sculptures – is to do little more than to claim that it does not (necessarily) involve illocutionary action. In order to provide the required positive account, the notion of a word-sculpture practice will have to be developed. The basic idea is that fictional composition involves producing a word-sculpture designed to play a certain role in what might be called the "fictional" or "fiction-centred" word-sculpture practice.

A practice, in the sense at issue here, is a pattern of behaviour sustained by a goal or goals. A commonplace example is the greeting practice wherein people verbally or non-verbally acknowledge certain others when they encounter them, and which serves the purpose of maintaining social relationships with those in what might be called one's "greeting circle." A word-sculpture practice is a practice in which word-sculptures play a central role. Examples include contractual practices, love note practices, academic essay practices, and fictional practices, as well the practice (or practices) of using word-sculptures to perform illocutionary acts of various kinds. Depending on the word-sculpture practice at issue, the sustaining goals can be the normal purposes of the creators of the word-sculptures, the recipients of the word-sculptures, or can be purposes shared by creators and recipients. The love note practice, for example, is sustained by the love note author's goal of generating feelings of romantic love in a desired lover. The fiction-centred practice, in contrast, is sustained by the goal of fiction recipients of having a certain kind of reading or appreciative experience.[19] And the illocutionary practice – of using word-sculptures to perform illocutionary acts – is sustained by the shared interest of creators and recipients (or more familiarly, speakers and listeners) in communication. Please note: the patterns of behaviour which in part constitute word-sculpture practices need not be strictly conventional;[20] nevertheless, most (if not all) word-sculpture practices presuppose (or otherwise depend on) the linguistic conventions which sustain the correlations between words and their meanings.

It is important to distinguish between two activities in which a participant in a word-sculpture practice might engage: composition and deployment. Composition is the activity of creating a word-sculpture; deployment is the activity of circulating it among other participants in the practice. What kind of word-sculpture one produces or how one goes about deploying it will, of course, depend on the nature of the word-sculpture practice in which one is participating. Although paradigmatically the author of a word-sculpture subsequently goes on to deploy it herself, these activities are nevertheless independent: one can deploy a word sculpture one did not create. One might, for example, send a Shakespearean sonnet as a love note to a desired lover. And one can create a word sculpture without deploying it. Unpublished academic manuscripts come to mind as a personally worrying example.

The tendency to inadequately attend to the distinction between these activities – which arguably underlies illocutionary analyses of composition of the kind rejected in chapter 1 – presumably stems from the fact that in the spoken variant of the illocutionary practice these two activities normally occur simultaneously. More precisely, in oral conversation compositional acts are typically performed improvisationally during the act of deployment. Nevertheless, this is an inessential feature of the illocutionary word-sculpture practice. Speakers sometimes do compose the sentences they mean to use in assertions, requests, etc., ahead of time; consider, for example, someone temporarily incapable of speech communicating using handwritten notes, or someone preparing herself for an expected confrontational conversation. Moreover, improvisational composition also occurs, albeit less frequently, in word-sculpture practices in which the composition/deployment distinction is uncontroversial; consider, for example, improvised storytelling and off-the-cuff academic presentations.

Before going on to look at composition and deployment in more detail, it is worth noting that, on the view on the table, word-sculptures are categorized in terms of the practices for which they are designed and in which they are deployed. Other things being equal, a word-sculpture counts as a contract, for example, just in case it is designed to satisfy the kinds of goals that sustain the contractual practice and deployed in a way pursuant of those goals.[21] Practices, however, do not have sharp boundaries. Practices can overlap or be nested in one another, and whether a particular action occurs as part of one or the other (or both) practices can be simply indeterminate. Moreover, practices can both evolve over time and be displaced by successor practices; but there are (arguably) no determinate diachronic identity conditions for practices and, as a result, it may be indeterminate whether or not a practice existing at one time is the same practice as one existing at another. Thus, according to the account on offer, there will be a corresponding vagueness in the categorization of word-sculptures. I take this to be a virtue, not a vice, of this account.

Composition is the activity of producing or generating word-sculptures. It is an intentional activity, performed by an author, whose goal is the creation of an artifact – a fictional work, an academic essay, a question, or a request. Paradigmatically, it involves the selection and recording of sequences of words and sentences, although in improvisational composition, as occurs in ordinary speech, selected sentences are normally deployed without being systematically recorded.[22] Except when engaging in the improvised illocutionary practice, a composing author refrains from illocutionary commitment: in selecting and recording as she does, she does not intend to produce an effect in an audience by means of their recognition that she intend that they do so. The question that has heretofore exercised us, however, is what, over and above so refraining, do authors intend to do when they produce word-sculptures of various kinds. The answer is that they intend to produce a word-sculpture appropriate to some word-sculpture practice or another; that is, authors design the word-sculptures they produce to play certain kinds of roles in various word-sculpture practices. Contracts, for example, are designed to legally oblige their signatories to engage in specified courses of action; and fictional works are designed to produce (or facilitate) certain sorts of appreciative experiences in those who read/listen to them.

There are two further features of compositional activity worth noting at this time. First, although the artifacts they produce are designed to play a certain role in a word-sculpture practice, authors need not intend to deploy them in the practice. An author may, for example, intend to produce a philosophical essay without ever intending to present or publish it. This is true even of word-sculptures designed for the illocutionary practice: someone might prepare a question they never mean to ask or a request they never mean to make; but what they have produced is not any less a question or a request for that reason.[23] And second, an author's compositional intentions – to create an artifact capable of playing a certain kind of role in a word-sculpture practice – can be unsuccessful as a result of either the content or the style of the word-sculpture she produces.

Producing a grocery list as a love note would be a failure of content: except under highly specialized circumstances, a grocery list will not express the author's feelings toward a desired lover, nor will it incline this person to enter into a romantic relationship with the author. And producing a contract in a loose vernacular rather than Legalese – or, perhaps, a love note without poetic language – counts as a failure of style. Like failures of content, such failures may interfere with the effectiveness with which the word-sculpture plays its intended role.

Deployment is the activity of circulating word-sculptures to various people. Paradigmatically, word-sculptures are deployed by their authors, but they can be deployed by others. Consider, for example, someone who enters into a contractual agreement by simply signing her name to a document she found online. The manner in which a word-sculpture is appropriately deployed will depend on the word-sculpture practice in which it is deployed. Two broad distinctions in the manner of deployment are worth noting. The first concerns to whom a word-sculpture is circulated – an individual or a group. And the second concerns how a word-sculpture is deployed – by means of an oral performance or by presenting its recipients with a written copy. Of course, many kinds of word-sculptures can be deployed both orally and via the presentation of a written copy to both individuals and groups. Differences will remain, however, in which individuals or groups they are circulated to and in both the contexts of their oral presentation and the vehicles of their written circulation. Academic papers are predominantly circulated among (other) academics, orally at academic conferences and in written form by means of academic journals available through university libraries; fictional stories are circulated among the fiction-reading public, orally at largely non-academic public readings by their authors and in written form by means of bound manuscripts available through commercial booksellers. Please note: not only is it not necessary that a word-sculpture be deployed by its author, it need not be deployed in the word-sculpture practice for which it was designed; a Shakespearean sonnet used as a love note again counts as a nice example.

As with composition, the deployment of word-sculptures is a goal-directed activity. Normally, the goal of a word-sculpture deployer coincides with the sustaining goals of the practice in which she deploys her word-sculpture. So, for example, the typical goal of someone who circulates a love note is that of generating feelings of romantic love in a desired lover, which is the sustaining goal of the love note practice; and the typical goal of someone who deploys a contract is that of legally obliging various signatories to specified courses of action, which is the sustaining goal of the contractual practice. It is worth noting that in addition to problems stemming from the failure to compose a word-sculpture with the right content or in the appropriate style, the goals of word-sculpture deployers can be frustrated by deployment errors. This occurs not only when a word-sculpture reaches the wrong audience, as when a love note is misdirected, but also when it reaches the right audience in the wrong manner. I have in mind here examples such as academic papers orally presented in a comedic style and written copies of novels labelled as non-fiction. Finally, the deployment of a word-sculpture can be insincere in the sense that someone lacking the practice-sustaining purpose might deploy it with the intention of deceiving the recipient or recipients into believing that she does. Someone might, for example, give a love note to a person whose affection she does not desire or pass off an intentionally falsified account of her life as autobiography.

At this point it might be rejoined that although the composition of word-sculptures need not involve the performance of any illocutionary acts, their deployment inevitably does. After all, not only do the goals of deployment coincide with the illocutionary purposes of speech acts of various kinds, acts of deployment are capable of the very same sorts of infelicities as are illocutionary acts. As a result, my claim that illocutionary action is just one among many modes of deployment of word-sculptures is misguided. Despite their similarities, however, illocutionary action and the more general word-sculpture deployment are distinct in three important respects. First, recall that what is characteristic of illocutionary action is the intention to produce an effect in an audience by means of the latter's recognition of this intention. In contrast, at least some word-sculptures are deployed with the intention that an effect be achieved by means of the recipient's recognition not of the intention that this effect be achieved, but rather of his recognition of the kind of word-sculpture with which he has been presented. Someone who deploys a contract, for example, intends that the recipient commit himself to a course of conduct not because he recognizes that she intends that he do so, but because he recognizes that it was a contract that he signed. Second, although the illocutionary purposes of certain speech acts may coincide with the sustaining purposes of a word-sculpture practice, someone who deploys a word-sculpture in this practice may be unaware of this coincidence. Suppose, for example, that reading a word-sculpture as fiction involves imagining or making-believe the propositions expressed by its constituent sentences. An author of fiction might nevertheless intend that the recipients of her work read it as fiction without realizing that this involves imaginative activities of this kind. As a result, deploying a word-sculpture in the fiction-centred practice cannot be identified with inviting or requesting (or what have you) an audience to imagine the requisite propositions. And third, one can distinguish between the overall purpose of a stretch of discourse – a series of illocutionary actions – and the purposes of the individual speech acts that make it up. Paradigmatically, when engaging in illocutionary interaction, the overall goal of the discourse is intended to be achieved by means of achievement of the purposes of the constituent actions. And while deployers of especially longer written word-sculptures may share the overall goals of those engaging in extended illocutionary discourse, they need not (and typically do not) share the sentence by sentence illocutionary purposes of the latter.

One might argue that although the circulation of written variants of word-sculptures does not always involve the performance of illocutionary actions, their oral deployment inevitably does. I am sympathetic to this line of reasoning; in my view, illocutionary pretense and *sui generis* fictive illocutions find their proper homes as accounts of storytelling performances rather than as accounts of fictionality *per se*. Nevertheless, a couple of complications remain. First, exactly what illocutionary action one performs by means of the oral deployment of a word-sculpture depends on the word-sculpture practice in which it is deployed. For example, a sentence used to make an assertion when orally deployed in the illocutionary practice would be used to engage in illocutionary pretense or perform a fictive illocutionary act if orally deployed in the fictional practice. And second, exactly what kind of speech act is performed by means of the oral deployment of a word-sculpture depends on who deploys it.[24] Consider, for example, a love note which includes the sentence "I love you." If the author of the love note were to orally deploy it – perhaps reciting it to her desired lover – she would (arguably) thereby assert that she loves the object of her desire. If, however, someone else orally deployed the note – perhaps a proxy enjoined by a shy love note author to recite it on her behalf – he would neither assert that he loves the author's desired lover nor assert that the author does so (even though he might, under the right circumstances, pragmatically imply the latter).[25] Although he might perform some kind of illocutionary pretense, or perhaps some kind of *sui generis* proxy illocutionary act, he does not make any kind of assertion.

3.3 THE FICTION-CENTRED PRACTICE

Let us turn now to the fiction-centred practice – the word-sculpture practice for which fictional works are designed and in which they are deployed. The first thing to note is that rather than being a single practice with well-delineated boundaries, the fiction-centred practice is actually a cluster of related practices which lack clear boundaries. There is, roughly, a distinct word-sculpture practice – or, perhaps better, subpractice – corresponding to each kind of fictional work there is. And not only are there numerous distinct categories of fictional works – novels, poems, plays, songs, oral epics, etc. – there are also a number of distinct genres of fiction – mysteries, romances, fantasies, etc. Moreover, not only is it not always a determinate matter whether a fictional work falls into one category or genre or another, it is also not always a determinate matter whether a work counts as fiction or non-fiction. Historical fiction, for example, is sometimes hard to distinguish from historical non-fiction in which the author creatively fills in details left open by the historical record.

Within any practice, there are a number of roles that a participant in the practice can occupy. In, for example, the greeting practice noted above, there exist the roles of greeter and greeted which the same person can occupy on different occasions. Like all word-sculpture practices, the fiction-centred practice includes authorial and recipient roles: occupants of the former role compose fictional works; occupants of the latter read or listen to them. In addition, there are stable distributive and evaluative roles: publishers and booksellers act as middlemen in the transfer of works from authors to fiction recipients; critics influence the choices among fictional works that recipients make. It is worth noting, however, that fictional works are often disseminated informally by authors to reader/listeners, without mediation by publishers and critics.

Corresponding to each of the distinct roles participants in the fiction-centred practice can occupy are characteristic or paradigmatic goals associated with those roles. For example, the paradigmatic goal of the distributive role(s) might be financial gain, whereas the goal associated with the evaluative role might be influence over recipient choices. Nevertheless, the goal that ultimately sustains the whole fiction-centred practice is the paradigmatic recipient goal: reader/listener engagement with fictional works (or, perhaps, the pleasures derived thereof). It is only (or, perhaps better, mostly) because many people desire to read or listen to fictional works, and take pleasure in so doing, that authors are moved to produce such word-sculptures. Moreover, this desire on the part of the recipients is what enables distributors to achieve financial gain through their actions and is a background presupposition without which the goal associated with the evaluative role would be empty.

Strictly speaking, it is not the desire to read or listen to fictional works per se that ultimately sustains the fiction-centred practice, but rather the desire to read or listen to them as fiction. An account of reader engagement with fiction will be developed in detail in chapter 4; nevertheless, a few comments are in order at this point. First, when reading/listening to a word sculpture as fiction, concern with truth and justification fades into the background. This is not to say that engaged readers have no concern with such things: textual accuracy is one measure of works in certain genres, such as historical novels; and to fully appreciate a satirical work, for example, one might have to recognize who or what is being satirized. Nonetheless, truth is largely irrelevant to the pleasure one derives from reading/listening to works of fiction, and is more often than not motivationally inert in the decision to engage in said activity. And second, while I agree with Walton, Currie, and others that reading/listening to a work as fiction is an imaginative activity of some sort – one which requires of fiction recipients that they imagine or make-believe various things – my account of this activity differs from the received view in a number of important respects. One difference worth emphasizing is that, contra Currie and Walton,[26] reading/listening to as fiction involves *de re* but not *de se* imaginings: engaged reader/listeners imagine *de re* of fictional texts that they are reports of actual events but do not (or need not) imagine *de se* reading such reports. And contra Currie and Lewis,[27] readers need not imagine the reporter to be a fictional teller. Rather, they need only imagine the work to be the product of a figure I call the "narrative informant" who may, but need not, inhabit the (fictional) world regarding which she makes her report.

At this point, we are ready to address the central goal of this chapter: providing an account of what fictional composition consists in over and above producing a word-sculpture while refraining from illocutionary commitment. In section 3.2 above, a generic answer was given: in addition to refraining from illocutionary commitment, composers intend that the word-sculptures they produce be appropriate to the word-sculpture practice in which they are participating; in the case at hand, this involves producing a word-sculpture that is designed to be read or listened to as fiction. Given the sketch of reading as fiction, the upshot is that composition consists in (intentionally) producing a word-sculpture that is designed to be imagined by its recipients to be a report of a narrative informant. It is worth noting, however, that an author need not intend to disseminate or otherwise deploy the product of her labours: it need only be designed for this kind of appreciation; it need not actually be so appreciated nor intended to be so.[28]

As it stands, the account of fictional composition on the table presupposes the existence of the fiction-centred word-sculpture practice. What is required is that an author produce a word-sculpture that is designed to be read as fiction – that is, read in the way in which word-sculptures deployed in the fiction-centred practice are read – whether or not she knows in what that consists. One might wonder whether or not someone could engage in fictional composition in the absence of this practice. Wilder argues that this is not possible: "Authors may sometimes have intentions to write fiction, but these intentions can only be framed in particular historical circumstance: circumstances in which a tradition of writing fiction already exists and is recognized by writers and readers as existing."[29] There are, however, three ways of understanding Wilder's point: logically, conceptually, and historically. In my view, only the latter interpretation is defensible and, as we shall see, it is compatible with fictional composition in the absence of the fiction-centred practice.

To say an intention depends logically on a practice is to say that the intended goal essentially depends on the practice and cannot be specified independently of it. The goal of checkmating one's opponent's king, for example, depends on the practice of chess in this sense. But there is no reason to think that the goal of producing an object designed to be imagined to be a report of a narrative informant depends in this way on the fiction-centred practice. After all, this goal can be, and just has been, specified without making mention of the practice.

Wilder's view seems to be that the fictional composition depends conceptually on the fiction-centered practice: "Fiction only became possible in Western Europe … due to shifts in the material and intellectual context: e.g., the development of secular and humanistic concepts of authorship …"[30] The idea here is that the concepts required to read or listen to a word-sculpture as fiction, or to intend that others do so, although specifiable independently of the fiction-centered practice, were nevertheless dependent on or (in some sense) presupposed by it. The model here is the role the practices of science and engineering play in the possession of propositional attitudes toward television sets or quantum mechanics and the like. Prior to the advent of modern science and engineering, humans simply lacked the conceptual wherewithal to believe quantum mechanics or desire television sets. But the concepts required of fictional composers by the present account – of informants, reports, and imagination – lack this technical character and were presumably widely available prior to the advent of the fiction-centred practice.

It is, however, presumably true that the intention to produce an object designed to be imagined to be a report of a narrative informant depends historically on the fiction-centred practice. The possession of this authorial goal in the absence of the fiction-centred practice is not only intelligible; authors had the conceptual wherewithal to desire it – and readers had the conceptual wherewithal to satisfy it – prior to the advent of the practice. Nevertheless until the fiction-centred practice emerged, recipients of word-sculptures as a matter of fact did not read them in this way nor did authors intend that they do so. Only with the presumably gradual emergence of the practice did these intentions and activities become widespread. But what is important to note, for present purposes, is that despite the fact that authors did not (except rarely if at all) intend that the products of their labours be appreciated in this way prior to the existence of the fiction-centred practice, they could in its absence have done so.

3.4 THE WEAK INSTITUTIONAL THEORY OF FICTIONALITY

What remains is to offer an account of fictionality, that is, an account of what features a word-sculpture needs to have in order to count as fictional. In what follows, fictionality will be treated primarily as a property of those word-sculptures which count as works; occurrences of texts can be fictional but not texts themselves – after all, a given text can have both fictional and non-fictional occurrences. There are, broadly speaking, three approaches to fictionality that have been defended in the literature: speech act theories,[31] functional theories,[32] and institutional theories.[33] As we have seen in chapter 1, speech act theories run into insuperable difficulties largely because there are simply multitudes of fictional works whose composition and subsequent deployment do not involve the performance of substantial speech acts of any kind. In what follows, I will be developing a version of the institutional theory. But before doing so, it will be worth saying a few words about Walton's functional theory, both to situate and motivate my alternative. According to Walton, "[w]orks of fiction are … works whose function is to serve as props in games of make-believe,"[34] where "[a] thing may be said to have the function of serving a certain purpose, regardless of the intentions of its maker, if things of that *kind* are typically or normally meant by their makers to serve that purpose."[35] There are two features of Walton's view which are relevant for present purposes. First, it is worth noting that aside from our disagreement regarding the role of *de se* imagining in engaged reading and listening, Walton's account of the function of fiction more or less coincides with my account of the sustaining purpose of the fiction-centred word-sculpture practice. But second, Walton's view runs into difficulties – which, as we shall see, my alternative avoids – by invoking an intention-independent notion of a kind of work. Given that works of fiction and non-fiction can, in principle, share all stylistic and content properties, the kind into which a work falls will have to depend on its extrinsic or relational properties.[36] And it is far from clear in what, aside from authorial intentions, these properties could plausibly consist.

An institutional theory defines fictionality in terms of the fiction-centred practice. A strong institutional definition entails that nothing could count as fiction in the absence of this practice. A weak institutional theory, in contrast, although it defines fictionality in terms of features of the practice, is nevertheless compatible with the existence of fictional works in circumstances in which the practice does not and never has existed. The version of the institutional theory on offer here defines fictionality in terms of authorial compositional intentions. In particular, it defines fiction in terms of the intention to produce word-sculptures designed to be read/listened to as fiction, that is, in the way in which they are read/listened to by word-sculpture recipients in the fiction-centered practice. But, given that, as above, such intentions depend only historically, and not logically or conceptually, on the practice, this opens up two distinct ways in which something can count as fictional.[37]

All fictional works, on my view, share the following feature: they are composed with the intention that they be objects designed to be read/listened to as fiction where, as above, reading/listening to a word-sculpture as fiction involves imagining it to be the report of a narrative informant. The difference between the two sorts of fictional works – which is reminiscent of Donnellan's referential/attributive distinction[38] – hangs on how an author conceives of the goal of her compositional intention. In the first case, the author intends to produce something designed to be read or listened to as fiction, whatever that might be. That is, she conceives of her goal as that of producing something designed to be appreciated in the way in which word-sculptures deployed in the fiction-centred practice are appreciated; and she may, but need not, realize what that mode of appreciation is. As should be obvious, an author could not have such an intention in the absence of the practice.[39] In the second case, the author conceives of the goal of her compositional intention to be the production of an object designed to be imagined to be the report of a narrative informant. And she may, but need not, realize that this is what reading or listening to a word-sculpture as fiction consists in. Again, as should be obvious, an author could have such an intention in the absence of the fiction-centred practice.

Before looking at the implications of this picture vis-à-vis certain puzzle cases, it is worth considering a couple of potential objections. First, one might worry that if word-sculpture practices can survive diachronic changes in their sustaining purposes, then there might be no fact of the matter as to whether or not a work which counts as fiction in the second, practice-independent way. Suppose, for example, that I am right that reading/listening to a work as fiction currently consists in *de re* but not *de se* imagining. But suppose that in the future readers and listeners have a practice of reading and listening to word-sculptures in which they engage in both *de re* and *de se* imagining, and suppose that this practice counts as the continuation of the fiction-centred practice rather than the displacement of it by a new practice. This seems to prevent taking a word-sculpture designed for *de re* but not *de se* imagining to be either fiction or some kind of non-fiction. My first inclination is to resist the suggestion that a word-sculpture practice could survive this kind of diachronic change, but it is not clear how to adjudicate this issue and I will not attempt to do so here. Nevertheless if it turns out that such change is possible, I will retreat to a time-relativized account of fictionality, at least as it applies to practice-independent works. So, for example, a work designed for *de re* but not *de se* imagining would count as fiction relative to the present time but not relative to some future time in which the fiction-centred practice has evolved in the way sketched above.[40]

Second, one might worry that the definition of fictionality on offer is too loose in the sense that it requires only that authors of fiction have the right kind of intentions and not that these intentions be successful in any sense. As long as an author produces a word-sculpture with the intention that it be designed to be read as fiction it counts as fiction, whether or not it is suitable for this purpose; even a grocery list or phone book would count, as long as it was produced with the right intentions. The first thing to note is that the main alternatives to this approach also fail to address this worry. As it stands, a grocery list or a phone book would count as fictional, according to speech act analyses, as long as the author engaged in illocutionary pretense or *sui generis* fictive illocutionary action in producing it. But second, and more importantly, in my view the notion of success in this sense finds a better home as part of a theory of the value of fiction rather than a theory of fictionality *per se*. There is no reason to suppose that a grocery list could not be fictional, but it might nevertheless be bad fiction.

I turn now to a couple of puzzle cases. There are, broadly speaking, two sorts of cases of interest for present purposes: cases in which the author of a putative work of fiction did not intend it to be read as fiction, and so called naturally occurring or authorless fiction. I will consider each in turn. First, often works intended by their author to be read as some kind of non-fiction come to be widely read as fiction. Fraudulent memoirs, such as James Frey's *A Million Little Pieces*, are a nice example.[41] In my view, there is a distinction between being fiction and being read as fiction; and despite their widespread use in the fiction-centred practice, such works retain their status as non-fiction. Consider the following analogy. In a pinch, butter knives make serviceable screwdrivers and they are widely used as such. Nevertheless, they do not literally become transformed into screwdrivers for that reason. They remain butter knives which happen to be used as screwdrivers. Similarly, the fact that works of non-fiction come to be read as fiction does not transform them into works of fiction: they remain works of non-fiction that happen to be used as fiction.[42]

Finally, one might worry about the implications of my view vis-à-vis (hypothetical) naturally occurring fictions – erosion patterns orthographically very similar to written texts and noises produced by winds phonographically very similar to spoken texts. Now while it is true that, at least in principle, such phenomena could be read or listened to as fiction, it is an implication of my view that nevertheless they are not fictions. Not only do they fail to be the products of intentional activity at all – let alone the right kind of intentional activity – they do not even consist of words. Words, like the word-sculptures of which they are constituents, are artifacts – products of intentional activity. And even a naturally occurring phenomenon intrinsically identical to (an occurrence) of a word or a sequence of words would not, for that reason, be a word or word-sequence itself. Nevertheless nothing would prevent someone who happened across it from reading it as fiction.[43]

3.5 CONCLUSION

The central goal of this chapter was two-fold: to give an account of compositional activity that explains what authors of fiction do over and above refraining from illocutionary commitment, and to give an account of fictionality commensurable with this account of composition. To this end, the word-sculpture model, with the concomitant notion of a word-sculpture practice, was developed. The application of this model to the accounts of composition and fictionality, however, presupposed the heretofore underdeveloped notion of reading and listening to a work as fiction. The time has come for this particular cheque to be cashed.

4

Narrative Informants

In this chapter, I develop a positive account of reader and listener engagement with literary fiction. At the core of this account lies a figure I call the "narrative informant." Readers and listeners imagine of fictional texts both that they are reports made by narrative informants and what narrative informants reveal by means of their reports. As should be obvious, this picture requires of reader/listeners that they engage in *de dicto* and *de re* imagining. But it does not require any *de se* imaginative activity. In the course of developing this view, accounts of both the nature of the narrative informant and the contents of her revelations need to be given.

A few preliminary comments are in order. First, unlike authors of fiction, narrative informants are fact-tellers rather than fiction-tellers. Moreover, although narrative informants can be identified with explicit narrators in those works that have them, engaged reading involves imagining the text to be the product of a narrative informant even in works which lack fictional narrators. And second, like all informants, what a narrative informant reveals can depart significantly from what she says. Not only does she (normally) reveal more than she says, if she is unreliable, some of what she reveals may conflict with what she says.

The account of reader/listener engagement developed in the first part of this chapter will serve as a basis of an account of fictional truth, understood here as truth in fiction as opposed to truth through fiction. It is worth noting that what readers and listeners ought properly to imagine at certain points in the reading or listening process can depart substantially from fictional truth. Consider, for example, fictional works with twists or surprise endings and those with narrators whose unreliability is not exposed until late in the work. In such works, prior to the point at which the twist occurs, or when the narrator's unreliability is exposed, engaged reader/listeners are often intended to imagine what is fictionally false. On the view defended here, this phenomenon can be handled by taking engaged reader/listeners at a given point in the reading/listening process to imagine what the narrative informant has revealed to that point, and identifying fictional truth with what she reveals by means of her entire report.

This chapter consists of seven sections. In the first two sections an account of engagement with written and spoken fictions is developed. As above, at the core of this picture is the idea that engaged readers and listeners imagine of what they read or listen to that it is the product of a narrative informant. In the middle three sections, the ubiquity of narrative informants – the thesis that all fictional works have narrative informants, or, more precisely, that engagement with them requires imagining this to be so – is defended. And in the final two sections, an account of fictional truth in terms of the revelations of narrative informants is developed and defended against its competitors.

4.1 LISTENING TO STORIES

In this section I develop an account of engagement with oral or spoken fictions. Since, on the view on the table, this engagement involves imagining of what one hears that it is a report, we would do well to begin with a discussion of what listening to actual reports consists in. Engaged "report-listening" consists in attentive listening to a report as a report.[1] And this requires having a cluster of doxastic attitudes, including believing *de re* of what one is listening to that it is a report, roughly a unified stretch of discourse intended (or claimed) to describe some part or aspect of reality. In addition, it includes believing *de re* of the speaker that she is acting (or purporting to act) as an informant vis-à-vis the subject matter of the report and, accordingly, believing *de re* of her utterances that they are illocutionary actions largely of the assertoric type. It is worth noting, however, that engaged report-listening also presumably involves a certain kind of *de se* belief – in particular, believing *de se* oneself to be listening to a report. To lack attitudes of these kinds is, in effect, to fail to recognize what one is listening to and, hence, to miss the point of the speaker's words.

In addition to the *de re* (and *de se*) beliefs presupposed by engaged report-listening, listeners typically acquire a number of *de dicto* beliefs as a result of the process of listening. However, this is not in general simply a matter of believing the propositions expressed by the sentences an informant asserts. Instead, an engaged (and receptive) listener will (or at least ought to) come to believe what her informant reveals by means of what he says, which can depart from what he says for three separate reasons. First and most obvious, informants can pragmatically impart propositions which they do not assert by means of the interplay between what they say and conversational maxims of various kinds.[2] An informant discussing a recent bank heist who, for example, says,

Jones has been throwing money around like water,

may thereby reveal, without asserting, that (he believes that) Jones was involved.[3]

Second, listeners normally possess a body of background information on the subject matter of the reports to which they listen which can affect what a report reveals in two ways. First, often some of the asserted or implied content of a report will clash with this background. In such circumstances, a listener has to determine whether the report or the background information with which it conflicts is erroneous, or simply withhold judgment about part of the content of the report (and some of her background information). And second, the content of a report and background information can together imply some further propositions which neither individually implies. For example, given background information about the amount of precipitation required for certain sorts of crop yields, a meteorological report can reveal information about the farming prospects in a certain region. There will, however, have to be some kind of relevance constraint on the background information which contributes to the revelations of a report. Otherwise, given the background fact that a listener's friend, Mary, will not attend picnics during inclement weather, a meteorological report would have to be said to include revelations about Mary's future picnicking behaviour.[4]

Third, informants are not always reliable: they can lack competence vis-à-vis the subject matters of their report, they can be dishonest, or both.[5] If an informant is reliable, a listener can straightforwardly believe the (asserted and implied) content of his report, at least as long as it does not clash with the background information the listener brings to the table. If, however, an informant is unreliable, then a listener should disbelieve some or all of what he says. If an informant's unreliability is local – restricted, for example, to his own role in a broader narrative – or systematic, then a listener may be able to adopt *de dicto* beliefs on the basis of his report. But if his unreliability is global and patternless, then a listener may be able to draw few conclusions from what he says.

In order to determine what has been revealed by a report she has heard, and what she should, as a result, believe, a listener needs to develop a theory of the report's subject matter which, in her judgment, best fits what the informant has said and implied, the evidence concerning his sincerity and expertise, and relevant background information. If there is reason to suppose the informant is reliable, or at least no reason to think him to be unreliable, and nothing he says clashes with the listener's background information, this theory will consist of the content of the report together with the joint implications of this content and relevant background information. But if there are grounds to be suspicious of the informant, or if what he says clashes with background information, the content of the report and the content of the listener's theory may be very different. And in such circumstances, we would say that what the informant said and what he revealed were distinct. It should be emphasized that the listening process sketched here is a dynamic one. Rather than developing a theory of this kind only after the report is complete, the listener develops one as she goes. At any point in the course of the report, the listener has a provisional theory based on the report content she has heard and the evidence as to the informant's reliability that she has acquired to that point. And as the report continues, she can modify her theory quite substantially, not only to accommodate the richer report content with which she comes to be acquainted but also in light of new evidence as to the informant's reliability (or lack thereof).

The fundamental goal of this section, however, is to provide an account of engaged listening to fiction, not of listening to factual reports. And the core idea of the theory on offer is that this consists in imagining the fictional text to which one is listening to be a factual report. Let me elaborate. First, engaged fiction-listeners – those listening to fiction as fiction – are not deluded: they believe *de re* of what they are listening to that it is fiction. But second, engaged listeners imagine *de re* of the fictional texts to which they listen that they are reports, that is, that they (putatively) describe some aspect of reality. Moreover, fiction-listeners imagine *de re* of the storytellers to whom they listen that they are informants – narrative informants – and of the utterances they make that they are assertions and other illocutionary actions.[6] It is worth noting that if the fictional story to which she is listening has a fictional narrator, this is who the listener imagines the storyteller to be; otherwise she imagines him to be reporting circumstances and events in which he does not figure.[7] And third, although listeners imagine *de re* of the fictional texts to which they listen that they are reports, they do not imagine *de se* listening to these reports. The only *de se* attitudes a listener need have on this view is that of believing *de se* herself to be listening to fiction. As a result, not only does a listener imagine a fictional story to be describing a world she does not actually inhabit; she does not imagine herself inhabiting that world.

As above, the *de dicto* imaginings of an engaged fiction-listener cannot simply be identified with the content of the report she imagines the fictional text to be. Narrative informants, like all informants, pragmatically imply various things by means of what they say. The contents of their reports can either clash with or imply various things in unison with background information, which in the fictional case can include genre conventions, "inter-fictional carryover" from other stories, authorial and critical discussions of the story, etc. And narrative informants can vary in their degree of reliability; like all informants they can be more or less honest and more or less competent vis-à-vis the topics of their reports. As a result, what a narrative informant reveals, and what engaged listeners imagine, is a product of the theory which best fits what the informant has said and implied, the evidence concerning her sincerity and expertise, and relevant background information. If he is reliable, and what he says does not clash with the relevant background information, what is revealed will consist of the (asserted and implied) content of his report (together with the joint implications of this content and relevant background information). But if he is unreliable or what he says clashes with background information, what he reveals, and the listener imagines, can depart significantly from the report's content. As before, what a listener imagines at various points in the listening process can differ substantially as the revelations of her narrative informant evolve.[8]

4.2 READING STORIES

I turn now to engagement with written fiction. As might be expected, according to the view on offer, here engaged reading involves imagining of what one reads that it is a report. So, again, we will begin with an account of actual report-reading. Like listening to reports, engaged report-reading requires having a cluster of doxastic attitudes. These include believing *de re* of what one is reading that it is a report, believing *de re* of the author that he is (or was) acting as an informant on the subject matter of the report, and believing *de se* oneself to be reading a report. Moreover, as with oral reports, written reports can clash with or imply things in unison with background information, and report-authors can vary in their degree of reliability. As a result, the *de dicto* beliefs report-readers acquire as a result of the reading process are a result of the theory which best fits what the informant has said and implied, the evidence concerning his sincerity and expertise, and relevant background information. It is worth noting, however, that unlike report listening, and for reasons discussed in chapter 3, readers do not (or should not) believe that in producing the sentences that make up his report, or by means of disseminating it, the author performed any illocutionary actions.

Engaged fiction-reading, too, requires having a number of doxastic attitudes. Readers believe *de re* of what they read that it is fiction and of their authors that they wrote fiction. Moreover, they believe *de se* themselves to be reading fiction. This is, of course, more or less obvious. The substantial claim being made here is that, like listening to fiction, fiction-reading involves imagining *de re* of what one reads that it is a report, without imagining *de se* reading a report.[9] Fiction-reading does, however, differ from fiction-listening in two important respects: it typically does not involve imagining *de re* of the sentences one reads that they are illocutionary actions; and it, again typically, does not involve imagining *de re* of the (actual) author that he wrote a report. I will consider each in turn.

First, the reason that in reading fiction one does not typically imagine of the sentences one reads that they are illocutionary actions is that, normally, one imagines of what one reads that they are written sentences[10] and, as above, authors do not perform illocutionary actions by means of writing or disseminating their written works. The reason, however, readers only typically refrain from imagining of the sentences they read that they are illocutionary actions is because in some cases it is part of the story that the words one in fact reads are spoken and not written;[11] and in such cases it is incumbent upon readers to imagine the sentences they read to be illocutionary actions.[12] But it is important to note, and central to the view on offer here, that imagining *de re* of the words one reads that they are spoken simply does not require imagining *de se* listening to them.[13]

Second, although it is a part of the view on offer here that engaged readers imagine *de re* of what they read that they are reports and that they were written by narrative informants, they need not, and normally do not, imagine *de re* of actual authors that they are the informants behind these reports.[14] Unlike the storytellers to whom appreciators of spoken fictions listen, authors of fiction are neither in the presence of readers nor do they pretend to be reporting anything. Moreover, even though naturally occurring phenomena and, more generally, authorless objects orthographically (or phonographically) similar to fictional works, are not themselves fictions, they nevertheless can be read (or listened to) as fiction. This is, of course, incompatible with any requirement that fiction-readers imaginatively identify narrative informants with authors. The exceptions are cases in which it is part of the (fictional) story that the actual author is the story's narrator. Only in these and similar cases is there any requirement that engaged readers imagine actual authors to be narrative informants.

One might worry that even the requirement that a reader imagine of what she reads that it was written by a narrative informant, without further requiring that she imaginatively identify this figure with the actual author, is too strong. After all, there are, or at least could be, fictional works in which it is part of the story that the text is authorless. I have in mind here cases in which it is stated or otherwise revealed by the text that the text itself is an erosion pattern or some other natural phenomenon. A particularly crude example might be a story which starts out as follows:

> This sequence of marks and those that follow are part of an erosion pattern.

The difficulty for the view on offer is that such works seem to require that readers not imagine what they read to be the words of any speaker, which, of course, rules out imagining them to be written by a narrative informant.

The first thing to note is that works of this kind pose difficulties for any account of fictional engagement, and not just the view defended here. This is because they seem to impose requirements on readers that would leave them in a state of imaginative incoherence. The problem is that unless a sequence of marks is understood to be the product of intentional activity, it cannot be understood to consist of words and sentences, let alone meaningful words and sentences. And if it does not consist of meaningful words and sentences, it cannot express the claim that it is authorless, or any claims at all for that matter. As a result, imagining a text to be a naturally occurring phenomenon which states this fact about itself requires both imagining that it is meaningful and imagining that it is not.

On the view defended here, however, there is a compelling solution to this problem. As will become clear below, the narrative informant need not be an inhabitant of the fiction world on which he reports. In the normal case, if the narrative informant is not fictional, neither are his words. But an elegant solution to the difficulty at hand can be found by supposing that in such cases, although the informant does not occupy the fictional world he describes, the words he uses to describe it do occupy the fictional world. An erosion pattern can literally be the words of a narrative informant. But since his intentional activity occurs outside the fictional world he describes using it, in the fictional world it remains a meaningless series of scratches. Rather than requiring readers to engage in a single imaginative project fraught with the threat of incoherence, on my view readers engage in two related but distinct imaginative projects – one directed toward the nature of the fictional world described, the other directed toward the report which describes it. Certainly a mystery remains concerning how the informant's words come to be so manifested in the world he describes. But the institution of fiction is rife with mysteries about how fictional stories come to be presented to readers.

Finally, it is worth reiterating that the *de dicto* imaginings of an engaged reader are the product of the theory which best fits what the informant has said and implied, the evidence concerning her sincerity and expertise, and relevant background information. And again, what one imagines at various points in the reading process evolves with the revelations of her (narrative) informant.

4.3 UBIQUITOUS NON-ACTUAL FACT-TELLERS: CON

A central feature of the view developed here is that it entails that every fictional work has a narrative informant or, more precisely, that engaged reader/listeners of all literary fictions are required to imagine of what they read or listen to that it is written or told by some such figure. And while one might naturally suppose that works with explicit narrators, or in which the narrative voice appears unreliable, have narrative informants, there might seem to be little reason to suppose the same of works written in a "plain third-person omniscient narrative style."[15] Andrew Kania has, in fact, developed an argument against views of this kind which may prove instructive here.[16] The target of Kania's argument is what he calls the "ubiquity thesis": the view that every literary narrative necessarily has a fictional narrator – an agent who tells the narrative and who exists on "the same ontological level" as the characters and events described by the narrative.[17] Kania proceeds by attempting to show that the main argument offered in support of the ubiquity thesis – the ontological gap argument – establishes no such thing.[18]

As Kania reconstructs it, the ontological gap argument has a positive and a negative stage. The positive stage consists of the claims (i) that understanding a literary narrative requires an account of how readers and listeners acquire information about the fictional world it describes and (ii) that the only adequate account is one according to which this information is provided to us by an agent of some kind. And the negative stage consists of the argument that this agent must be a fictional narrator because otherwise she would not be related cognitively to the characters and events in the story so as to be able to coherently provide us with information about them "as if they were real."[19]

Kania criticizes both stages of this argument. He criticizes the positive stage by pointing out that if understanding a literary narrative requires an explanation of how we acquire information about the fictional world it describes, it presumably also requires an explanation of how the fictional narrator – who provides us with it – goes about acquiring and transmitting this information to us. But in many works no such explanation is forthcoming: the process by which the information is acquired and transmitted by the narrator is indeterminate or even incoherent.[20] And he criticizes the negative stage by arguing that if there is a genuine epistemic gap between fictional worlds and the actual world, then even if fictional narrators could acquire information about the worlds they inhabit, they could not transmit this information to actual readers and listeners. Kania's conclusion is that the ubiquity thesis ought to be abandoned and that fictional narrators should be posited on a case by case basis when so doing yields a better understanding of the work under consideration.

Although Kania's objections may undermine the ubiquity of certain sorts of tellers, or at least one argument for the same, they undermine neither the ubiquity of narrative informants nor the arguments I offer in their favour. The first thing to note is that Kania explicitly acknowledges only two categories of tellers – actual tellers and fictional tellers:[21] "[we] can thus distinguish between the *actual* telling of the fictional story, which John Barth engages in, and the *fictional* telling of the story engaged in by Horner."[22] There is, however, a pair of orthogonal distinctions that can be drawn among tellers – one tripartite and one bipartite – which together yield six categories rather than Kania's two. First, following Kania, one can distinguish ontologically between tellers that are actual and those that are non-actual; but, departing from Kania, one can subdivide the latter category into fictional and non-fictional (but still non-actual) tellers. By an actual teller, I mean a teller who performs her act of telling – speaking or writing – in the actual world; an actual teller is a real person whose act of telling really occurs. A fictional teller, in contrast, is a teller whose act of telling occurs in a fictional world, that is, the world generated by a fictional work wherein the events described in the work unfold; fictional characters who engage in dialogue, for example, count as fictional tellers.[23] A non-actual/non-fictional teller is one whose act of telling occurs neither in the actual world nor in a fictional world, but rather in some alternative distinct from both of them. Figures who hypothetically or counterfactually perform acts of telling to that extent count as non-actual/non-fictional tellers. Second, one can distinguish linguistically between narrators who engage in factual discourse – or "fact-telling" – and those who engage in fictional discourse – or "fiction-telling." Fact-telling is what authors do when they write (and disseminate) non-fictional reports of various kinds and speakers do when they engage in what Searle calls "serious" discourse.[24] Fiction-telling, in contrast, is what authors do when they write (and disseminate) fictional stories and storytellers do when they perform them.[25]

Of the six categories of tellers generated by this pair of distinctions, three – actual fact-tellers, actual fiction-tellers, and fictional fact-tellers – are quite familiar. Actual fact-tellers are simply real people who actually write non-fictional reports and perform ordinary sorts of speech acts; authors of non-fiction, among numerous others, are included in this category. Actual fiction-tellers are real people who engage in fiction-telling, and include, most prominently, authors of fiction. Fictional fact-tellers are inhabitants of fictional worlds who write reports or engage in serious discourse; this typically includes several of the characters that appear in a given fictional work including the explicit narrator, if there is one.

Less familiar are fictional and non-actual/non-fictional fiction-tellers. Fictional fiction-tellers are simply inhabitants of fictional worlds who engage in fiction-telling, such as characters who are themselves storytellers or authors of fiction. A potentially problematic example is a storytelling narrator – an explicit narrator who clearly indicates that the story being presented is fictional.[26] Non-actual/non-fictional fiction-tellers are tellers of fictional stories whose speech acts occur neither in the actual world nor in fictional worlds. The primary examples of such tellers are idealized author figures of the sort invoked for various theoretical purposes by hypothetical intentionalists.[27]

For present purposes, however, the important category is the least familiar one – that of the non-actual/non-fictional fact-teller. Such tellers, like fictional narrators, write non-fictional reports or make assertions describing the goings on in fictional worlds; but unlike fictional narrators, they do not inhabit those worlds, nor do they inhabit the actual world. In contrast to the other categories, there are no well-known examples of non-actual/non-fictional fact-tellers; part of the goal of this essay is to establish the theoretical need for such a figure. Nevertheless, given that it is generated by the pair of distinctions developed above, it remains a possible category into which a teller might fall. And even if Kania is right that fictional (fact- or fiction-) tellers are not ubiquitous, it still could be true that every literary narrative must have a non-actual fact-telling narrator, that is, either a fictional narrator or a non-actual/non-fictional fact-teller. And this is exactly what I claim of narrative informants.

The second thing to note is that Kania addresses not one but two ontological gap arguments: an epistemic argument and a doxastic argument. The epistemic argument, if successful, establishes that a fictional work must have a fictional narrator; the doxastic argument, in contrast, aims only to establish that it must have a non-actual fact-teller. Moreover, it is easy to show that the arguments Kania marshals undermine only the epistemic argument and leave the doxastic argument untouched.

Kania is addressing the epistemic argument when he says, "the artist cannot present the fictional world to us because he or she does not stand in the right relation to it … [this] problem is solved by positing an agent at the fictional level, who thereby *does* stand in the right epistemic relation to the fictional world."[28] This argument can be fairly reconstructed as follows:

(1_E) Understanding a fictional work requires the supposition that it has a teller who is so cognitively related to the fictional world as to be able to provide readers with the information about it she in fact provides.

(2_E) The only kind of teller who is appropriately cognitively related to a fictional world is a fictional narrator.

(C_E) Understanding a fictional work requires the supposition that it has a fictional narrator.

And as should be clear, Kania's positive stage criticisms bring (1_E) under suspicion and his negative stage criticisms undercut (2_E).

Kania is addressing the doxastic argument when he says, "though at first glance it might seem that actual authors narrate their novels, this is incoherent, because they cannot make the assertions about the fictional world that are clearly being made … Graham Greene is clearly not asserting this; he of all people should know that neither Wilson nor the Bedford Hotel exist … [anyone] prepared to make the assertion about Wilson and the Bedford must be at the fictional level and Graham Greene is simply not."[29] This argument can be reconstructed as follows:

(1_D) Understanding a fictional work requires the supposition that it is told by a fact-teller.

(2$_D$) There are no actual fact-tellers of fictional works.
(C$_D$) Understanding a fictional work requires the supposition that it is told by a non-actual fact-teller.

There are two points worth noting here. First, the doxastic argument does not conclude that every fictional work has a fictional teller, but rather that every work has a non-actual teller – either fictional or non-actual/non-fictional. Given his rather more coarse-grained taxonomy of tellers, Kania is forced to conclude that if a teller is non-actual then he must be fictional. And second, Kania's objections to the epistemic argument gain no purchase here. As long as (1$_D$) is not invoked to explain how we acquire information about a fictional world, Kania's positive-stage criticisms do not count against it. And because (2$_D$) is motivated simply by the fact that the only actual tellers of fictional works are fiction-tellers and not fact-tellers, rather than to ensure that these narrators stand in the right kind of cognitive relations to fictional worlds, Kania's negative-stage criticisms are impotent here as well.[30]

4.4   UBIQUITOUS NON-ACTUAL FACT-TELLERS: PRO

It is, of course, one thing to establish that an argument is immune to a certain line of criticism and another to show that there are good grounds to accept the argument. In the case at hand, although the second premise,

(2$_D$) There are no actual fact-tellers of fictional works,

seems incontestable,[31] the first premise,

(1$_D$) Understanding a fictional work requires the supposition that it is told by a fact-teller,

is, as it stands, sorely lacking in motivation. There are, however, compelling grounds for accepting it. In a nutshell, the argument for this claim is that (i) understanding a fictional work involves understanding the propositions generated by it (or true in it),[32] (ii) some of the propositions generated by a work are not expressed by sentences which occur in it, (iii) (some) unexpressed propositions are generated by pragmatic implicature, and (iv) the generation of unexpressed propositions by this means presupposes that the teller is a fact-teller.[33]

Consider, by way of illustration, the following (very short) fictional story:

> King Leopold's reign was rather short lived. He ascended the throne on his eighteenth birthday after his father's untimely demise. Shortly thereafter he made his virtues known, chief among which was the infrequency with which he cheated at cards. His most notable policy initiative involved the termination of military pensions. He used the savings to the public purse to fund a lavish and extended celebration of the monarchy. He was dead within the year. Leopold was buried with all due honours somewhere in the southern part of the kingdom.

In addition to the propositions expressed by the sentences that make it up, a correct understanding of this story requires imagining a number of unexpressed propositions including that Leopold murdered his father, that he had no virtues, that he was assassinated by the military, and that he was secretly buried in an unmarked grave.

Now if this story is imagined to be the report of a narrative informant – a non-actual fact-teller – then an account of how these propositions come to be generated by the text is easy to come by: through the interplay between the informant's acts of telling and Gricean conversational maxims. For example, the narrative informant might be thought to implicate that Leopold was assassinated by the military in virtue of the fact that he must be assumed to believe this in order to reconcile his statement that Leopold terminated military pensions with the maxim of relation.[34] And he might be thought to implicate that Leopold was buried in an unmarked grave in virtue of the fact that the infringement of the first maxim of quantity – make your conversational contribution as informative as is required – he commits by his vagueness about the location of Leopold's grave can best be explained by supposing that to say more would have involved a violation of the second maxim of quality – do not say that for which you lack adequate evidence.[35]

Byrne argues, however, that acts of fiction-telling, here understood as invitations to make-believe, can generate unexpressed propositions by the very same mechanisms: "Now what the Author invites the Reader to make-believe may not be explicitly stated in the text. But just as implicit assertions in non-fiction can be recovered by pragmatic inference, so can implicit invitations to make-believe in fiction."[36] The trouble with Byrne's argument is that the familiar Gricean conversational maxims govern acts of fact-telling but do not govern acts of fiction-telling. This is clearest in the case of Grice's maxims of quality:

(1) Do not say what you believe to be false.
(2) Do not say that for which you lack adequate evidence.[37]

Although fact-tellers are obligated to refrain from making false or unjustified claims, fiction-tellers are not. A fictional author or storyteller may invite appreciators to imagine any proposition she likes – insofar as this is what fiction-tellers do – regardless of the evidence she has for it, or even whether or not she believes it. This is also relatively clear in the case of Grice's maxims of quantity:

(1) Make your contribution to the conversation as informative as necessary.
(2) Do not make your contribution to the conversation more informative than necessary.

Acts of fiction-telling, unlike acts of fact-telling, are not designed to be informative in any substantial sense.[38] As a result, they can neither be too informative nor insufficiently informative. Even Grice's maxim of relevance,

Be relevant,

arguably applies only to acts of fact-telling, at least insofar as it is relevance to the truth of what has been said that it is at issue. Minimally, it is unclear in what sense invitations to make-believe can be relevant to one another. The upshot is that since acts of fiction-telling are not governed by conversational maxims, no pragmatic inferences can be drawn from fiction-tellers' failure to conform to them.

Byrne might, of course, rejoin that acts of fiction-telling are governed by communicative maxims specific to fictional discourse and that pragmatic inferences, similar to those that arise in factual discourse, are generated by the interplay between fiction-telling acts and these maxims. An example might be something like

F-QUALITY: do not invite readers to make-believe what you do not intend to be fictionally true.[39]

Although I have no decisive objection to this strategy, there is reason to balk. In lieu of an independent argument for the existence of such maxims, this strategy is simply ad hoc. Moreover, since the right sorts of pragmatic implications are generated by the Gricean maxims and the supposition that fictional texts are the products of non-actual fact-tellers, fiction-specific maxims are going to have to be tailored to generate the same results. This, I take it, would make the charge of ad hoc-ness even more telling.

An alternate strategy that the opponent of ubiquitous fact-tellers might invoke would be to eschew the role of pragmatic implication in the generation of unexpressed fictional propositions altogether. Kania, for example, suggests that certain very general principles – the Reality Principle and the Mutual Belief Principle, among others – which govern the practice of fictional interpretation are by themselves sufficient.[40] Following Walton, we can formulate the Reality Principle as

> if $p_1, \ldots, p_n$ are the propositions expressed by a fiction work, w, then a proposition q is fictional in w if and only if, if it were the case that $p_1, \ldots, p_n$ then it would be the case that q,[41]

and the Mutual Belief Principle as

> If $p_1, \ldots, p_n$ are the propositions expressed by a fiction work, w, then a proposition q is fictional in w if and only if it is mutually believed in the author's society that if it were the case that $p_1, \ldots, p_n$ then it would be the case that q.[42]

Now it is arguably true that these principles, or their kin, are required to generate certain unexpressed propositions in fictional works. The Reality Principle (or something like it), for example, seems required to generate fictional propositions to the effect that Leopold was human, that his kingdom was not on the moon, that he was not adept at sorcery, etc. But what is important here is that neither it nor the Mutual Belief Principle can generate all of the unexpressed propositions that in part constitute the story described by a fictional work. Consider again King Leopold's tale. It is simply not the case that were the propositions expressed by the story true, it would be true that Leopold murdered his father, that he had no virtues, that he was assassinated by the military, and that he was secretly buried in an unmarked grave, nor is this mutually believed in the author's – that is my – society. For example, the closest world to our own in which a monarch was buried with all due honours in some location in the southern part of his kingdom is not one in which he was secretly buried in an unmarked grave, even a monarch of whom the propositions expressed by the sentences which make up the story are true. And the closest world in which a monarch ascends to the throne after the premature death of his father is just as likely one in which the latter died of natural causes, or in battle, as one in which he was assassinated by his successor, if not more so. Nor is the contrary mutually believed in my society.

Facts about the world and the shared beliefs of the author's community are included in the background information that contributes to the content of a fictional work. The Reality and Mutual Belief principles offer plausible accounts of how this information is incorporated into a work's content. But, on my view, the propositions that get into the antecedents of the counterfactuals these principles deploy include not simply the propositions expressed by the sentences which constitute fictional works but also the propositions pragmatically imparted by them; together, as I cast it, these two sets of propositions make up the contents of narrative informants' reports. If this is right then this latter set of propositions clearly cannot be generated by these principles.

4.5 UBIQUITOUS FICTIONAL FACT-TELLERS: CON

The argument of the previous section is compatible not only with my own narrative informant figure but also with Currie's fictional author – a fictional fact-teller.[43] Given that fictional fact-tellers are more familiar than those which are neither actual nor fictional – as are some narrative informants – and questions do not arise as to how they come to be in position to report about worlds they do not inhabit, one might wonder whether Currie's figure ought to be preferred. Before addressing this question, it is worth saying a bit more about the distinction between the two figures. There are three central differences worth emphasizing here. First, as above, although both narrative informants and fictional authors are fact-tellers, all fictional authors, but only some narrative informants, are fictional – inhabitants of the fictional worlds on which they report. Some narrative informants are instead non-fictional (but not actual) fact-tellers – reporting on (fictional) worlds they do not inhabit.

Second, unlike fictional authors, narrative informants are identified with fictional narrators in those works that have them. So, for example, the title character himself is the narrative informant of "Memoirs of Barry Lyndon, Esq., written by Himself."[44] But in works without fictional narrators, narrative informants are not themselves fictional. Fictional authors, in contrast, are not identified with fictional narrators even in those works that have them.[45] Rather the fictional author is a hypothetical member of the actual author's community who inhabits the fictional world generated by the work and who, unlike the latter, tells the story as known fact. And if the work contains a fictional narrator, the fictional author tells the story by speaking in the voice of, or writing in the words of, the narrator.

And third, unlike fictional authors, narrative informants are, or at least can be, unreliable. Their beliefs about the circumstances on which they report can be erroneous, they can be dishonest, or both. Moreover, on the view being defended here, narrative unreliability is understood in terms of deviations between what narrative informants report and what they reveal by means of what they report. Fictional authors, in contrast, are authoritative figures. Not only are they incapable of unreliability, their beliefs and intentions are the determinants of fictional truth in the stories they tell: what it is for a proposition to be fictional in a given work is for it to be believed by the fictional author.[46] Please note: rather than understanding narrative unreliability in terms of disparities between the reports of fictional narrators and the beliefs of fictional authors,[47] Currie takes it to be the product of complex intentions of fictional authors: a fictional narrative is unreliable when the fictional author intends that superficial evidence will suggest her intention was one thing but a better, more reflective grasp of the evidence will suggest her intention was something else.[48]

There are a number of difficulties that arise for the claim of the ubiquity of fictional authors that do not arise for the similar claim regarding narrative informants. I will focus on two objections here, one to the ubiquity of any kind of fictional fact-teller, and the other specifically to the ubiquity of Currie's fictional author.

The first difficulty concerns the phenomenon of mindless fiction. By mindless fiction, I mean fictional stories in which there are no intelligent beings. Since tellers are intelligent beings,[49] such stories cannot have fictional tellers.[50] As a result, since there are at least some fictional works which lack any sort of fictional tellers, any claim of the ubiquity of fictional fact-tellers in general, or fictional authors in particular, must be false.

Now if Currie's view were correct, then mindless fictions, or, more generally, fictions which exclude a teller, would be contradictory. Currie himself simply embraces this consequence: "[on] my theory mindless fiction generates a game of make-believe in which we are called upon to make believe contradictory things: that it is told as known fact and that there is no one there to tell it."[51] Although I do not have a decisive objection to

Currie's manoeuvre, two objections are worth making here. First, as with Radford's analogous response to the paradox of fiction, the suggestion that readers and listeners of mindless fictions imagine contradictory propositions, or are, at least, called upon to do so, is not entirely satisfactory. Not only does it entail that proper engagement with such fictions is a lot more difficult than it actually is – imagining contradictory things being no easy task – it entails a heretofore unnoticed inconsistency in the imaginative projects of large numbers of readers and listeners. And second, as should be clear, there is no contradiction between the propositions that a story is told as known fact and that there is no one there to tell it if the teller in question is my narrative informant rather than Currie's fictional author.[52]

The second difficulty arises specifically for the ubiquity of Currie's fictional author and not for the ubiquity of fictional fact-tellers more generally. The problem is that, on Currie's view, in works with fictional narrators, not only does the fictional author inhabit the same world as the narrator, she speaks in the voice, or writes in the words, of the narrator. And given that the fictional author is supposed to be a (presumably embodied) hypothetical member of the actual author's community and not some kind of disembodied possessing spirit, it is not entirely clear what readers and listeners are supposed to imagine vis-à-vis the relation between the narrator and the fictional author.[53] In some works, the fictional author could be thought to have certain sorts of psychic powers or, perhaps, just a high degree of influence over the narrator. But such possibilities are ruled out in works of realistic fiction, or in works in which the narrator is immune to such influence.[54] Now it is, of course, true that there are often puzzles involving the source and nature of the text in works with fictional narrators: it can be indeterminate whether the narrator spoke, wrote, or thought the text, and it may simply be impossible for her to have produced it by any means. But what is important to note is that not only does the ubiquity of fictional authors entail that this phenomenon is a lot more widespread than has previously been thought – arising in works that lack fictional narrators – it also entails that in works with narrators there is an extra heretofore unnoticed layer of puzzles of this kind. If, however, the ubiquity of fictional authors is abandoned in favour of the ubiquity of narrative informants, this problem does not even arise: the narrative informant is, after all, identical to the fictional narrator in those works that have one.

4.6 TRUTH IN FICTION — NEGATIVE

The focus of the remainder of this chapter is on fictional truth, here understood as truth in fiction rather than truth through fiction. In particular,

I will be looking at accounts of fictional truth that draw on the act/attitude analyses of engagement with fiction that I have been discussing. Unlike the non-fictional case, there is no realm of independently existing fictional facts to which appreciators' psychological states may or may not correspond, or so I would claim.[55] As a result, the accounts of fictional truth at issue are formulated in terms of psychological states of ideal appreciators, or the psychological states ordinary appreciators ought to have, rather than in terms of any kind of correspondence relation.

The problem addressed by a theory of fictional truth is that of providing a general account of the conditions under which a sentence of the form

In fiction F, S

is true. A natural first suggestion is to identify fictional truth with what is explicitly reported, by means of spoken or written acts of fact-telling, in the text. There are, however, a number of familiar objections to this suggestion. First and foremost, the sentences which constitute fictional texts are not normally used to make reports at all. Felicitous reporting presupposes belief on the part of the speaker or writer in the truth of what is said. But neither authors of fiction nor storytellers (normally) believe what they say, and their acts of telling are not for that reason considered defective. One might, of course, rejoin by identifying fictional truth with what is reported by the fictional narrator rather than by the author of the fictional work. The trouble, however, is that what fictional narrators report is neither necessary nor sufficient for fictional truth. It is not necessary because there are many fictional truths that are not (explicitly) reported by the narrators of the works in which they occur. Watson, for example, nowhere says that Holmes wears underpants, yet it is true in the Holmes stories that he is so clad. And it is not sufficient because fictional narrators are often unreliable: they report things that are not true – even in the story.

Despite these difficulties, many philosophers have found the basic idea underlying this suggestion to be promising.[56] This idea is that fictional truth is correctly analysed in terms of the speech acts or propositional attitudes of tellers of fictional works. As we have seen, taking the relevant act/attitude to be assertion, or more generally, reporting, leads to insuperable difficulties, but it remains open to analyse fictional truth in terms of other acts/attitudes such as belief[57] or some kind of *sui generis* fictive speech act.[58] The views considered below differ in this respect, but also in respect of who the relevant teller is taken to be – the author, the narrator, or some third figure. As a result, it may prove fruitful to identify the following shared form of the various analyses under consideration:

"In fiction F, S" is true if and only if **a** V's <p>,

where **a** is a teller, V is an act/attitude, and <p> is a proposition expressed by (or otherwise suitably related to) "S."[59]

In this section, three accounts of fictional truth will be considered and found lacking: Lewis's possible-worlds analysis,[60] Currie's analysis in terms of the beliefs of fictional authors,[61] and Byrne's appeal to the fictive illocutionary acts of ideal authors.[62] In section 4.7, a positive account in terms of the revelations of narrative informants will be defended. Some of the difficulties that arise for these accounts of fictional truth have already been discussed in earlier sections of this chapter and elsewhere in this essay. Nevertheless, it may prove fruitful to revisit them in this context.

Lewis's theory retains the idea that fictional truth is to be analysed in terms of the reports of a fictional fact-teller – the narrator, if there is one – who tells the fictional story as known fact.[63] What is unique about Lewis's view is that it embeds this core idea within a counterfactual analysis. Lewis in fact offers two distinct counterfactual analyses of fictional truth:

> LEWIS-1: "In fiction F, S" is true if and only if there exists a world w in which F is told as known fact and "S" is true, which is closer to the actual world than any world in which F is told as known fact and "S" is not true[64]
>
> LEWIS-2: "In fiction F, S" is true if and only if for all worlds w, if w is a collective belief world of the author's community, then there is a world w' in which F is told as known fact and "S" is true, which is closer to w than any world in which F is told as known fact and "S" is not true,[65]

where the collective belief worlds of a community are those worlds in which the (overt) beliefs shared by most members of the community are true.[66] So, for example,

> Holmes is the offspring of human parents

comes out true on Lewis's analyses because there are worlds where the Holmes stories are told as known fact and Holmes is the offspring of human parents which are closer to actuality, and to the collective belief worlds of Doyle's community, than any world in which the stories are told as known fact and Holmes had less typical origins.

Despite its virtues, Lewis's analysis falls prey to insuperable difficulties. First, it entails the ubiquity of fictional fact-tellers. After all, the closest worlds in which a story is told as known fact are worlds in which someone so tells it. As a result, it runs afoul of the problem of mindless fiction discussed in section 4.5. Moreover, Lewis's analysis is incommensurable with the possibility of an unreliable narrator. At any world in which a work is told as known fact, all the claims contained in the work will automatically be true. Hence, it trivially follows that, for any claim contained in the text, there is a world where the text is told as known fact and the claim is true which is closer than any told-as-known-fact world in which it is false. Lewis, as usual, is aware of this difficulty and suggests that works with unreliable narrators require a separate treatment: "In these exceptional cases also, the thing to do is to consider those worlds where the act of storytelling really is whatever it purports to be – ravings, reliable transmission of a reliable source, or whatever – here at our world."[67]

Now it may well be possible to develop this idea to cover these sorts of cases.[68] But narrative unreliability is a more common phenomenon than Lewis acknowledges and cannot be set aside as a mere marginal case. And, other things being equal, a univocal theory is preferable if one can be found.

One of the virtues of Lewis's theory is that it can accommodate fictional truths that are not explicitly stated in the text. For example, despite not being explicitly stated in the Holmes stories,

Holmes wears underpants[69]

comes out true on Lewis's analysis because worlds where the Holmes stories are told as known fact and Holmes wears underpants are closer to the actual world, and the collective belief worlds of Doyle's community, than any world in which the Holmes stories are told as known fact and Holmes does not wear underpants. The difficulty that arises for Lewis's account of unstated fictional truth is that it is too permissive: it entails of any given fictional work that there are a multitude of fictional truths which intuitively are not true in that work. The trouble is that both the actual world and the collective belief worlds of an author's community contain a lot of facts – about the distant past, about spatially remote regions of the universe, about the microphysical constitution of things, etc. – which are almost always irrelevant to the events described in a fictional work. And a world where a text is told as known fact and this extraneous fact obtains will be closer to the actual world, or the author's community's collective belief worlds, than a world where it is told as known fact and the extraneous fact does not obtain (as long as it is not explicitly ruled out by the text).

As a result, all this extraneous fact will be true in fiction if Lewis's analysis is correct. But it is intuitively implausible to suppose that, for example, the fact that Julius Caesar had a certain number of hairs on his head when he died is true in the Holmes stories.[70]

Moreover, even if these extraneous fictional truths are tolerable in realistic fiction, they are not tolerable in non-realistic fiction, such as fantasy and (some) science fiction. Consider, for example, a story in which the use of magic plays a prominent role or in which the world rests on the back of a giant turtle. Even if it is not explicitly stated in the text, it may well be fictionally true that the world is non-quantum or that the events described do not occur in our universe. However, the closest told-as-known-fact world to the actual world or the author's community's collective belief worlds might nevertheless prove to be quantum worlds or worlds consisting of our universe.

Lewis suggests that such worries can be alleviated by appeal to "inter-fictional carry-over" from other stories in the same genre: "If Scrulch [a dragon] does breathe fire in my story, it is by inter-fictional carry-over from what is true of dragons in other stories."[71] But although the notion of inter-fictional carry-over has intuitive appeal, it needs to be much more fully developed to be of use here. Minimally, an account of exactly what information gets carried over from (and to) which fictional works is required, as well as an account of how this information is to be balanced with information derived from the actual world or the collective belief worlds of the author's community.

Finally, Lewis's analysis runs afoul of the problem of inconsistent or impossible fiction. If a work of fiction contains an inconsistency, then there is no possible world in which it is told as known fact. As a result, Lewis originally acknowledged that, on his analysis, "anything whatever is vacuously true in an impossible fiction."[72] Lewis subsequently attempted to solve this problem by dividing inconsistent fictions into consistent fragments and characterizing truth in an inconsistent fiction as truth in at least one of the fragments.[73] Currie has argued, however, that this strategy cannot accommodate a fictional work in which, for example, the protagonist has refuted Gödel's theorem: since there will be no consistent fragment in which the protagonist has done so, it will not prove to be true in the work that she has refuted Gödel.[74]

Rather than analysing fictional truth in terms of what would be the case, or would be believed to be so by the author's community, were the story told by a fictional fact-teller, Currie analyses fictional truth in terms of the beliefs of such a figure – the fictional author:

CURRIE-1: "In fiction F, S" is true if and only if it is reasonable for the informed reader to infer that the fictional author of F believes that S.[75]

Given that "the teller – the fictional author – is a fictional construction, [who] has no private beliefs, no beliefs that could not reasonably be inferred from text plus background,"[76] this is essentially equivalent to the simpler

CURRIE-2: "In fiction F, S" is true if and only if the fictional author of F believes that S.

So, for example, since the fictional author of the Holmes stories is a member of Doyle's community and, as such, would presumably believe that respectable detectives wear underpants,

Holmes wears underpants

is true, on Currie's analysis, despite its non-occurrence in the text.

In addition to accommodating fictional truths not explicitly stated in the text, Currie's analysis avoids some of the difficulties that beset Lewis's theory. By distinguishing fictional authors from explicit narrators, and identifying fictional truth with the beliefs of the former, Currie's analysis can easily handle the difficulties posed by unreliable narrators. Although the assertions and beliefs of an explicit narrator may be a poor guide to fictional truth, the beliefs of a fictional author – "an unobtrusive narrator who, by putting words in the mouth of the explicit narrator in a certain way, signals his scepticism about what the explicit narrator says"[77] – are not. And Currie's analysis can also accommodate inconsistent fictions. In order for contradictory propositions to be true in a fictional work, all that is required is that the fictional author believe both of them.[78] Inconsistent beliefs are, after all, a hazard faced by many of us.

Nevertheless, Currie's analysis does run into serious difficulties. First, because the fictional author is a member of the actual author's community, she will presumably share beliefs prevalent among members of this community. And many of these beliefs will be simply irrelevant to the fictional story. But, as with Lewis's second analysis, Currie's view implies that such beliefs are true in fiction. Second, as Byrne points out,[79] typical members of, for example, Doyle's community would have had significant gaps in their knowledge, as well as mistaken beliefs, about the relative locations of landmarks in turn-of-the-century London. As a result, given that the fictional author of the Holmes stories is herself a (typical) member of Doyle's community, Currie's analysis entails that the London of the Holmes stories differs geographically from the real London in significant (but unspecified) ways. And finally, as noted in section 4.5, not only does Currie's analysis run afoul of mindless fictions, it is faced with the puzzle of explaining exactly how a (hypothetical) member of the author's community could manage to put words in the mouths (or pens) of fictional narrators.

Byrne's alternative analysis of fictional truth differs from those discussed above not only with respect to the act/attitude deployed but also with respect to the subject of this act/attitude: not only is this subject not fictional, she is not any kind of fact-teller at all. But rather than invoking an actual fiction-teller – in particular, the author – Byrne invokes a non-actual/non-fictional fiction-teller or ideal author. Byrne's motivation here is the thought that what a text means – roughly sentence meaning – and what an author means by a text – speaker meaning – can come apart, and fictional truth is a function of the former.[80] The ideal author, in contrast, is a hypothetical construct whose intentions regarding the meaning of the text are by definition satisfied. Please note: the objections to Byrne's view raised in this section do not depend on the ideality of the author figure Byrne invokes, and would weigh equally against a similar view which invoked instead the actual author.

The act/attitude in terms of which Byrne analyses fictional truth is that of inviting readers to make-believe. This yields the following:

BYRNE-1: "In fiction F, S" is true if and only if the ideal reader could infer that the ideal author of F is inviting the ideal reader to make-believe that S.[81]

But given that "the [ideal author] intends to say precisely what the ideal reader … thinks the actual author intended to say,"[82] this is effectively equivalent to the simpler

BYRNE-2: "In fiction F, S" is true if and only if the ideal author of F invites the ideal reader to make-believe that S.

So, for example, the ideal author of the Holmes stories invites readers to make-believe that Holmes is a respectable nineteenth-century London detective. As a result, the social conventions of respectable London society of the time, such as those governing the use of undergarments, are salient; we would expect to be told if the London of the Holmes stories differed significantly in its social conventions from nineteenth-century London itself. Since the ideal author has not told us this, she has strongly contextually implied that we are to imagine that actual conventions are in effect. Hence,

Holmes wears underpants

is true, on Byrne's analysis, despite its non-occurrence in the text.

In addition to accommodating certain fictional truths not explicitly reported in the text, Byrne's analysis also avoids many of the difficulties that arose for the alternatives we have considered. First, it is specifically designed to avoid the problem of mindless fictions. Since the ideal author is not fictional, Byrne's account does not entail that in every fictional work it is fictionally true that the story is told as known fact and, hence, that mindless fictions are inconsistent. Second, since nothing prevents an author from inviting a reader to make-believe a contradiction, Byrne's analysis has no difficulty handling inconsistent fictions. And third, since the ideal author of a fictional work is distinct from the explicit narrator, narrative unreliability poses no difficulty for Byrne's view, at least as long as there is no reason to identify the reliable invitations of the former with the unreliable assertions of the latter.

Nevertheless, like the alternatives discussed to this point, Byrne's view runs into some serious difficulties. First, as discussed in section 4.4, Byrne's view cannot accommodate pragmatically imparted implicit fictional truths without making an ad hoc appeal to conversational principles specifically governing fictional discourse. And second, there are grounds to reject the supposition that author figures make invitations to make-believe to readers or listeners at all. As we saw in chapter 3, what authors who non-verbally disseminate works of fiction intend is that their works be read or listened to as fiction. And even if reading or listening to as fiction involves imagining or making-believe various propositions – as it arguably does – this does not suffice to establish that by disseminating her work, an author invites readers and listeners to do so, even if she is aware of what reading or listening to as fiction consists in. Moreover, in chapter 6 I will argue that even authors who engage in storytelling performances fail to make invitations of this kind, or perform *sui generis* fictive illocutionary acts with the same perlocutionary goals, but rather engage in illocutionary pretense.

4.7 TRUTH IN FICTION – POSITIVE

In this section, I defend an account of fictional truth in terms of the revelations of the narrative informant. As above, what an informant reveals by means of her testimony cannot, in general, be identified with what she says; rather, it is a function of the theory which best fits what she says and implies, the evidence of her reliability, and relevant background information. In the non-fictional case, the revelations of informants cannot be identified with truth; after all, to put it crudely, some of the propositions entailed by a given revelation-theory may simply fail to correspond to the facts. In the fictional case, in contrast, there are no extra-theoretical fictional facts to which claims about fiction may or may not correspond. As a result, there is no impediment to identifying fictional truth with what the narrative informant reveals.

Of course, fictional truth cannot be simply identified with whatever actual readers and listeners happen to imagine but, rather, with what they ought to imagine. And this requires defining it in terms of the relevant evidence and theory that best fits it and not merely the evidence reader/listeners judge to be relevant and the theory they judge to have the best fit. As a result, the definition of fictional truth on offer here is as follows:

> ALWARD-1: "In fiction F, S" is true if and only if the theory which best fits what the narrative informant of F says and implies, the evidence for her reliability, and relevant background information includes the proposition that S,

or, more simply,

> ALWARD-2: "In fiction F, S" is true if and only if the narrative informant of F reveals that S,[83]

where the notion of revelation is understood in the normative sense sketched above. Consider again the sentence

> Holmes wears underpants.

The narrator of the Holmes stories – Dr Watson – by mentioning dates and places, pragmatically implies that the events he is describing occurred in nineteenth-century England. He gives every indication of being a reliable informant about these events except, perhaps, exaggerating his own contribution to them. Since the relevant background information includes the fact that respectable detectives in nineteenth-century England wore underpants, and Watson has neither said nor implied anything to the contrary regarding Holmes, the theory which best fits the facts entails that Holmes was so clad. Hence, this is something that Watson reveals.

As should be obvious, this analysis has little trouble accommodating unreliable narrators: it is, in fact, designed to do so. Nor does it run afoul of the problem of mindless fiction. The narrative informant, in terms of whose revelations fictional truth is defined, is a non-actual fact-teller, and not a fictional fact-teller like Currie's fictional author. Hence, in a mindless fiction this figure can be understood to be neither actual nor fictional but nevertheless reporting on a fictional world she does not inhabit. Since the mindlessness in question is restricted only to the world on which she reports, and does not extend to the world she inhabits – from which she reports – the threat of contradiction is forestalled. And any worry about the intelligibility of reporting about worlds one does not inhabit can be obviated by noting that appreciators of fiction commonly make reports about the very same fictional worlds that narrative informants report on, also without inhabiting them.

This analysis can also easily handle the problem of inconsistent fictions. Consider, again, a work in which it is reported that the protagonist has refuted Gödel's theorem. In order for it to be fictionally true, on the revelation analysis, that Gödel's theorem has been refuted all that is required is that this proposition be revealed by the narrative informant, that is, that it be included in the theory that best fits the evidence. There are, however, a couple of reasons one might balk here. First, one might worry that given that the refutation of Gödel's theorem is impossible, a theory according to which the narrative informant is reliable and Gödel's theorem was refuted will inevitably fit the evidence less well than one according to which she is unreliable and Gödel's theorem was not refuted. This worry presupposes, however, that the proposition that actual mathematics holds constitutes an unrevisable part of the background information of all fictional works. But not only are no background propositions immune to revision, there is no reason to suppose that this proposition – or any propositions for that matter – has this kind of privileged position as part of the relevant background information in all fictional works. Consider, for example, a work in a series centred around impossible mathematical breakthroughs. And second, one might worry that since the proposition that Gödel's theorem has been refuted is self-contradictory, it entails everything – at least unless classical logic is abandoned – and, hence, as with Lewis's analysis, everything will turn out to be vacuously fictionally true on the revelation analysis. What is important to note, however, is that, like "believes," "reveals" is an intensional operator. As a result, from the fact that the narrative informant of some work reveals a proposition P which entails some other proposition Q, it does not follow that the narrative informant reveals that Q.

A potential difficulty for the revelation analysis is presented by the phenomenon of storytelling narrators.[84] A storytelling narrator, recall, is an explicit narrator who clearly indicates that the story being presented is fictional and, hence, that she is a fiction-teller rather than a fact-teller. But, the objection goes, since narrative informants are fact-tellers, they cannot be storytelling narrators. Moreover, since fiction-tellers do not reveal anything by means of their utterances, fictional truth, in works with storytelling narrators, cannot be identified with narrators' revelations.

This worry can be dispelled, however, by noting that fictional works with storytelling narrators are best understood to generate stories within stories. The outer, and typically much thinner, story concerns the narrator's act of fiction-telling and related events, if there are any; and the inner story is the story the narrator relates by means of this act. Now, on my view, when she tells the outer story, the narrator engages in fact-telling, reporting about who she is and what she is doing – namely, fiction-telling – and the like. And when she tells the inner story, the narrator either pretends to be a fact-teller – in particular a non-actual (from her perspective)/non-fictional fact-teller – if her act of fiction-telling is oral, or she produces a manuscript she intends to be imagined to be authored by some such figure if her act of storytelling is written. As a result, fictional truth in the outer story can be identified with the revelations of the story-telling narrator, whereas fictional truth in the inner story can be identified with the revelations of the narrative informant the storytelling narrator either pretends to be or of whose efforts she intends her manuscript be imagined to be the product.

Finally, a word needs to be said about fictional objectivity. What the revelation analysis provides are truth conditions for fictional claims; but unless these conditions determinately obtain, this does not suffice for objective fictional truth. There are two separate reasons why the revelation analysis might fail to yield fictional objectivity. First, there could in principle be multiple distinct theories which equally well fit the evidence. And second, there may be no determinate fact of the matter regarding what constitutes the evidence; in particular, there may be no fact of the matter about what the relevant background information is. In response to the first worry, I am simply inclined to note that while there is always a theoretical possibility of ties, as a practical matter this is rarely the case. Moreover, in those cases in which genuine ties between competing theories do occur, I will happily concede that there is no fact of the matter about which theory is correct. After all, there is no reason to believe that fictional objectivity holds across the board.

An adequate response to the second worry will require briefly revisiting the role background information plays in the revelation analysis. Please recall: sources of background information include genre conventions, inter-fictional carry-over, and authorial and critical discussions of story, as well as facts about the actual world and beliefs prevalent among members of the author's community. And background information contributes to the revelations of narrative informants both through what is jointly implied by this information and the contents of informants' reports and through clashes between the two. The problem is that what and how much, if any, information is relevant in any given case is controversial. The role of information about or provided by the author, for example, remains especially controversial. One might hope that a process of reflective equilibrium, along the following lines, would suffice to resolve such disputes: (i) identify some relatively uncontentious fictional truths; (ii) working backwards, discern what background information is required to yield such truths; (iii) inductively develop general principles relating background information to fictional works; and (iv) test these principles by applying them to further cases. Whether or not such a procedure is even promising is, I take it, an open question. But in lieu of some such procedure, we may be left with no determinate fact of the matter regarding the relevance of background information. And if so, fictional objectivity will have to be abandoned, if the revelation analysis is accepted, in favour of a kind of fictional relativity according to which fictional truth is relative to decisions about what background information is relevant. But, arguably at least, fictional truth is relative to decisions about the relevance of exactly this sort of information. And if this is right, the failure of fictional objectivity is a virtue, and not a vice, of the revelation analysis.

PART THREE

Fictional Names and Fictional Talk

5

Empty Revelations

In this chapter, I develop a theory of the contents of fictional names – names of fictional people in particular, and of fictional entities more generally. The fundamental datum that must be addressed by such a theory is that fictional names are, in an important sense, empty: the entities to which they putatively refer do not actually exist.[1] Nevertheless, they make substantial contributions to the truth conditions of sentences in which they occur. Not only do such sentences have truth conditions but sentences that differ only in the fictional names they contain differ in their truth conditions. The central problem of fictional names is that of reconciling their emptiness with their substantial contributions.

A common approach to fictional names involves taking them to fall within the scopes of intensional fictionality operators and offering a broadly Fregean analysis of referring expressions that occur within sentence frames of that kind.[2] Fregean analyses of fictional names, however, run into serious difficulties. In particular, the analyses heretofore on offer seem to imply that fictional names of what are intuitively the same fictional characters but which occur in different fictional stories must inevitably differ in content. As a result, speakers whose uses of fictional names are derived from different stories are inevitably talking past one another. A subsidiary problem of fictional names, at least for theorists of a Fregean bent, therefore, is that of showing how names which occur in distinct fictional stories can have the same contents, at least when they are intuitively of the same fictional characters.

It is worth noting, again, that the sense of content at issue here is illocutionary content – what is asserted, or requested, or commanded, etc., by means of an utterance. The content of a fictional name is its contribution to the illocutionary content of a sentence in which it occurs. Illocutionary content is a property of utterances or sentence tokens and, as such, is to be distinguished from sentence meaning or character – a property of sentence types.[3] And insofar as there is a distinction between the semantic content of an utterance and what is said or requested, etc., by means of it, it is the latter which is at issue here.[4]

This chapter consists of five main parts. First, the intensional fictionality operator approach to fictional names defended here, as well as the Fregean analysis of expressions occurring within the scopes of such operators, will be motivated. Second, the difficulty for this approach sketched above will be developed and shown to undermine both Lewis's and Currie's variants of it. In the remaining three sections, an alternative to these theories will be defended. In the third section, cognitive relations and their intra- and intersubjective collections, which lie at the core of the analysis developed here, will be introduced. Fourth, a theory which takes the contents of names in epistemic sentence frames to be intersubjective collections of cognitive relations will be developed and applied to revelation reports made of actual informants. Finally, this theory will be adapted to the revelation reports of narrative informants in terms of which claims about fiction are analysed – at least on the theory defended here – and shown to avoid the difficulties which undermined its competitors.

5.1 MOTIVATIONS

The focus in this chapter is the contents of fictional names in metafictive claims – claims concerning the goings on in particular fictional stories. Broadly speaking, there are two distinct positions that can be taken regarding the logical forms of metafictive sentences containing fictional names: fictional names can be treated as if they occur within extensional sentence frames; or they can be treated as if they occur within the scopes of fictionality operators of some kind. A sentence frame can be thought of a sentence with one or more holes or gaps in it. When these gaps are filled with expressions of the appropriate grammatical category, a grammatically well-formed sentence is produced. A sentence frame is extensional if its gap(s) does not fall within the scope of an intensional sentential operator. Paradigmatic intensional operators include modal – "it is necessary that," for example – and epistemic – "Fred believes that," for example – operators. An important feature of extensional frames is that they are open to substitutivity: an expression that occurs within some such frame can be replaced by any co-extensive expression without affecting the truth-value of the overall sentence. Consider, for example, the occurrence of the name "Professor Alward" in the (I hope) false sentence

Professor Alward has poor personal hygiene.

Since "Professor Alward" and "Peter All-weird" (unfortunately) co-refer, and the sentence frame

… has poor personal hygiene

is extensional,

Peter All-weird has poor personal hygiene

must be false as well.

In the period since Kripke's devastating attacks on descriptivism,[5] Millianism has become the received view of the contents of referring expressions in extensional sentence frames.[6] According to the Millian view, the content of a name just is its referent. Given that fictional names lack actual referents,[7] the Millian who thinks fictional names have extensional occurrence has to claim that they either lack contents[8] or have non-actual referents which serve as their contents.[9] And neither alternative is altogether satisfactory. If the former is correct, then (utterances of) sentences containing fictional names lack contents as well. But it is not clear how this can be reconciled with the (intuitive) truth or falsity of such sentences.[10] And not only does the latter bring with it an unpalatable metaphysic of impossible objects but how fictional names come to stand in referential relations to such causally isolated entities remains a mystery.[11]

Even if such worries could be alleviated, it is important to note that no appeal to fictional names is required to motivate the fictional-operator analysis of talk about fiction; rather, appeal to fictional immigrants is by itself sufficient. Fictional immigrants are actual people, places, or events which appear in fictional stories in *propria persona*. The problem posed by fictional immigrants is that they have at least some features in the fictional works in which they appear that differ from the features they have in actuality. As a result, unless (true) claims describing their fictional features are understood to occur within the scopes of fictionality operators, they will straightforwardly contradict (true) claims describing their actual features. Consider the following claim:

(1) Captain Broke took a fugitive spy on board the *Shannon* immediately prior to his action against the *Chesapeake*.

Understood as a description of the events depicted in *The Fortune of War*,[12] this claim is true; but as a matter of fact it is false.

The most obvious strategy for avoiding the implication that the very same claim can be both true and false is to recast the metafictive use of (1) as

(2) It is *The Fortune of War* fictional that Captain Broke took a fugitive spy on board the *Shannon* immediately prior to his action against the *Chesapeake*.

There is after all no contradiction in supposing that (1) is false and (2) is true. Unless the fictionality operator is properly interpreted, however, this manoeuvre will not by itself solve the problems that arose for extensionalism. Minimally, what is required is that the fictionality operator be interpreted in such a way that (i) the truth-value of a sentence of the form "Fp" – where "F" is the fictionality operator – can differ in truth-value for the embedded sentence "p" and (ii) the contents of referring expressions occurring within the scope of the fictionality operator can differ from their contents in extensional sentence frames.

A promising approach to finding an interpretation of the fictionality operator which meets these conditions involves appeal to some variant of the act/attitude analysis of fictional discourse. On this approach, metafictive claims are analysed as attributions of speech acts or propositional attitudes to a teller of some kind, normally an author or narrator figure. Variants of this approach include Currie's analysis in terms of the beliefs of the fictional author,[13] Lewis's analysis in terms of the assertions of a reliable fictional fact-teller,[14] and my own analysis in terms of the revelations of a narrative informant. The promise of this approach stems from the fact that speech act and propositional attitude attributions arguably have the two features we are requiring of the fictionality operator. I will consider each feature in turn.

First, it is commonplace to note that the truth-value of what someone might be judged to say or believe is independent of the truth-value of the judgment that she said or believes it. So, for example, the (putative) truth of

All unsullied snow is white

would be compatible with either the truth or the falsity of

Peter believes that all unsullied snow is white,

and of,

Peter said that all unsullied snow is white.

As a result, insofar as,

(2) It is *The Fortune of War* fictional that Captain Broke took a fugitive spy on board the *Shannon* immediately prior to his action against the *Chesapeake*,

is analysed as

(3) The fictional author of *The Fortune of War* believes that Captain Broke took a fugitive spy on board the *Shannon* immediately prior to his action against the *Chesapeake*,

or even,

(4) The narrative informant of *The Fortune of War* revealed that Captain Broke took a fugitive spy on board the *Shannon* immediately prior to his action against the *Chesapeake*,

the truth of (2) is compatible with the falsity of

(1) Captain Broke took a fugitive spy on board the *Shannon* immediately prior to his action against the *Chesapeake*.

Second, there are good grounds to think that the contents of names in act/attitude attributions cannot be their referents. As a result, if Millianism gives the correct account of their contents in extensional sentence frames, names can differ in content as between their act/attitude and extensional occurrences. The grounds I have in mind concern the role act/attitude attributions play in psychological explanations. Suppose, for example, that as the Watergate scandal was unfolding, Nixon sent some thugs to break into the offices of Woodward and Bernstein. Nixon's (hypothetical) behaviour might be explained as follows:

(a) Nixon desired to protect his presidency.
(b) Nixon believed that Deep Throat was a danger to his presidency.
(c) Nixon believed that in order to protect his presidency from people dangerous to it, he needed to discern their identities.

(d) Nixon believed that the identity of Deep Throat could be discerned by breaking into the offices of Woodward and Bernstein.

What is important to note is that if the content of "Deep Throat" in (b) is its referent, this pattern of reasoning does not in fact yield an explanation of Nixon's behaviour. Nixon stood in two distinct complex cognitive relations to the single person, Mark Felt. These can be called the "Felt-relation" and the "Deep Throat-relation." Nixon engaged in the pattern of behaviour that he did only because he believed Felt to be a danger while thinking about him by means of the Deep Throat relation. If Nixon had instead believed Felt to be a danger while thinking about him by means of the Felt-relation, he would have ousted him from his position as Associate FBI Director, or had him assassinated, rather than breaking into the offices of a couple of *Washington Post* reporters.[15] If the content of "Deep Throat" is simply its referent, the putative explanation makes no reference to either cognitive relation and so could not serve to explain either pattern of behaviour. But if the content is a Fregean entity – perhaps the Deep Throat-relation itself – the upshot is a genuine explanation of Nixon's behaviour.[16]

Consequently, on this approach the emptiness of "Stephen Maturin" in

(5) Captain Broke took Stephen Maturin on board the *Shannon* immediately prior to his action against the *Chesapeake*

can, at least arguably, be reconciled with its contentfulness in

(6) It is *The Fortune of War* fictional that Captain Broke took Stephen Maturin on board the *Shannon* immediately prior to his action against the *Chesapeake*,

at least insofar as (6) is analysed as an act/attitude attribution such as

(7) The fictional author of *The Fortune of War* believes that Captain Broke took Stephen Maturin on board the *Shannon* immediately prior to his action against the *Chesapeake*.

5.2 DESCRIPTIVE STASIS

In this section, a serious difficulty that arises for Fregean accounts of fictional names is developed. Lewis's and Currie's theories are the primary targets here, but the point is meant to be generalized. Despite their superficial differences, Lewis's and Currie's views share the same core idea – that the content of a fictional name consists of the set of descriptions predicated of its putative bearer by the fictional work in which it occurs. And it is to this core idea that I wish to object.

Consider, first, Lewis's theory. The contents of both fictional names and ordinary non-fictional names are, according to Lewis, functions from possible worlds to individuals. The distinguishing feature of the contents of fictional names is their behaviour at worlds in which the fictional stories in which they occur are told as known fact. Such worlds have two features which are worth emphasizing. First, the text, which is the product of acts of fiction-telling in the actual world, is the product of acts of fact-telling in such worlds. And second, since the story is told as known fact in these worlds, all the claims made in the story are true (and justified) in these worlds.

Now according to Lewis, at a world in which the fictional story in which a fictional name occurs is told as known fact, the value of the function which serves as the content of the name is the individual who has all the features and does all the things attributed to the bearer of the name by the story: "for any world w where the Holmes stories are told as known fact rather than fiction, the name denotes at w whichever inhabitant of w it is who there plays the role of Holmes."[17]

And at a world in which the fictional story is not told as known fact, the function which serves as the content of the fictional name has no value/denotation: "whenever a world w is not one of the worlds just considered, the sense of 'Sherlock Holmes' as we use it is such as to assign it no denotation at w."[18]

Consider the explicitly fictional sentence

It is *The Fortune of War* fictional that Captain Broke took Stephen Maturin on board the *Shannon* immediately prior to his action against the *Chesapeake*

(which, recall, we are supposing to be analysed as

The fictional author of *The Fortune of War* believes that Captain Broke took Stephen Maturin on board the *Shannon* immediately prior to his action against the *Chesapeake*,

or something along these lines). The content of the fictional name "Stephen Maturin" is, on Lewis's view, the function whose value at all worlds where *The Fortune of War* is told as known fact is the individual who does all the things attributed to the bearer of the name by the text and which lacks a value at all other worlds. Since *The Fortune of War* is told as fiction and not fact in the actual world, "Stephen Maturin" has no actual denotation on Lewis's view. In contrast, the name of a fictional immigrant, such as "Captain Broke," has a denotation in the actual world as well as in those worlds where *The Fortune of War* is told as known fact.[19]

Currie, in contrast, treats fictional names as implicit theoretical terms, and gives an account of their contents using Ramsey's technique for explicitly defining such terms.[20] According to Currie, a fictional story, S, can be viewed as a conjunction of claims containing a number of fictional names, $n_1, \dots, n_n$, which can be represented as

$$S(n_1, \dots, n_n).$$

Currie takes the content of the fictional story to be the contents of the "Ramsey sentence" generated by replacing each fictional name with a variable bound by an existential quantifier:

$\exists x_1 \dots \exists x_n \exists y [S(x_1, \dots, x_n)$ and y is responsible for the text T and T sets out y's knowledge of the activities of $x_1 \dots x_n$],[21]

where T is the text which constitutes the fictional story and the variable name "y" denotes Currie's fictional author figure. The content of a name, n_i, which occurs in story $S(n_1 \dots, n_{i-1}, n_i, n_{i+1}, \dots, n_n)$ is, on this view,

The unique x_i such that $\exists x_1 \dots \exists x_{i-1} \exists x_{i+1} \dots \exists x_n \exists y [S(x_1, \dots, x_n)$ and y is responsible for the text T and T sets out y's knowledge of the activities of $x_1 \dots x_n$].

Consider, for example, the following very simple (and short) fictional story:

T: Peter sat at his computer and wrote an article so boring it even put him to sleep,

in which "Peter" is fictional name. On Currie's view, the content of this story is

$\exists x \exists y (x$ sat at his computer and wrote an article so boring it even put x to sleep and y tells of the activities of x by producing T),

and the content of the name "Peter" is the content of the description

The unique x such that ∃y(x sat at his computer and wrote an article so boring it even put him to sleep and y is responsible for text T and T sets out y's knowledge of x).

Strictly speaking, what has been presented thus far is Currie's account of the contents of fictional names in metafictive claims only. When fictional names are used in fictive discourse – that is, when they are used in acts of fiction-telling – in contrast, "they are to be interpreted as bound variables"[22] in the Ramsey sentences generated from the fictional stories in which they appear. And when they occur in trans-fictive claims – claims concerning relations between characters and events from distinct fictional stories, or relations between fictions and non-fictional entities, or the like – their contents are roles: functions from worlds to individuals. The differences Currie draws between these distinct uses of fictional names are, however, at bottom differences of logico-syntactic category – bound variables, definite descriptions, logically proper names – rather than differences in the contributions of names to the contents of the sentences in which they occur. As a result, they are orthogonal to the objections developed below. If Currie's account of metafictive occurrences of fictional names falls prey to these objections, so too do his accounts of fictive and trans-fictive occurrences.

Despite their superficial differences, Lewis's and Currie's accounts of fictional names are nearly extensionally equivalent. At any world in which a fictional story is told as known fact there exists someone – in particular, the person who tells the story as known fact – who is responsible for the text of the story and whose knowledge is set out by the story. And at any such world, the object which satisfies the description Currie takes to serve as the content of a fictional name will be the very same object that is value at that world of the function which Lewis takes to be the content of the name: the object which has all the features and does all the things attributed to the bearer of the name by the story. Of course, insofar as there are worlds in which someone is responsible for the text of the story who nevertheless does not tell it, there will be worlds in which Currie's descriptions are satisfied but Lewis's functions lack values. But whether or not there are such worlds depends on how broadly or narrow one defines the notion of telling.

One reason to balk at what we might call the Lewis-Currie analysis is that it presupposes that every fictional story has a fictional teller – an inhabitant of the world described by the story who tells or is otherwise responsible for it.[23] The problem of interest here, however, remains even if we eliminate this element of the view and simply identify the content of a fictional name with the complex property attributed to the name's putative bearer by the fictional text. The basic difficulty is that the Lewis-Currie analysis seems to entail that occurrences of fictional names, intuitively of the same fictional characters, in distinct fictional stories differ in content. As a result, readers of distinct fictional works in which a character appears and who use the same name to talk about that character are inevitably talking past one another.

Consider Fred, who, on the basis of reading *The Fortune of War*[24] and no other books in the Aubrey-Maturin series, says,

Stephen Maturin is an ingenious spymaster.

And suppose that Mary, who has read only *Treason's Harbour*,[25] replies,

Stephen Maturin is a naive dupe.

Now according to the Lewis-Currie analysis, the content of "Stephen Maturin" in Fred's utterance is, roughly, the complex property of having the features and performing the actions attributed to the putative bearer of the name "Stephen Maturin" by *The Fortune of War*. And the content of "Stephen Maturin" in Mary's utterance is the complex property of having the features and performing the actions attributed to the putative bearer of the name by *Treason's Harbour*. But since these are distinct complex properties, the name differs in content in the two utterances.

Now the natural rejoinder would be that the content of a fictional name which occurs in multiple fictional stories is the complex property of having the features and performing the actions attributed to the putative bearer of the name by all the texts in question. So, according to this suggestion, the content of both Fred's and Mary's utterances of "Stephen Maturin" is the complex property of having the features and performing the actions attributed to the putative bearer of the name by *The Fortune of War* and *Treason's Harbour* (as well as, presumably, all the other novels in the Aubrey-Maturin series). As a result, the rejoinder goes, there is no reason to suppose that the Lewis-Currie analysis entails that Fred and Mary are talking past one another.

This rejoinder, however, is not ultimately tenable. This becomes clear when one considers that speakers can respond to utterances made long in the past. In particular, a speaker can disagree with something said using a fictional name on the basis of events depicted in a fictional story written subsequent to the original utterance. Suppose, for example, that Fred's utterance of

> Stephen Maturin is an ingenious spymaster

was made shortly after the original publication of *The Fortune of War* in 1979 and Mary's response,

> Stephen Maturin is a naive dupe,

was made only after the publication of *Treason's Harbour* in 1983. Now according to the rejoinder, the content of Mary's use of "Stephen Maturin" is the complex property attributed to the bearer of the name by *The Fortune of War* and *Treason's Harbour*. But what of Fred's use of the name? At the time he made his utterance, this complex property could not have served as content of his use of "Stephen Maturin"; after all, *Treason's Harbour* had not yet been written, and might not ever have been written. The alternative is to suppose that Fred's use of the name changed in content after the fact. But this is hardly palatable either: it renders what one says now, at least on matters fictional, hostage to the vicissitudes of future compositional decision making.

5.3 COGNITIVE RELATIONS AND THEIR COLLECTIONS

At the core of the account of fictional names that will be defended here is the notion of a cognitive relation. A cognitive relation is a relation in which a thinking subject stands to the (potential) objects of thought and talk. More to the point, the cognitive relations – as opposed to the non-cognitive relations – in which a subject stands to such objects are those relations in virtue of which she is able to think and talk about them. Cognitive relations include (i) experiential relations, such as seeing or hearing an object, (ii) reputational relations, such as hearing or reading about an object, and (iii) conceptual relations, thinking about objects by means of the deployment of concepts which uniquely denote them, as well as (iv) memory relations – remembering seeing, hearing about, etc., objects.

Cognitive relations, as I characterize them, are quite finely individuated. I am inclined to go so far as to suggest that no more than one entity can be the actual object of any given cognitive relation and, in the case of experiential and reputational relations, no more than one actual subject can be so related to that entity. (I am willing to concede, of course, that more than one subject can stand in the same conceptual relationship to a single entity). Nevertheless, again as I characterize them, cognitive relations are, for the most part, contingent.[26] This idea can be usefully formulated in terms of possible worlds as follows: experiential and reputational relations are instantiated by at most one subject-object pair at any given world, but may be instantiated by different subject-object pairs at different worlds;[27] at most one entity can be the object of a conceptual relation at any given world, but different entities can be its object at different worlds.[28]

One feature of cognitive relations, which may prove important later, is that they can fail to be actually instantiated. One can intelligibly speak of the experiential relation in which someone would (or could) have stood to an object had she been properly situated with respect to it, but in which no one, as a matter of fact, stood. Speculation regarding an unwitnessed crime is a nice example of what I have in mind. Or one can speak of an entity to which a subject would have been visually related, given her actual situation, had only it been properly situated. A subject might have seen – that is, been visually related to – the culprit fleeing the crime scene if only he had run the other way.

Folk psychological explanations of the behaviour of cognitive agents appeal to the properties they attribute to the objects of their cognitive relations. It is because she believes some such object has a certain property, or because she desires that it does, that a cognitive agent behaves as she does. But agents do not attribute properties in a piecemeal fashion to the relatum of each cognitive relation in which they stand. Rather, they attribute properties to what they take to be the shared relatum of a collection of cognitive relations. For example, an agent might believe that the object of her current visual experience is dangerous, not because of any of his current visual properties but because she remembers a visual experience of someone carrying a weapon and judges that the object of her current experience is the same person as the object of her remembered experience.

Such collections of cognitive relations do not map neatly onto objects in the world, however. This is the result of two sorts of errors to which cognitive agents commonly fall prey. First, cognitive agents can fail to realize that several of their cognitive relations share a relatum. An agent might, for example, simply fail to appreciate that a person she is currently being told about is the same person she saw earlier in the day. The upshot of this sort of error is that an agent's cognitive relations to a single object may end up falling within distinct collections of relations. Second, cognitive agents can erroneously judge that certain of their cognitive relations share a relatum. For example, an agent might incorrectly judge that the coat she sees on a bed at a party is the same item she remembers putting on when she left her own home. The upshot of this sort of error is a collection of cognitive relations whose members include relations to distinct objects. As a result, we might say that collections of cognitive relations correspond to an agent's notional objects – the objects she believes to occupy the world – rather than the actual furniture of the world.

Agents' collections of cognitive relations are better thought of as teams – let's call them "C-teams" – than sets. Sets are not only individuated in terms of their members, but have exactly those members essentially. As a result, they cannot survive diachronic, or counterfactual, changes in membership. That is, a collection to which one or more members are added, or from which one or more members are subtracted, is not the same set as the resulting collection. Nor are there any counterfactual circumstances in which a set exists but has different members. Teams, in contrast, regularly survive changes in membership. Consider, for example, a professional sports team that has traded away one of its players. And there are always counterfactual circumstances in which a given team exists with different members. This is important because agents' collections of cognitive relations continually undergo changes in membership. As an agent has new experiences, the experiential relations she thereby forges are added to pre-existing collections whenever she judges the experienced object to be one with which she is already familiar. And as her identity judgments are revised, or her memory fails, cognitive relations are subtracted from collections, or simply severed.

When a cognitive agent thinks or talks about one of her notional objects, one or more members of the corresponding C-team are typically salient. And any shared relatum these salient cognitive relations might have is the actual object of her thought and talk. Suppose, for example, that an agent, Lisa, has a visual experience of John at a party and an auditory experience of Gavin over the phone and judges that her two experiences are of a single person. Lisa thereby generates a C-team whose members include her visual relation to John and her auditory relation to Gavin. Suppose that while thinking about this notional person, her visual relation to John is salient. In such circumstances, her notional object of thought is a person whom she both saw at the party and spoke to on the phone, but her actual object of thought is John, a person with whom she has had no phone contact.

Thus far, we have been talking about intrasubjective teams of cognitive relations which correspond to the notional objects of individual speaker/thinkers. In what follows, however, the notion of conversationally generated intersubjective C-teams will prove to be equally important. By an intersubjective C-team, I mean a collection of cognitive relations in which distinct agents stand to objects in the world, bound together by the shared judgment that they have a common relatum. Such collections are conversationally generated in the following sense: cognitive agents stand in distinct cognitive relations to objects in the world; thus, in order to get a conversation about some object or other off the ground, potential conversational interlocutors need to establish that they are thinking/talking about the same thing – that is, they need to establish that their salient cognitive relations share a relatum.

The process by which intersubjective C-teams are conversationally generated can be illustrated as follows. Suppose the following conversation between Tom and Fred occurs while watching a tennis match in which Mary is participating:

Stage I:
    Tom: Mary is a good tennis player.
    Fred: Yes, she is.
Stage II:
    Tom: She is also a good philosopher.
    Fred: Yes, she is.
Stage III:
    Tom: Her talk on mental causation last Tuesday was excellent.
    Fred: Mary didn't give a talk last Tuesday. She was in Australia.

Underlying Tom's initial utterance is a salient cognitive relation in which he stands to Mary – let's say his experiential relation to Mary during the tennis match. Fred's initial response presupposes that the person to whom Tom referred is the same person as the object of the salient cognitive relation underlying his own utterance – Tom's own experiential relation to Mary at the tennis match. Once Tom comes to share this presupposition, as his subsequent utterance indicates he does, an intersubjective C-team has been generated consisting of both Tom and Fred's experiential relations to Mary at the tennis match.

By means of subsequent conversational moves, further cognitive relations can be added to this C-team and current members can be subtracted from it. Suppose, for example, the salient cognitive relation underlying Tom's utterance during the second stage of the conversation is his experiential relation to the speaker at a philosophy talk he attended the previous Tuesday and the salient cognitive relation underlying Fred's utterance at this stage is some reputational relation in which he stands to Mary. Insofar as Fred continues to judge that Tom is talking about the same person he has in mind and vice versa these new cognitive relations get added to the previously generated intersubjective C-team. At the third stage, however, Fred rejects the assumption that Tom is talking about the same person that he has been talking about. As result, if Tom accepts Fred's correction, his experiential relation to the speaker at the philosophy talk gets subtracted from the C-team, assuming, of course, this was the salient cognitive relation underlying his utterance at this stage.

It is worth noting that many conversations putatively about a single object take place between numerous conversational interlocutors over long periods of time and across great distances. Paradigmatically such conversations concern well-known historical figures, but most conversations concerning lesser known figures also share this form, albeit in a more limited way. The C-teams generated by such conversations are more complicated (and just messier) than the simple model discussed above. Conversational contributions rarely reach all participants in the conversation, rarely is there uniform agreement about the properties of the object under discussion or even that the same object is being referred to by all participants, the contributions of some participants are often held to be more authoritative than those of others, and it is not even generally true that all conversational participants are alive at the same time. As a result, the corresponding C-team is made up in large part of a patchwork of subteams of (sometimes radically) differing sizes and statures. And some cognitive relations – those regarding which there is substantial disagreement – are neither members nor non-members of a given C-team, having instead a kind of inactive status. Nevertheless, such C-teams are genuine entities encompassing real and important features of social reality. They are cultural artifacts with which we can engage and to which we can contribute. Merely having heard of the object at issue – that is, standing in a reputational relation to it – puts one in a position to enter into the conversation and contribute one's own cognitive relations to the corresponding C-team.[29]

5.4 CONVERSATIONS WITH, AND ATTRIBUTIONS TO, ACTUAL INFORMANTS

Suppose an informant, Fred, makes the following assertion about a subject, Mary, who is suspected of vandalizing a bakery:

(1) Mary spent the night at her home watching television.

In a subsequent meeting to discuss Fred's interrogation, the police stenographer makes the following report on Fred's verbal behaviour:

(2) Fred said that Mary spent the night at her home watching television.

Detective Smith, perhaps on the basis of Fred's nervous tone of voice, judges his assertion to be insincere and infers

(3) Fred believed that Mary did not spend the night at her home watching television.

Finally, Detective Jones, on the basis of his knowledge of Fred's general reliability vis-à-vis the whereabouts of people in his circle, and, perhaps, the lack of independent evidence corroborating Mary's presence in her home on the evening of the crime, concludes

(4) Fred revealed that Mary did not spend the night at her home watching television.

For broadly Kripkean reasons, I take the content of "Mary" in (1) to be its referent.[30] And in my view, the referent of some such use of a name is the object of the salient cognitive relation underlying it, or the shared object of the salient cognitive relations underlying it, if there is one.[31] As a result, if Mary is the object of the salient cognitive relation underlying Fred's utterance of (1) then she is the content of the occurrence of the name "Mary" in that utterance. Our central question, however, concerns the contents of names and other referring expressions in act/attitude reports. And there are two preliminary comments worth making at this point. First, as above, a Millian account of the contents of referring expressions in act/attitude reports, according to which their contents are their referents, is incommensurable with the role such reports play in psychological explanations; hence, the view developed here will be, broadly speaking, Fregean. And second, given the inferential relations that hold between (2), (3), and (4), a theory according to which referring expressions have the same contents in indirect discourse, belief reports, and revelation reports is desirable.[32]

The basic analysis of act/attitude attributions on offer here takes them to report that the subject of the attribution stands in a certain relation to a propositional object whose constituents are the contents of the referring and predicative expressions in the complement clause of the attribution. So, for example, an utterance of

Jennifer believes that Peter is a genius

is analysed as

Believes (Jennifer, <C('is a genius'); C('Peter')>)

(where "C('x')" abbreviates "the content of 'x'"). Now according to the Millian view, the contents of expressions in the complement clauses of sentences of this kind are just their ordinary referents. As a result, the Millian analysis of

Jennifer believes that Peter is a genius

is

Believes (Jennifer, <Being a genius; Peter>).[33]

On the view developed here, in contrast, the contents of expressions in the complement clauses of act/attitude ascriptions are teams of cognitive relations, or C-teams. As a result, our example sentence receives the following analysis:

Believes (Jennifer, $<CT^{\text{'is a genius'}}; CT^{\text{'Peter'}}>$),

where "$CT^{\text{'is a genius'}}$" denotes the C-team which is the content of "is a genius" in the belief report at issue, and "$CT^{\text{'Peter'}}$" denotes the C-team which is the content of 'Peter' in this sentence.

The question, of course, is exactly which team of cognitive relations serves as the content of an expression in the complement clause of an act/attitude attribution. Normally, it will be a C-team whose members are largely made up of cognitive relations in which the subject of the attribution stands. In particular, it will include those cognitive relations which played a salient role in producing the behaviour which prompted the attribution. Consider, again, the police stenographer's utterance of

(2) Fred said that Mary spent the night at her home watching television,

which, recall, was prompted by Fred's prior utterance of

(1) Mary spent the night at her home watching television.

Included in the content of "Mary" in (2) are the cognitive relations by means of which Fred was thinking of Mary when he uttered (1).

In addition to including cognitive relations in which the subject of the attribution stands, the C-team which serves as the content of a complement clause referring expression will also include cognitive relations in which the attributer stands. In particular, it will include those relations by means of which the attributor was thinking of the object of the attribution when making the attribution. When the police stenographer made his utterance of (2), he was thinking of the referent of his use of "Mary" by means of some of his own cognitive relations. Moreover, he judged these relations to share an object with the cognitive relations by means of which Fred was thinking of the referent of his previous use of "Mary." And these relations in which the stenographer stands are included among the members of the intersubjective C-team which serves as the content of "Mary" in (2).

What is important to note, however, is that with subsequent conversational moves the membership of these intersubjective C-teams can undergo change. In order to respond to a speaker's act/attitude attribution, a conversational interlocutor needs to judge that the referents of any names she uses share referents with those used by the speaker. And in so doing, she adds the cognitive relations by means of which she was thinking of the referents of the names she uses to the C-teams which served as the contents of the names the speaker used.[34] So, for example, when in response to the stenographer's utterance of (2), Detective Smith says,

(3) Fred believed that Mary did not spend the night at her home watching television,

she adds the cognitive relations by means of which she was thinking of the referent of "Mary" to the C-team which served as the content of the name in (2). And when Detective Jones responds to (3) with

(4) Fred revealed that Mary did not spend the night at her home watching television,

he too adds the cognitive relations by means of which he was thinking of the referent of "Mary" to the C-team in question, and this enriched C-team serves of the content of the name in his revelation report. Nevertheless, despite the changes in membership, the same C-team remains: just as sports teams can survive the gain or loss of members, due to trades, retirements, and the like, so too can teams of cognitive relations. As a result, the police stenographer's, Detective Smith's, and Detective Jones's uses of "Mary" all have the same content in their respective act/attitude attributions of Fred. After all, despite the differences in membership of the C-teams which serve as contents of "Mary" in their various utterances, it is nevertheless the same C-team.

Finally, suppose that a second informant, Joe, makes the following assertion regarding Mary's whereabouts:

(5) Mary was either at home watching television or loitering near Baker's Lane.

Detective Smith, on the basis of her judgment that Joe is both sincere and reliable, then infers

(6) Joe revealed that Mary was either at home watching television or loitering near Baker's Lane.

And, finally, by appeal to (4) and his basic logical acumen, Detective Jones concludes

(7) Joe and Fred (jointly) revealed that Mary was loitering near Baker's Lane.

Now according to the view on offer here, the content of "Mary" in (7) is the intersubjective C-team that was thereby generated, whose members include the salient cognitive relations underlying Fred's utterance of (1), the salient cognitive relations underlying Joe's utterance of (5), and the cognitive relations by means of which Detective Jones was thinking of the referent of "Mary" when he uttered (7) (as well as the salient cognitive relations underling Detective Smith's and the police stenographer's prior utterances).

One might wonder, however, how this could be compatible with the claim that the content of "Mary" is the same in (4), (6), and (7). After all, the C-team which is its content in (4) contains no cognitive relations in which Joe stands and, one might think, by parity of reasoning the C-team which is its content in (6) contains no cognitive relations in which Fred stands. But what is important to note is that given the different points at which they occur in the conversation, the reasoning vis-à-vis (4) and (6) need not be equivalent. When Detective Jones uttered (4), Joe's utterance had yet to occur, and so no judgments had been made to the effect that Joe's cognitive relations shared an object with other relations in which anyone else stood. But when Detective Smith uttered (6), (4) and its predecessors had already occurred as part of the ongoing conversation. As a result, insofar as Smith was continuing the discussion about the police suspicions regarding Mary's role in the bakery vandalism, she would have to judge that Joe's and Fred's (and her own) salient cognitive relations shared an object. And in so doing, she added Joe's salient cognitive relations to the C-team that served as the content of "Mary" in (4). But as before, C-teams can survive changes in membership; hence, there is no reason to believe that "Mary" differs in content in the various revelation reports in which it occurs.

5.5 NARRATIVE INFORMANTS AND FICTIONAL NAMES

What remains is to apply the account of referring expressions in act/attitude attributions developed above to the fictional case. And insofar as metafictive claims are analysed as act/attitude attributions, as we have been assuming, this is a more or less straightforward matter. There are, however, a few complications. Please note: the account of fictional names on offer here and the account of fictional truth in terms of the revelations of narrative informants, developed in chapter 4, are meant to be independent; the former could be applied to a distinct account of fictional truth, and the latter is compatible with distinct accounts of fictional names. Nevertheless, for purposes of expository simplicity, the account of fictional names will, in this section, be formulated in terms of the revelations of narrative informants.

Suppose Fred makes the (explicitly) metafictive claim

It is *The Fortune of War* fictional that Stephen Maturin is an ingenious spymaster,

which, we are assuming, is equivalent to

The narrative informant of *The Fortune of War* revealed that Stephen Maturin is an ingenious spymaster.

On the view on offer here, this revelation report can be analysed as,

$$\text{Revealed (NI}_{\textit{The Fortune of War}}, \langle\text{CT}^{\text{'is an ingenious spymaster'}}; \text{CT}^{\text{'Stephen Maturin'}}\rangle),$$

where, as above, "CT$^{\text{'Stephen Maturin'}}$" denotes the C-team which is the content of the fictional name "Stephen Maturin" (and "NI$_{\textit{The Fortune of War}}$" abbreviates "the narrative informant of *The Fortune of War*"). Now if we were to follow the model of the non-fictional case, the members of this C-team would include cognitive relations in which both the narrative informant and Fred stand to the character Stephen Maturin, as well as similar cognitive relations in which other speakers stand, if Fred made his claim in response to claims made by other readers of *The Fortune of War* with whom he was conversing. Given that access to fictional worlds is mediated by the reports of narrative informants, the cognitive relations in which readers and listeners stand to fictional characters would (normally) have to be reputational.[35] The exception would be when narrative informants are themselves fictional characters, in which case reader/listeners would stand in experiential relations to them in virtue of experiencing (what they imagine to be) their words.

There are, however, a number of reasons one might balk at this picture as it stands. First, if, as I claim, fictional characters do not exist, it is far from clear how anyone – reader/listeners or narrative informants – can stand in cognitive relations to them. Second, both because they often fail to occupy the (fictional) worlds on which they report and because they too fail to exist, it is far from clear how narrative informants can stand in cognitive relations to fictional characters (or fictional entities more generally). And third, for similar reasons it is unclear how narrative informants can serve as intermediaries in reader/listeners' cognitive relations to fictional characters. One might think that the problems delineated here could be largely resolved by appeal to an ontology of non-existent objects.[36] The difficulty with this strategy – metaphysical qualms aside – however, is that it remains unclear whether and how thinking subjects could come to stand in any kind cognitive relation to such entities.

It will, I hope, prove fruitful to take two passes at this collection of problems. As a first pass, a solution can be found to them by appeal to uninstantiated – and trans-world – cognitive relations. As above, cognitive relations can be uninstantiated: we can speak intelligibly of the cognitive relation that would have obtained had there been a suitably situated subject or object (or both). Moreover, since the membership of C-teams consists of cognitive relations, and not the relata of these relations, there is no impediment to taking uninstantiated relations to be included among the membership of such collections. As a result, in place of instantiated cognitive relations in which the narrative informant of *The Fortune of War* stands to Stephen Maturin, the C-team which serves of the content of "Stephen Maturin" in metafictive claims includes the uninstantiated relations in which the narrative informant would have stood to the referent of "Stephen Maturin" had those two figures existed and had the former produced the text of *The Fortune of War* as a report on the activities of the latter. And in place of the instantiated complex cognitive relation, mediated by the narrative informant, in which a reader of *The Fortune of War* stands to Stephen Maturin, the C-team at issue includes the uninstantiated relation in which she would have stood to the referent of "Stephen Maturin" had the narrative informant and Maturin existed, had the former produced the text of *The Fortune of War* as a report on the activities of the latter, and had the reader read *The Fortune of War* as a work of non-fiction. Finally, as to the worry about narrative informants reporting on fictional worlds they do not inhabit, this presupposes that narrative worlds – from which they make their reports – are causally isolated from the fictional worlds on which they report. But even if there are grounds to deny non-fictional narrative informants the ability to intervene in the fictional worlds on which they report, there is no (general) reason to suppose they cannot stand in experiential relations to the events that occur therein, and hence that they cannot stand in perfectly ordinary cognitive relations to the inhabitants of those worlds.

There is, I think, something to be said for this solution to the difficulties that arose for applying the account of referring expressions in act/attitude attributions discussed in the previous section to the fictional case. There are also reasons to balk. First, in the non-fictional case, the members of a C-team which serves as the content of a name in an act/attitude attribution are cognitive relations in which the subject of the attribution and the attributor (or her conversational interlocutors) stand and which the latter judges to share an object. But not only is it odd that the membership of the C-teams that are the contents of fictional names consists of cognitive relations in which no one stands, if these relations lack objects they cannot be judged to share objects. Second, not only are the cognitive relations in question uninstantiated, they are of the wrong kind. They are the kinds of relations in which a subject with doxastic attitudes toward a text – who was reading or listening to it as a non-fictional report – would be expected to stand. But reader/listeners of fiction have imaginative – not doxastic – attitudes toward the texts with which they are engaged. And third, one might rightly point out that the cognitive relations in question are of the kind in which a reader/listener of fiction might imagine standing if she were thereby imagining reading or listening to a non-fictional report. But recall, on the view on offer here, engaged reader/listeners do not, or at least need not, imagine *de se* reading or listening to factual reports, or being or doing anything for that matter; rather, they simply imagine *de re* of what they are in fact reading/listening to that it is factual.

As a second pass, we might formulate matters in terms not of cognitive relations in which reader/listeners fail to stand but might imagine themselves standing, but rather in terms of the cognitive states in which they actually find themselves. And such states can be fruitfully modelled on those of audience members watching (and listening to) a stage play. Members of theatrical audiences stand in experiential relations to the actors (and props) onstage. And they imagine *de re* of these actors that they are the characters they are portraying. One might think that the audience members thereby stand in experiential relations to the fictional characters in question. This way of putting it, however, is misleading: one cannot, after all, literally see what does not exist. What one might loosely describe as standing in a cognitive relation to a fictional entity is best understood as a cognitive state in which one stands in a cognitive relation to an actor/storyteller, prop, or fictional work and imagines of it that it is thus and so.

On this model, in place of instantiated cognitive relations in which the narrative informant of *The Fortune of War* stands to Stephen Maturin – or uninstantiated relations in which the narrative informant would have stood to the referent of "Stephen Maturin" had those two figures existed – the C-team which serves of the content of "Stephen Maturin" in metafictive claims includes the reader/listener's cognitive state of imagining that there is (or was) a narrative informant figure who produced the text of *The Fortune of War* as a report on the activities of someone named "Stephen Maturin" (among other things) to whom he stood in various cognitive relations. And in place of the instantiated complex cognitive relation in which a reader of *The Fortune of War* stands to Stephen Maturin, the C-team at issue includes the reader/listener's cognitive state of imagining *de re* of the fictional text she is reading, or to which she is listening, that it is the report of a narrative informant figure on the activities of someone called "Stephen Maturin" to whom the former stands in various cognitive relations.[37] Finally, this model does not require that narrative informants stand in trans-world cognitive relations to fictional characters; rather it requires only that reader/listeners imagine that this be so.

What remains is to explain how this view avoids the difficulties that arose for the Lewis-Currie analysis. The first thing to note is that, as it now stands, the C-teams which serve as the contents of fictional names are collections of cognitive, and, in particular, imaginative, states. Moreover, distinct imaginative states come to fall within the same collection not when they are judged to share a relatum, but rather when they are judged to be same-character imaginings. Let me elaborate. A reader of *The Lord of the Rings* might at one point find herself in a state of imagining that the narrative informant is reporting on the activities of someone named "Gollum" – let's call this a "Gollum-imagining."[38] Subsequently, she might find herself in a state of imagining that the narrative informant is reporting on the activities of someone named "Smeagol" – let's call this a "Smeagol-imagining." If the reader judges (correctly) that Gollum-imaginings just are Smeagol-imaginings, then she has judged her two imaginative states to be same-character imaginings. As a result, they come to fall within the same (intrasubjective) collection of cognitive states.

Consider again Fred who, having read only *The Fortune of War*, says,

Stephen Maturin is an ingenious spymaster,

and Mary who, having read only *Treason's Harbour*, replies,

Stephen Maturin is a naive dupe.

Now the content of Fred's use of "Stephen Maturin" is an intersubjective C-team of cognitive states and relations, whose members include various of Fred's imaginative states – his Stephen Maturin-imaginings – that he judges to be same-character imaginings (as well as imaginative states of other speakers with whom he has previously discussed *The Fortune of War* regarding which he has made a similar judgment). Like Fred, Mary judges the imaginative states she finds herself in when the name "Stephen Maturin" occurs while reading *Treason's Harbour* to be same-character imaginings. But, in addition, because her utterance is made in response to Fred's prior utterance, she also judges these imaginative states and the members of the C-team which was the content of Fred's use of the name to be same-character imaginings, and in so doing, she adds the former states to this C-team. What is important to note is that this larger collection, which is the content of Mary's use of "Stephen Maturin," – is the same C-team as that which served as the content of Fred's prior utterance, despite the difference in membership. As a result, the content of Mary's use of the fictional name is the same as the content of Fred's.

5.6 CONCLUSION

The central goal of this chapter was to develop an account of fictional names compatible with both their emptiness and their substantial contributions to the sentences in which they occur. This was achieved by taking the metafictive claims in which they occur to be analysed as act/attitude attributions and giving a, broadly speaking, Fregean account of the contents of names in such contexts. In order to avoid the difficulties that undercut Lewis's and Currie's similarly Fregean views, however, a theory was required that did not simply identify the content of a fictional name with the collection of features attributed to the bearer of the name by the fictional story in which it occurs. The theory developed in this chapter achieved this result by (i) distinguishing between individual cognitive states and relations and teams of the same and (ii) taking only the latter to serve as the contents of fictional names. What remains is to embed this theory within a broader account of the various sorts of speech acts in which fictional names occur.

6

Fictional Discourse

This essay's final task is to provide an account of fictional discourse that draws on what has gone before. Such an account requires not only a characterization of the nature of the speech acts performed by someone engaging in speech of this kind but also an account of the truth conditions of her utterances, if they have any, as well as of the contents of the expressions she uses. This task is complicated, however, by the existence of a number of distinct varieties of fictional discourse. As above, we can distinguish between fictive discourse – the sentences which constitute fiction texts – metafictive discourse – claims about the goings on in particular fictional stories – and trans-fictive discourse – claims relating fictional characters and events to things external to the stories in which they occur. Moreover, speaker/writers of at least the latter two forms of discourse can be either imaginatively engaged or disengaged.

The focus here will depend on the variety of fictional discourse at issue. The discussion of fictive discourse focuses on the nature of the speech acts performed by fiction-tellers of various kinds. Given that speakers of meta- and trans-fictive discourse more or less uncontroversially perform assertions, the discussion of these kinds of fictional talk will focus instead on the truth-conditions of such assertions. Please note: although the distinction between fictive discourse, on the one hand, and meta- and trans-fictive discourse, on the other, will prove to be significant, the distinction between the latter two – and their engaged and disengaged variants – will prove to be less so. As we shall see, all varieties of talk about fiction are, on the account offered here, unified by their relation to the core analysis of engaged metafictive discourse.

This chapter consists of eight sections. In the first three sections, fictive discourse – and in particular, storytelling performance – is discussed. The main thrust of this discussion is a defence of the pretense model of story-telling[1] against both the fictive illocution account[2] and the game model.[3] In the middle two sections, metafictive discourse is addressed. In addition to developing the picture introduced in chapters 4 and 5, Walton's alternative is critiqued.[4] The topic of the final three sections is trans-fictive discourse. The sections concern, in turn, two sorts of imaginative projects in which engaged speakers/writers might be involved, as well as the trans-fictive utterances of imaginatively disengaged speakers.

6.1 FICTIVE DISCOURSE — COMPOSITION
AND STORYTELLING REVISITED

Fictive discourse includes both the products of compositional activity and the sentences used in storytelling performances. And although composition and storytelling can coincide, for example, in improvised performances, they are nevertheless very different sorts of activities. Composition has been largely discussed in chapters 1 and 3, but before going on to address storytelling, it may prove fruitful to briefly revisit the results of that discussion. On the view defended here, the goal of fictional composition is the production of a fictional work – a word-sculpture designed to be read/listened to as fiction. Moreover, in selecting and recording the sentences which constitute fictional works they compose, authors need not, and rarely do, perform illocutionary acts of any kind or engage in any kind of illocutionary pretense.

Not only do authors refrain from performing illocutionary acts when they compose their fictional works, the sentences they produce, in an important sense, lack truth conditions. After all, rather than writing sentences which may or may not "correspond" to a pre-existing set of fictional facts, by means of their compositional acts authors instead create the fictional facts. Moreover, there are grounds for thinking they also lack propositional content.[5] The content of a sentence is fixed by its character or sentence meaning and features of the context in which it is uttered. But because a context of composition is not a context of utterance, at least insofar as authors refrain from illocutionary commitment, the sentences which constitute fictional works typically remain ambiguous between multiple propositional contents. [6] One might, of course, identify the content of a composed sentence with the proposition the author intends that reader/listeners imagine upon reading/listening to it. But not only do some authors fail to have intentions of these kinds vis-à-vis the imaginative states of their reader/listeners, given that what an author intends her audience to imagine can be distinct from the proposition that the sentence literally expresses in any context of utterance – especially if the narrator the author creates is unreliable – this could hardly be identified with the content of the sentence in any ordinary sense of the term.

One might, of course, suppose that by means of disseminating or otherwise deploying her completed work, an author thereby performs substantial (and contentful) speech acts. But as we have seen, in circulating her completed work among friends, or sending it to a potential publisher, an author does not thereby perform illocutionary acts corresponding to each of the sentences which constitute the work, even if in so doing she intends that the recipients of her work read or listen to it as fiction. But given that in a storytelling performance, the author – or someone else – utters each sentence that makes up the work in turn, it remains open for her to thereby perform substantial speech acts of some kind. And the nature of such storytelling speech acts will be the topic of the next two sections of this chapter.

6.2 STORYTELLING – NEGATIVE

There are three central theories of fictional storytelling: Searle's illocutionary pretense account,[7] Curry's *sui generis* fictional illocution account,[8] and Saltz's game model.[9] In this section, the latter two approaches will be developed and subjected to critical scrutiny. In the next section, a variant of the former will be developed and defended. The question here concerns the kind of speech acts authors and others make during their storytelling performances. A naive first suggestion is that storytellers perform genuine and familiar kinds of illocutionary acts by means of their utterances of the sentences which make up the stories they tell. So, for example, on this view, if someone uttered,

> Case picked at a shred of bacon that had lodged between his front teeth,[10]

during a storytelling performance of William Gibson's *Neuromancer*, she would thereby have asserted that Case – or, perhaps, someone named "Case" – had picked at a shred of bacon that had lodged between his front teeth. The trouble with this suggestion, however, is that the genuine performance of an illocutionary act of a given kind requires that a number of criteria be satisfied, several of which are not satisfied by the utterances of storytellers.

The criteria of interest here are the illocutionary-intention criterion and the sincerity-obligation criterion. According to the illocutionary-intention criterion, in order to perform an illocutionary act of a certain kind, a speaker's utterance needs to be prompted by an illocutionary intention appropriate to acts of that kind – in general, the intention to produce some effect upon the listener by means of his recognition of this intention.[11] So, for example, in order to assert that most unsullied snow is white, a speaker needs to intend that her listener come to believe this to be the case by means of his recognition of her intention that he believe it.[12] And according to the sincerity-obligation criterion, a speaker who makes an illocutionary act of a certain kind is under an obligation to be in a mental state corresponding to the effect she intends to produce in listeners. So, for example, a speaker who asserts that most unsullied snow is white, and thereby intends to produce a belief that most unsullied snow is white in her listeners, is under an obligation to believe it herself.[13]

There are three separate reasons for thinking that the utterances of storytellers fail to satisfy these criteria. First, as a matter of fact, storytellers need not and typically do not find themselves in the requisite mental states. An author who uttered,

> Case picked at a shred of bacon that had lodged between his front teeth,

during a storytelling performance would not ordinarily either believe that someone named "Case" picked at a shred of bacon that had lodged between his front teeth, or intend to instill this belief in the listening audience. Second, there is no reason to think that when they engage in their performances, storytellers are under sincerity obligations, that is, that they are obligated to believe their storytelling assertions, to keep their storytelling promises, etc. Not only do listening audiences refrain from criticizing storytellers who fail to believe what they say, etc., in most ordinary cases they would be surprised if they did. And third, when a speaker makes a genuine illocutionary act, her utterance is caused by her illocutionary intention. But except when they are engaged in improvisational storytelling, the utterances of storytellers are caused instead by the texts they are performing. A storyteller who utters the sentence,

> Case picked at a shred of bacon that had lodged between his front teeth,

while performing *Neuromancer* does so because it occurs in the text and not because of any illocutionary intentions she might have.

According to Currie, authors (and others), when they make their storytelling utterances, perform *sui generis* fictive illocutionary actions distinct from and irreducible to familiar illocutions such as assertions and requests.[14] This fictive illocution is distinguished from other sorts of illocutionary action in terms of the intended effects on listeners. Whereas the illocutionary intention characteristic of assertion, for example, is that the listener come to believe the asserted proposition by means of his recognition of the speaker's intention that he do so, the perlocutionary goal of fictive illocutionary action is that the listener imagine or make-believe the proposition expressed by her utterance. Although this approach presupposes that storytellers' utterances are prompted by illocutionary intentions and governed by sincerity-obligations, the intentions and obligations characteristic of *sui generis* fictive illocutions are more plausibly attributed to storytellers than the intentions and obligations characteristic of more familiar illocutionary actions. A storyteller who utters the sentence

> Case picked at a shred of bacon that had lodged between his front teeth.

need only intend that her audience imagine what she says and not believe it; and she is obligated only to desire that her audience imagine what she says, not to believe it herself.

As we have already seen, however, the appeal to *sui generis* fictive illocutions runs into insuperable difficulties, as do the related views that storytellers make commands, suggestions, or invitations with similar perlocutionary goals. As argued in chapter 1, while this account of storytelling may be commensurable with what we might term "storytelling assertions," such as

> It was a dark and stormy night,

it is far from clear that storytelling questions, such as

> Was it a dark and stormy night?

or storytelling requests,

> Listen closely, dear reader, to my tragic tale,

could similarly have as their perlocutionary goals that listeners imagine or make-believe their propositional contents. And as we saw in chapter 4, this view cannot accommodate the pragmatic implications storytellers generate by means of their utterances except by ad hoc appeal to conversational principles specifically governing fictional discourse.

In addition, insofar as storytelling performances are best understood as a species of theatrical performance, as I would argue they are,[15] the strategy of appealing to *sui generis* fictive (or theatrical) illocutionary action fails as an account of a phenomenon that arises, not just for theatrical speech but for theatrical action more generally. By means of their actions, actors make it fictionally the case that the characters they portray behave thus and so. Laurence Olivier, for example, by his actions made it fictionally true that Hamlet kissed Gertrude and stabbed Polonius.[16] In some cases, actors can do so by actually performing the actions their characters perform. So, for example, Olivier made it fictionally true that Hamlet kissed Gertrude by actually kissing Eileen Herlie.[17] Sometimes, however, for moral or metaphysical reasons,[18] or simply as a result of directorial decision, actors cannot generate fictional truths in this way: it would have been morally inappropriate, for example, for Olivier to make it fictionally true that Hamlet stabbed Polonius by means of actually stabbing Felix Aylmer. In such cases, the natural thing to say is that actors engage in theatrical pretense – performing acts which count as stabbings, for example, within the conventions of the theatrical productions in which they are involved. Moreover, there is no temptation here to think instead that actors engage in a *sui generis* theatrical kind of action – that rather than actually stabbing Aylmer or pretending to do so, Olivier instead subjected him to a uniquely theatrical kind of stabbing. As a result, deploying this strategy in the case of storytelling/theatrical speech seems ad hoc.

A more promising approach to storytelling might be thought to be provided by Saltz's game model.[19] Strictly speaking, what Saltz offers is an account of the speech acts actors make during their theatrical performances. This view can, however, be fruitfully applied to the utterances of storytellers, especially insofar as storytelling is understood, as above, to be a species of theatrical performance. On this view, storytellers perform genuine and familiar illocutionary actions prompted by game intentions and subject to game obligations. In games a number of goals are associated with a number of distinct roles. In chess, for example, associated with each player role is the goal of capturing the other player's king. As a result, a player who occupies a game-role and who desires to play the game properly will adopt the goals associated with this role. Moreover, during a game a player is under an obligation to adopt the ends associated with the role she occupies: a chess player who does not intend to capture her opponent's king is violating her obligations by throwing the game. What is important to note, however, is that a player remains motivated to pursue such goals and is subject to such obligations only as long as she occupies her game-role. Once the game is over, or she has stopped playing, game intentions and obligations no longer apply.

Now according to the game model, the role of storyteller that someone might adopt is analogous to the roles occupied by game-players. In particular, associated with the storytelling role are a number of goals and other intentional states; and the conventions of the practice of storytelling require of storytellers that they adopt these goals and act accordingly.[20] The intentional states in question are those of the narrator, or narrative informant, of the story in question; in effect, on this model, a storyteller is an actor who portrays this figure. And just as rules of chess attach the goal of capturing the opponent's king to the player-roles, the conventions of storytelling attach to the storytelling role the goal of achieving the narrative informant's ends or goals. And so, for example, if the narrator of a story desires to deceive his audience as to the extent of his participation in the events on which he reports, a storyteller who portrays him is required by the conventions in question to so desire as well; failure to do so, in effect, counts as throwing the "storytelling game."[21] As should be obvious, this model entails that the utterances of storytellers are both prompted by their illocutionary intentions and subject to storytelling-game obligations; as a result, they count as genuine illocutionary acts, at least insofar as storytelling-game obligations can be identified with sincerity-obligations. Contra Currie, however, these are familiar sorts of illocutionary acts like assertions and requests rather than *sui generis* fictive illocutionary acts. But contra the naive view critiqued above, because these acts are motivated only by game intentions and subject only to game obligations, storytellers have these intentions and are subject to these obligations only during their storytelling performances.

For present purposes, I will leave aside worries about the analogy between storytelling and game playing, as well as concerns about the putative contents of the conventions of storytelling; even if these presuppositions of the game model on these matters are granted, it still runs into serious difficulties. First, despite superficial appearances to the contrary, the game model does not fare any better vis-à-vis the sincerity-obligation criterion of genuine illocutionary action than did the naive view considered above. Being under an obligation to adopt the goals of a narrator figure she portrays simply does not suffice to place a storyteller under an obligation to believe what she says, desire what she requests, etc. This is clearest in the case of the performance of a story with a dishonest narrator figure whose goals include the deception of his audience. In such circumstances, an obligation to adopt the narrator's goals would require that a storyteller disbelieve what she says, rather than believe it as would be required by any sincerity-obligations she might be under. But even if the narrator informant is sincere – and hence an obligation to adopt his desires obligates a storyteller to believe what she says, desire what she requests, etc. – this does not suffice to place the storyteller under sincerity-obligations. After all, it is only happenstance that her storytelling-game obligations coincide with the obligations she would have were she under sincerity-obligations. Consider, by way of analogy, a child who is under an obligation to a parent to attend university as a result of a promise he has made. Even though his obligations coincide with the obligations he would have had had he promised a friend to attend university, we would not be tempted to say for that reason that he had an obligation to his friend to engage in that course of action.

And second, although the game model may provide an adequate account of what prompts authors' utterances during improvised storytelling performances, it runs afoul of the causal role of the text in non-improvised performances. Insofar as a storyteller performs genuine illocutionary actions, as the game model would have it, her utterances are caused or motivated by her illocutionary intentions rather than the text of the story she is telling. But in non-improvised performances, it is the text which causes the storyteller's utterances. Saltz attempts to alleviate this worry by suggesting that during the process of rehearsing for her performance, a storyteller can try out various hypotheses about the mental states of the narrator figure she is to portray and various ways of uttering the text, in the hope of discovering a set of ends which, if adopted, would cause her to utter the sentences which constitute the fictional text. And once, after sufficient rehearsal, she is able to reliably adopt such ends, she can engage in performances wherein her speech acts are caused by her illocutionary intentions but at the same time conform to the text.[22] The trouble with this suggestion is that it mischaracterizes the obligations of storytellers in non-improvised performances. On Saltz's view, an actor's obligation is to act in accordance with her adopted ends. And although an appropriate process of rehearsal can render it highly likely that doing so will yield verbal behaviour that conforms to the text, if unforeseen circumstances arise,[23] a storyteller may be obligated to depart from the text in order to act in accordance with her adopted ends. But as a matter of fact, the obligations of a story-teller are to conform to the text under such circumstances.[24]

6.3 STORYTELLING — POSITIVE

Although in chapter 1 the claim that fictional composition consists in pretending to perform illocutionary acts of various kinds was found lacking, this view does provide a promising account of storytelling performances. Rather than actually making assertions, requests, etc., by means of their utterances, according to this view, storytellers merely pretend to do so. Now in order to pretend to do something an agent needs to actually do something, but the type of action in which she actually engages is typically distinct from the action-type she pretends to perform.[25] And a general account of pretending-to-do requires an account of the conditions that need to hold in order for an agent to pretend to engage in an act of one type by means of actually engaging in an act of another type. Our somewhat more delineated task is to determine the conditions that need to hold in order for storytellers to pretend to make familiar sorts of speech acts of various kinds by means of the utterances they actually make during their storytelling performances.

Searle has suggested that a necessary condition of pretending to do something is that the act in which the agent actually engages be a constituent part of the act in which she pretends to engage: "It is a general feature of the concept of pretending that one can pretend to perform a higher order or complex action by actually performing lower order or less complex actions which are constitutive parts of the higher order or complex action."[26] For example, one can pretend to eat an apple by holding one's empty hand by one's mouth while moving one's jaw as if masticating. Saltz, however, rightly balks at the generality of this suggestion. Children, for example, often pretend to shoot one another "by pointing their index finger at their victims with their thumbs upward, and shouting the word 'bang'"[27] but these behaviours are not constitutive parts of the higher order behaviour of genuinely shooting someone. Alternatively, one might suppose that an agent needs to imitate an action in order to pretend to engage in it, or, equivalently, that a necessary condition of pretending to do something is that the agent perform an act that resembles it. But again, as Saltz points out, it is possible to pretend to engage in an action by actually doing something which bears no non-trivial resemblance to it. Consider, for example, a play or children's game of make-believe in which saying "Cheep, cheep!" counts as flying.[28]

Saltz does, however, make a positive suggestion about "theatrical pretense" which may ultimately prove fruitful. On his view, an actor who pretends to murder "is (really) committing an action which *counts* as murder within the conventions of the play."[29] The core general idea is that pretense requires the existence of conventions according to which actually performing an action of one type counts as pretending to engage in an act of another type. These conventions can be local, as in the case of the conventions of a particular production of a given play or a once-played game of make-believe, but they can also hold quite generally. In my view, the appeal of Searle's "constitutive action" analysis of pretense, as well as the imitation account, is due to the existence of very general conventions according to which one can pretend to engage in an action by engaging in a constituent part of it or by imitating it. It should be noted, however, that an agent's pretense can be facilitated by such conventions only if they are operative in the context in which she acts. This is why one can always pretend to fly by imitating or engaging in a constituent part of flight behaviour but one can do so by means of uttering "Cheep, cheep!" only if one is performing in the right kind of play.

Illocutionary pretense typically involves general conventions that are operative in a very wide range of contexts.[30] One can always, or almost always, pretend to make an assertion or request, etc., by means of producing an utterance which is highly similar to the kinds of utterances speakers use to make genuine assertions, etc.[31] Of course, by means of the very same kind of verbal behaviour in the very same sorts of contexts speakers can also make genuine illocutions. The difference between the two cases is that in the former speakers invoke or deploy the requisite pretense-conventions whereas in the latter they do not. It is worth noting that, on Searle's view, pretense-conventions are "horizontal conventions" which suspend the normal requirements of "vertical" linguistic conventions which establish connections between language and the world.[32] Invoking these horizontal pretense-conventions both enables a speaker to avoid actually performing the illocutionary action she would otherwise perform and to successfully pretend to perform it. On my view, in contrast, one can refrain from illocutionary commitment by just making one's utterance without having illocutionary intentions. Pretense-conventions simply serve to enable speakers to pretend to perform illocutionary acts of various kinds by their (illocutionary-intention free) utterances.

What needs to be addressed, however, is how one goes about invoking such conventions. Searle's view seems to be that what is required is the intention to do so on the part of a speaker: "[one] cannot truly be said to have pretended to do something unless one intended to pretend to do it."[33] And while I agree with Searle that this is all that is required, I think, contra Searle, that this requirement opens the door for deceptive illocutionary pretense which is to be distinguished from other sorts of deception like lying (and other failures to satisfy one's sincerity obligations).[34] Let me elaborate. Normally when engaging in illocutionary pretense, a speaker indicates to her audience that she is doing so. This can involve explicit statements to that effect, various kinds of gestures, shifts in tone of voice, or characteristic turns of phrase such as "once upon a time." The important thing to note is that one can intentionally invoke pretense-conventions without giving one's audience any indication to that effect. And in so doing a speaker deceives her audience. But rather than lying or, more generally, attempting to get them to falsely believe that she has satisfied her sincerity-obligations, such a speaker deceives her audience by attempting to get them to believe she is genuinely making an assertion or a request, etc., and, hence, is even under sincerity-obligations. Orson Welles's famous radio broadcast of *The War of the Worlds* arguably counts as a deception of this kind as opposed to an outright lie.

As should be obvious, the illocutionary pretense account of storytelling avoids the difficulties which beset its competitors. First, since, on this view, storytellers do not make genuine illocutionary actions at all, it simply side-steps any requirement that they have appropriate illocutionary intentions or be under sincerity-obligations. In order for a storyteller who says,

> Case picked at a shred of bacon that had lodged between his front
> teeth,

during a storytelling performance to thereby pretend to assert that some-one named "Case" had picked at a shred of bacon that had lodged between his front teeth, she need neither intend to produce this belief in her audience nor be under any obligation to believe it herself; she need only (refrain from illocutionary commitment and) intentionally invoke the relevant pretense-conventions. Second, again because storytellers do not make genuine illocutionary actions, there is no reason to suppose that their utterances are caused by anything other than the text in non-improvised performances. And third, since the illocutionary actions they pretend to perform are governed by the familiar conversational maxims, storytellers can pretend to generate pragmatic implications by means of the interplay between these maxims and their acts of illocutionary pre-tense. So, for example, because a belief that King Leopold was assassinated by the military is required to reconcile the assertion that Leopold died within a year of terminating military pensions with the maxim of relation, by means of pretending to make the latter assertion a storyteller can thereby pretend to make the former implication.

6.4 ENGAGED AND DISENGAGED METAFICTIVE DISCOURSE

I turn now to metafictive discourse, that species of talk about fiction wherein speakers are concerned to describe the goings on within particular fictional stories. The first thing to note is that metafictive utterances normally take one of two forms: an explicitly fictional form and an extensional form. In the explicitly fictional form, descriptions of fictional goings on occur within the scopes of fictionality operators, as in,

> It is *The Last Chronicle of Barset* fictional that Josiah Crawley was accused of stealing twenty pounds.[35]

In the extensional form, descriptions of fictional goings on have extensional occurrence, outside the scope of any intensional operators, as in

> Josiah Crawley was accused of stealing twenty pounds.

If the view defended here is correct, one could also make a metafictive claim using reports of the revelations of narrative informants, such as,

> The narrative informant of *The Last Chronicle of Barset* revealed that Josiah Crawley was accused of stealing twenty pounds.

At present, however, this is rarely if ever done.

The second thing to note is that – again, according to the view on offer – metafictive utterances in the extensional form are elliptical for their explicitly fictional or revelation reporting analogues. The reason for this is twofold: speakers make genuine assertions, rather than engaging in assertive pretense or the like, by means of both their explicitly fictional and extensional metafictive utterances;[36] and non-elliptical extensional assertions have actual world truth-conditions. As a result, the truth-value of an extensional (putatively) metafictive utterance without any fictional names, such as

> Captain Broke took a fugitive spy on board the *Shannon* immediately prior to his action against the *Chesapeake*,

would depend on what actually happened – in this case, Broke's real behaviour – and not what happened in a fictional story; and an extensional (putatively) metafictive utterance with fictional names, such as,

Josiah Crawley was accused of stealing twenty pounds,

would lack a truth-value, because fictional names lack actual referents. Finally, as noted above, speakers who make metafictive utterances can be either imaginatively engaged or disengaged. And what sort of sentences extensional metafictive utterances are best understood to be elliptical for depends on which state the speaker who produces the utterance found herself in. In what follows, I will consider the metafictive utterances of engaged and disengaged speakers in turn.

Consider, first, the metafictive utterances of imaginatively engaged speakers. Please recall: on the view defended in chapter 4, engaged readers/listeners imagine *de re* of the words they read, or to which they listen, that they constitute a report made by a non-actual fact-teller – the narrative informant – but they refrain from imagining *de se* reading or listening to this report. This is important for two reasons. First, speakers who are engaged in games of make-believe, or other *de se* imaginative activities, do not, and arguably cannot, perform genuine illocutionary actions unless they temporarily discontinue their imaginative role-playing; instead they are capable of only illocutionary pretense. After all, such speakers normally fail to satisfy the illocutionary-intention and sincerity-obligation criteria of genuine illocutionary action; a speaker who uttered,

Josiah Crawley was accused of stealing twenty pounds,

during a game of make-believe, for example, would be unlikely to intend to instill this belief in either his co-players or any non-participating observers, and would certainly not be obligated to believe it herself. But, because engaged reader/listeners refrain from *de se* imagining on the view on offer here, there is no similar impediment to their making genuine assertions by means of their metafictive utterances.

And second, the extensional metafictive utterances of engaged readers/listeners need to be understood to be elliptical for revelation reports. After all, such speakers are, in effect, describing the contents of their imaginative states which, as above, consist of imagining *de re* that they are reading/listening to the report of a narrative informant and imagining *de dicto* what this figure has revealed. Please note: on this view, an explicitly fictional metafictive utterance, such as

It is *The Last Chronicle of Barset* fictional that Josiah Crawley was accused of stealing twenty pounds,

made by an imaginatively engaged speaker is elliptical for

> The narrative informant of *The Last Chronicle of Barset* revealed that it is *The Last Chronicle of Barset* fictional that Josiah Crawley was accused of stealing twenty pounds.

And an utterance of this kind is true only if the work in question consists of a story within a story.

Finally, as discussed in chapter 5, the content of a name – fictional or otherwise – in the metafictive utterance of an engaged speaker is a C-team whose members include various cognitive states of the speaker, as well as similar states of her conversational interlocutors who spoke previously and, perhaps, cognitive relations in which various speakers stand to these cognitive states. And, as discussed in chapter 4, a metafictive assertion by an engaged reader/listener is true just in case the proposition it expresses is included in the theory which best fits what the narrative informant of the work in question says and implies, the evidence for his reliability, and relevant background information.

I turn now to the metafictive utterances of imaginatively disengaged speakers. This includes both speakers who have previously been imaginatively engaged in the fictional stories they are discussing but are not so at the time of their utterances, and speakers who have never been caught up in these stories, knowing of them only by reputation. The first thing to note is that by means of such utterances, speakers (normally) make assertions.[37] At the very least, there is no impediment to their doing so. And second, rather than being about the contents of their imaginings, the assertions of disengaged speakers concern the actual world – the properties of actual works of fiction. As a result, the extensional metafictive utterances of disengaged speakers are elliptical for explicitly fictional utterances rather than revelation reports. Moreover, a report of the revelations of a narrative informant figure made by an imaginatively disengaged speaker, such as

> The narrative informant of *The Last Chronicle of Barset* revealed that Josiah Crawley was accused of stealing twenty pounds,

is, on this view, elliptical for an explicitly fictional metafictive utterance, such as

It is *The Last Chronicle of Barset* fictional that the narrative informant of *The Last Chronicle of Barset* revealed that Josiah Crawley was accused of stealing twenty pounds,

which is true only if the work contains a fictional narrator.[38]

Finally, as in the case of their engaged cousins, the contents of names in the metafictive utterances of disengaged speakers are collections of cognitive states and relations. But if the speaker knows of the work she is discussing only by reputation, only her cognitive relations to the cognitive states of others, and not any (non-relational) cognitive states of her own, will be included among the members. The truth conditions of the metafictive utterances of disengaged speakers are a slightly trickier issue. The difficulty stems from the fact that, because narrative informants do not actually exist, reports of their revelations are truth-valueless. As a result, the truth conditions of an explicitly fictional metafictive utterance, such as

It is *The Last Chronicle of Barset* fictional that Josiah Crawley was accused of stealing twenty pounds,

cannot simply be identified with those of the corresponding revelation report:

The narrative informant of *The Last Chronicle of Barset* revealed that Josiah Crawley was accused of stealing twenty pounds.

Nevertheless, this difficulty can be avoided by noting that an explicitly fictional metafictive utterance is true in the actual world just in case the corresponding revelation report is true in the narrative world – the world in which the text is a report produced by the narrative informant. As a result, it is a relatively simple matter to analyse explicitly fictional utterances in terms of revelation reports. One strategy for doing so involves (i) taking revelation reports of the form

The narrative informant of S revealed that p

to express relations between subjects and propositions, as in

Revealed (N_S, p),

(ii) taking explicitly fictional claims to express monadic properties of propositions, as in

F(p),

and (iii) offering an analysis of the fictionality property in terms of the revelation relation which entails

$F_a(p)$ iff $Revealed_n$ (N_S, p)

(where the subscripted "a" and "n" denote respectively the actual world and the narrative world). More could be said here, but this will suffice for present purposes.

6.5 METAFICTIVE DISCOURSE AND MAKE-BELIEVE

Before going on to discuss trans-fictive discourse, it may prove fruitful to pause briefly to compare the account of the metafictive utterances of engaged speakers presented above with accounts that embrace the make-believe model of engagement. Please recall: what is characteristic of the latter account of engagement with fiction is that it prescribes that appreciators engage in *de se* imaginative activities of various kinds. For reasons adverted to above, speakers who are playing games of make-believe do not perform genuine illocutionary acts by means of their metafictive utterances; rather, they engage in illocutionary pretense or, as Walton would have it, participate verbally in these games of make-believe.[39] Now although, as a result, the metafictive utterances of engaged speakers cannot strictly speaking be true or false, they can nevertheless be appropriate or inappropriate. An utterance of

Josiah Crawley was accused of stealing twenty pounds,

made while playing an authorized game for *The Last Chronicle of Barset*, a game in which it is the function of this work to serve as a prop, is appropriate, according to Walton, just in case the speaker thereby makes it fictional of herself that in the game she speaks truly.[40] Please note: on this view, the extensional metafictive utterances of engaged speakers are not normally elliptical for their explicitly fictional analogues. After all, an explicitly fictional metafictive utterance is appropriate only if, in the story, the (actually fictional) work is a work of fiction.

The account of engagement, and the corresponding account of engaged metafictive discourse, on offer here possesses one advantage over the competing make-believe accounts; it entails that despite being caught up in fictional stories, engaged reader/listeners retain the ability to make genuine assertions about these stories. Consider, for example, a whispered conversation between a pair of listeners at a (very long) storytelling performance of *The Last Chronicle of Barset* about whether or not the false accusations against Josiah Crawley were something he brought on himself. Walton suggests, however, that such speakers can simultaneously engage in pretended and genuine assertion: "Appreciation (participatory appreciation) and criticism are intimately intertwined, and so are the activities of pretending to describe the real world and actually describing a fictional one. Indeed we often do both at once."[41]

Moreover, according to Walton, what an engaged speaker asserts by means of her utterance of, for example,

Josiah Crawley was accused of stealing twenty pounds,

when engaging in some such "dual performance" can be paraphrased as follows:

> *The Last Chronicle of Barset* is such that one who engages in a pretense of kind K in a game authorized for it makes it fictional of herself that in the game she speaks truly,

where the speaker's utterance itself fixes the referent of "K" by means of being an instance of the relevant kind.[42]

It is far from clear, however, that this suggestion is ultimately satisfactory. Walton attempts to motivate it by appeal to examples from outside fiction: "In other contexts also it is not uncommon for one to pretend to say one thing by way of actually saying something else. A diner jokingly remarks that he could eat a rhinoceros, in order to indicate, seriously, that he is hungry. Smith declares in a sarcastic tone of voice, 'Jones is a superhero,' thereby implying or suggesting or asserting that Jones thinks thus of himself."[43]

But it is not clear that Walton's description of these cases as instances wherein a speaker simultaneously pretends to assert one thing and genuinely asserts another is accurate. First, rather than asserting that he is hungry or that Jones thinks highly of himself, the diner and Smith respectively pragmatically impart these propositions by means of what they say. And second, it is far from clear that what the diner and Smith actually say counts as assertive pretense rather than genuine assertion. The fact that neither seems to be committed to the proposition literally expressed by the sentence he utters does not suffice to establish that they are engaged in pretense. Moreover, it is not clear that speakers can genuinely pragmatically impart information by means of merely pretending to make assertions. That the utterances in question violate conversational maxims which govern them is essential to the mechanisms by which they convey the information that they do. It is only because his remark violates Grice's maxim of quality – do not say what you believe to be false – for example, that the diner is able to thereby pragmatically convey that he is hungry.[44] But acts of assertive (or more generally illocutionary) pretense are not governed by Grice's maxims and so information cannot be imparted by means of clashes between such speech acts and maxims. One could, of course, pretend to pragmatically impart something by means assertive pretense, but that would not help Walton's case.

6.6 ENGAGED TRANS-FICTIVE DISCOURSE – ONE-WORLDERS

Trans-fictive discourse includes a variety of different kinds of claims. A fruitful taxonomy of such claims includes the following four categories: (i) claims relating fictional characters/events from different fictional works; (ii) claims relating fictional characters/events to actual persons/events; (iii) claims identifying fictional characters/events in one work either with characters/events in another work or with actual persons/events; and (iv) claims involving the fictional status of characters/events in one or more fictional works. Examples of sentences falling in category (i) include

Holmes is less loquacious than Poirot

and

Gandalf the Grey is a more experienced spell-caster than Harry Potter.

Category (ii) includes sentences such as

Josiah Crawly is more honest than Jimmy Swaggert.

Category (iii) includes both

Sam Spade is Philip Marlowe

and

Gandalf is Tolkien's father.

And finally, category (iv) includes sentences such as

Holmes is fictional

as well as sentences like

Tolstoy first made Anna fall in love before visiting her brother; then he made her visit her brother before falling in love.[45]

What unifies the sentences from these various categories is that their truth (or falsity) depends in part on facts independent of the goings on in the works to which the fictional entities at issue belong. And, as a result, the analysis of metafictive discourse developed above cannot be directly applied to them. Even if it is true that Holmes is less loquacious than Poirot, the narrative informant of neither the Holmes stories nor the Poirot stories revealed any such thing. Please note: normally trans-fictive utterances have an extensional form; but they are, on the view defended here, always elliptical for more complex sentences whose constituents include fictionality or revelation operators.

As with metafictive utterances, we can distinguish between the trans-fictive utterances of imaginatively engaged and disengaged speakers. Unlike the metafictive cases, however, there are two distinct imaginative projects in which those making trans-fictive utterances might be engaged: they might imagine that the entities they are discussing occupy distinct fictional worlds; and they might imagine them to occupy the same world. A speaker who utters,

Gandalf is a more experienced spell-caster than Harry Potter,

for example, might either imagine Gandalf inhabiting the fictional world described in *The Lord of the Rings* and Harry occupying the world described in *Harry Potter and the Philosopher's Stone*[46] or she might imagine them both inhabiting a single fictional world distinct from, but related to, the aforementioned work worlds – perhaps an amalgam of them. In this section, the trans-fictive utterances of engaged speakers who imagine a single world – one-worlders – will be addressed. In the next two sections, the trans-fictive utterances of engaged speakers who imagine two worlds – two-worlders – and of disengaged speakers will be addressed. Since the utterance of category (iv) trans-fictive sentences by imaginatively engaged speakers of either kind makes sense only when there is a story within a story, I will reserve my discussion of them for the section on disengaged speakers.

Consider, first, an imaginatively engaged one-worlder who utters a category (i) trans-fictive sentence. Such a speaker imagines the narrative informants of two or more fictional works to be reporting on a single fictional world and so imagines the characters and events they describe all to occur within that single world. Except insofar as the works contradict one another, the characters and events from each work are imagined to have the same properties in this more robust world that they do when each work is considered individually. Any conflicts there might be between the works are resolved in the same way one normally handles conflicting reports from informants: some of the claims of one or both of the informants are rejected, or the world they are jointly describing is imagined to be a contradictory one.

For reasons discussed in section 6.4, such a speaker is capable of making genuine assertions and, as a result, normally does so by means of her trans-fictive utterances. And again, for reasons discussed in this same section, her extensional trans-fictive utterances are best understood to be elliptical for complex revelation reports of the sort presented below. In the case at hand, the subject of this revelation report cannot be one or the other of the narrative informants of the fictional works at issue. After all, the narrative informant of *The Lord of the Rings*, for example, revealed nothing about the activities of Harry Potter, nor did the narrative informant of *Harry Potter and the Philosopher's Stone* reveal anything about the activities of Gandalf the Grey. Rather, the two fictional texts will have to be treated as making up a single fictional work with multiple narrators, and the trans-fictive sentence the speaker utters will have to be taken to be elliptical for a report of revelations jointly made by the narrative informants of both constituent works. So, for example, the category (i) trans-fictive sentence

Gandalf is a more experienced spell-caster than Harry Potter

is, on this view, elliptical for

The narrative informant of *The Lord of the Rings* and the narrative informant of *Harry Potter and the Philosopher's Stone* (jointly) revealed that Gandalf is a more experienced wizard than Harry Potter.

Finally, since, on this view, fictional names occur within the scopes of revelation operators, there is no reason to amend the thesis that their contents are collections of cognitive states and relations.

Consider, second, an imaginatively engaged one-worlder who utters a category (ii) sentence. Rather than imagining the characters and events described in distinct works to occur within a single world, she imagines the fictional entity and the actual entity she relates by means of her utterances to occupy a common world. Again, although this world is distinct from the fictional world described by the work in which the former occurs and the actual world inhabited by the latter, except insofar as the work conflicts with actuality, the properties these entities are imagined to have in this world are for the most part the same as in their respective home worlds. But unlike the previous case, the speaker cannot be thought of as imagining that the narrative informants of distinct works are describing a single world; there is, after all, no narrative informant who mediates our access to actuality.[47]

Nevertheless, category (ii) sentences are amenable to a treatment similar to that to which category (i) sentences were subjected. Consider a police informant who reveals that the chief suspect is over six feet tall. Since I am less than six feet tall, there is a sense in which the informant has revealed that the suspect is taller than me. The reason we do not judge the informant to have revealed this fact in a strict sense is that information about me and my height is irrelevant to the investigation the police are carrying out. It is only if we allow this irrelevant information to count as background information that we get the result that the informant revealed anything at all about me. This suggests that we can distinguish between two senses of revelation, a narrow sense – $revelation_N$ – and a broad sense – $revelation_B$. An informant $reveals_N$ a proposition p just in case the theory which best fits the informant's reports, the evidence for her reliability, and *relevant background* information includes p. And an informant $reveals_B$ that p just in case the theory which best fits the informant's reports, the evidence for her reliability, and *both relevant and (certain) irrelevant background information* includes p.

This manoeuvre allows us to continue to characterize fictional truth in terms of the $revelations_N$ of fictional narrators. But it also allows us to analyse the category (ii) trans-fictive utterances of engaged one-worlders in terms of the $revelations_B$ of narrative informants. For example, on this picture the category (ii) trans-fictive sentence

Josiah Crawly is more honest than Jimmy Swaggert

is elliptical for

> The narrative informant of *The Last Chronicle of Barset* revealed$_B$ that
> Josiah Crawly is more honest than Jimmy Swaggert.

Finally, as before, the contents of fictional names when they occur in such sentences are collections of cognitive states and relations. And since they occur, as well, within the scope of revelation operators, the contents of names of actual individuals are also collections of cognitive relations. But rather than including imaginative states of the speaker, the members of such collections consist solely of relations in which the speaker and her interlocutors (actually) stand to the actual entities at issue.

Consider, finally, category (iii) trans-fictive sentences, again uttered by engaged one-worlders. Given our accounts of category (i) and (ii) utterances by similar speakers, an analysis of such sentences will not prove hard to find. A category (iii) sentence identifying entities from distinct fictional works, such as

> Sam Spade is Philip Marlowe,

can be treated as elliptical for

> The narrative informant of *The Maltese Falcon* and the narrative informant of *Farewell, My Lovely* (jointly) revealed that Sam Spade is Philip Marlowe.

And a category (iii) sentence identifying a fictional entity with an actual entity, such as

> Gandalf is Tolkien's father,

can be taken to be elliptical for

> The narrative informant of *The Lord of the Rings* revealed$_B$ that Gandalf is Tolkien's father.

As above, in both cases the contents of names, both fictional and actual, can be taken to be collections of cognitive states and/or relations. Nevertheless, the revelations in question should not be taken to be that these collections of cognitive states are identical. Rather, it should be understood to be that the members of these distinct collections are same-character imaginings, if fictional characters are identified, or that the character-imaginings that make up one collection are *de re* imaginings of the shared relatum of the cognitive relations which make up the other collection, if a fictional entity is identified with an actual entity.[48]

Before pushing on to discuss the trans-fictive utterances of engaged two-worlders and disengaged speakers, it is worth pausing for a moment to compare the view offered here with the account of trans-fictive utterances favoured by Walton. According to Walton, a speaker who utters a trans-fictive sentence "S" (of category (i), (ii), or (iii)) relating entities from fictions $F_1, \ldots, F_n$, asserts the following:

> $F_1, \ldots, F_n$ are such that one who engages in a pretense of kind K [of which the speaker provides an instance by her utterance of "S"] in an unofficial game of such and such sort makes it fictional of herself that in the game she speaks truly,[49]

where the decision as to what unofficial game is implied in a given case is based on a principle of charity – requiring one to refrain, if possible, from interpreting an utterance in a way which renders it blatantly false or trivial or stupid – as well as precedent – relying on more or less standard patterns of implication.[50] So, for example, on Walton's view, the assertion a speaker makes by uttering,

> Gandalf the Grey is a more experienced spell-caster than Harry Potter,

can be paraphrased as

> *The Lord of the Rings* and *Harry Potter and the Philosopher's Stone* are such that one who engages in a pretense of kind K [of which the speaker provides an instance by her utterance of "Gandalf the Grey is a more experienced spell-caster than Harry Potter"] in an unofficial game of such and such sort makes it fictional of herself that in the game she speaks truly,

and the assertion a speaker makes by uttering,

> Gandalf the Grey is Tolkien's father,

can be paraphrased as

The Lord of the Rings is such that one who engages in a pretense of kind K [of which the speaker provides an instance by her utterance of "Gandalf the Grey is Tolkien's father"] in an unofficial game of such and such sort makes it fictional of herself that in the game she speaks truly.

What is important to note is that despite the differences in detail, Walton's strategy for handling the trans-fictive utterances at issue is at bottom the same as my own. After all, an unofficial game in which a participant can fictionally speak truly by saying,

Gandalf the Grey is a more experienced spell-caster than Harry Potter,

is a game/world in which Gandalf and Harry are imagined to co-exist.

6.7 ENGAGED TRANS-FICTIVE DISCOURSE – TWO-WORLDERS

I turn now to the trans-fictive utterances of engaged two-worlders – speakers who imagine that the entities they are discussing occupy distinct fictional worlds. In effect, such speakers make trans-world comparisons of entities occupying distinct fictional worlds, or fictional worlds and the actual world. As a result, treating the uttered sentences as if they fall within the scopes of revelation (or fictionality) operators is not an option. Moreover, insofar as we continue to eschew allowing fictional entities to serve as the contents of (actual uses of) expressions, taking fictional names to fall outside the scopes of revelation operators is also off the table.[51] A natural suggestion, then, is to take fictional names in such trans-fictive sentences to fall within the scopes of revelation operators and take the sentences themselves to involve quantification into said operators.

Consider a category (i) sentence, uttered by some such speaker, of the form "aRb," where "a" is the name of a character in a work *A* and "b" is the name of character in a work *B*. The basic analysis I wish to propose here is one which takes a sentence of this form to be elliptical for the following:

$$(\exists P)(\exists Q)(\text{Revealed } (N_A, <a \text{ is } P>) \,\&\, \text{Revealed } (N_B, <b \text{ is } Q>) \,\&\, PR^*Q),$$

where "N_A" abbreviates "the narrative informant of A" and "P" and "Q" denote variables ranging over properties. R^* is a second-order relation related to R as follows:

$$(\forall P)(\forall Q)(PR^*Q \equiv (\forall x)(\forall y)((x \text{ is } P) \,\&\, (y \text{ is } Q) \supset xRy)).$$

The idea here is that two fictional entities stand in a given relation just in case it is true in their respective stories that they have properties which are such that any entities which bear them stand in said relation.[52]

On this view, a category (i) trans-fictive sentence such as

Gandalf the Grey is a more loquacious than Harry Potter,

when uttered by an engaged two-worlder, is elliptical for

$(\exists P)(\exists Q)$(the narrative informant of *The Lord of the Rings* revealed that Gandalf is P & the narrative informant of the *Harry Potter and the Philosopher's Stone* revealed that Harry Potter is Q & anyone who is P is more loquacious than anyone who is Q).

One may, but need not, be more specific about the properties in question, perhaps taking them to be degrees of loquaciousness.

The analysis of category (ii) trans-fictive sentences when uttered by engaged two-worlders is exactly the same except that the names of actual entities need not be taken to fall within the scope of a revelation operator. So, for example,

Josiah Crawly is more honest than Jimmy Swaggert

is, on this view, elliptical for

$(\exists P)(\exists Q)$(the narrative informant of *The Last Chronicle of Barset* revealed that Josiah Crawly is P & Jimmy Swaggert is Q & anyone who is P is more honest than anyone who is Q).

One might be tempted to offer a similar analysis of such utterances of category (iii) sentences, taking

Sam Spade is Philip Marlowe,

for example, to be elliptical for

$(\exists P)(\exists Q)$(the narrative informant of *The Maltese Falcon* revealed that Sam Spade is P & the narrative informant of *The Big Sleep* revealed that Philip Marlowe is Q & anyone who is P is identical to anyone who is Q).

There are, however, a number of reasons to balk here. First, it is far from clear that there are properties of the requisite sort – guaranteeing identity between their possessors. And second, unlike genuine identities, the putative identities that hold between fictional entities, or between fictional and actual entities, are not a function of the properties of the entities. Rather, they are a function of a certain sort of genetic relation that holds between distinct fictional texts, or between fictional texts and actual events or entities, when a character is based on a character from a previous text or an actual person. As a result, a better analysis takes the utterance at issue to be elliptical for

> The Spade-revelations of the narrative informant of *The Maltese Falcon* are G-related to the Marlowe-revelations of the narrative informant of *The Big Sleep*,

and

> Gandalf is Tolkien's father

to be elliptical for

> The Gandalf-revelations of the narrative informant of *The Lord of the Rings* are G-related to Tolkien's father,

where G-relatedness just is the aforementioned genetic relation.[53] Moreover, insofar as we understand an expression of the form "the a-revelations of the narrative informant of A" to be a complex name of a class of propositions whose members include the contents of the complement clauses of all true sentences of the form

> The narrative informant of A revealed that … a …,

there is no impediment to continuing to take the contents of fictional names in category (iii) sentences to be collections of cognitive states and relations.

6.8 DISENGAGED TRANS-FICTIVE DISCOURSE

It remains to consider utterances of trans-fictive sentences of all categories by imaginatively disengaged speakers. What is characteristic of such speakers is that they are describing the actual world rather than describing imagined worlds or comparing imagined worlds with one another or the actual world. On my view, the trans-fictive utterances of such speakers should be handled in the same way as were the metafictive utterances of disengaged speakers; that is, rather than being treated as involving quantification into revelation reports, they should be taken to involve quantification into explicit fictional sentences. On this view, a category (i) sentence of the form "aRb," where "a" is the name of a character in a work A and "b" is the name of character in a work B, is analysed as

$$(\exists P)(\exists Q)(F_A(\text{<a is P>}) \,\&\, F_B\,(\text{<b is Q>}) \,\&\, PR^*Q),$$

when uttered by a disengaged speaker, rather than

$$(\exists P)(\exists Q)(\text{Revealed}\,(N_A, \text{<a is P>}) \,\&\, \text{Revealed}\,(N_B, \text{<b is Q>}) \,\&\, PR^*Q).$$

So, for example, a category (i) sentence such as

Gandalf is more loquacious than Harry Potter

should be taken to be elliptical for

$(\exists P)(\exists Q)$(It is *The Lord of the Rings* fictional that Gandalf is P & it is *Harry Potter and the Philosopher's Stone* fictional that Harry Potter is Q & anyone who is P is more loquacious than anyone who is Q)

when uttered by a disengaged speaker. Please note: the fictionality operator can be defined in terms of the revelation operator as per section 6.4 above. Similarly, the category (ii) sentence

Josiah Crawly is more honest than Jimmy Swaggert

is elliptical for

$(\exists P)(\exists Q)$(it is *The Last Chronicle of Barset* fictional that Josiah Crawly is P & Jimmy Swaggert is Q & anyone who is P is more honest than anyone who is Q),

and the category (iii)

Sam Spade is Philip Marlowe

is elliptical for

The Spade-fictional-truths generated by the author of *The Maltese Falcon* are G-related to the Marlowe-fictional-truths generated by the author of *The Big Sleep*,

in both cases when uttered by a disengaged speaker.[54]

Heretofore, no mention has been made of category (iv) trans-fictive utterances. As above, except under unusual circumstances, they are sensibly uttered only by disengaged speakers. There is, however, no impediment to treating them as involving quantification into explicit fictional sentences. A sentence such as

Holmes is fictional

can be analysed as

$(\exists P)(\exists W)$(It is W-fictional that Holmes is P),

where "W" denotes a variable ranging over fictional works and, as above, "P" denotes a variable ranging over properties.[55] And a sentence such as

Tolstoy first made Anna fall in love before visiting her brother; then he made her visit her brother before falling in love

can be analysed as

$(\exists W)(\exists W')$(Tolstoy first made it the case that in W, Anna falls in love before visiting her brother and then Tolstoy made it the case that in W', Anna visits her brother before falling in love),

as long as we assume that included in the range of the variables are the various drafts of any given fictional work.

Howell, however, balks at analyses of this sort on the grounds that "from such a rendering … we cannot infer that there is any single character, Anna, who is such that first Tolstoy makes her fall in love before visiting and then Tolstoy makes her fall in love after visiting."[56]

Howell's objection presupposes that the content of the name of a fictional character in the scope of a fictionality operator is a complex property that an object bears just in case it satisfies all the descriptions true of the character in the work in question. As a result, if there are different descriptions true of a character in one work than are true of a character in another work, or in distinct drafts or editions of a single work, then the contents of the names of these characters must differ. So, for example, if a character named "Anna" falls in love before visiting her brother in one work, and a character named "Anna" visits her brother before falling in love in another, then the content of the name "Anna" differs as between these two works.[57]

The view on offer here, however, avoids Howell's objection by refraining from making this presupposition. On this view, the contents of such expressions are teams of cognitive states and relations whose membership can undergo change. As a result, the fact that different descriptions are true of a character in one work than are true of a character in another is compatible with (uses of) the names of those characters having the same content. Moreover, in the case at hand, Tolstoy's intention to write about the same character in the two drafts of *Anna Karenina* renders the Anna-fictional-truths in the two drafts G-related. And, on my view, this suffices for the truth of the trans-fictive identity judgment

> Anna is Anna

where the first occurrence of the name refers to the draft in which the character named "Anna" falls in love before visiting and the second occurrence of the name refers to the draft in which the character named "Anna" falls in love after visiting.

Finally, one might worry that the account of trans-fictive discourse on offer here rather radically fails Howell's requirement of a "smooth and uniform" treatment of such sentences.[58] After all, even though I have offered a reasonably uniform treatment of all four categories of sentences when uttered by a single kind of speaker, there are marked differences between their treatments when uttered by speakers engaged in different kinds of imaginative projects. Nevertheless there is greater unity, if not uniformity, here than there superficially appears to be. This stems from the fact that the treatments of both the utterances of disengaged speakers and engaged one-worlders are dependent on the treatment of the utterances of engaged two-worlders. Given that, as above, the fictionality operator is defined in terms of the revelation operator, the treatment of the utterances of disengaged speakers is clearly so dependent. And given that the joint revelations of narrative informants from different works are determined by their individual revelations in the works to which they belong, and that the revelations$_B$ of narrative informants are determined by their revelations$_N$, the treatment of the utterances of engaged one-worlders is also so dependent. Thus a primary and unifying analysis of trans-fictive discourse is yielded by the treatment of the utterances of engaged two-worlders.

Conclusion

There are four central themes running through this essay. The first theme is that a sharp distinction needs to be drawn between compositional acts and acts of storytelling. As we have seen, failure to attend to this distinction has led to fruitless attempts both to analyse fictional truth and to draw the fiction/non-fiction boundary in terms of substantial speech acts – *sui generis* fictive illocutionary acts or illocutionary pretense, for example – in which authors of fiction do not characteristically engage. Composition is best understood as the production of a text or word-sculpture – a sequence of utterances or inscriptions – designed for deployment in the fiction-centred word-sculpture practice. And storytelling, which does involve the performance of substantive speech acts, is best understood as one of several methods of deploying some such artifact within this practice.

The second theme is that storytelling is a species of theatrical speech. A storyteller is, in effect, an actor portraying a character – the narrative informant of the fictional work in question. The narrative informant normally engages in fact-telling discourse, making genuine assertions and other illocutionary acts. The storyteller portrays this figure by means of engaging in assertive or, more generally, illocutionary pretense. Not only does this picture facilitate a unified account of literary and theatrical fiction, it reconciles the fact that storytellers fail to make genuine assertions with the fact that the fictional truths they generate by their performances include propositions pragmatically imparted by what they say.

The third theme is that engaged readers/listeners of literary fiction need only engage in *de re* and *de dicto* imaginative activity – imagining *de re* of the text that it is a report of actual events and *de dicto* what is thereby revealed. They need not, however, engage in any kind of *de se* imagining;

in particular, they need not imagine reading or listening to the report they imagine the text to be. As we have seen, engagement of this kind suffices to explain readers' emotional reaction to the plights of fictional characters. And unlike *de se* imagining, it is compatible with the performance of genuine assertions on the part of engaged readers. *De se* imagining may, of course, be required for appropriate engagement with some fictions, such as role-playing games; it is, however, not required for engagement with literary fictions.

Finally, the fourth theme is that reader access to the fictional worlds generated by the works they read is mediated by a non-actual fact-teller: the narrative informant. Such mediation enables us to distinguish between fictional truth and what is stated in the text, as we must do to accommodate both unreliable narration and implicit fictional truths. Moreover, this picture yields an account of fictional truth in terms of the acts/attitudes of this figure which reconciles the meaningfulness of fictional claims of various kinds with the non-existence of fictional entities. This idea is, of course, hardly original: Currie and others have invoked similar figures to serve similar ends. Unlike Currie's fictional author, however, my narrative informant may, but need not, be an inhabitant of the world she describes, and her reports may or may not be reliable; and the act/attitude in terms of which fictional truth is analysed is revelation rather than belief.

One might worry, however, that this latter theme impedes the generalization of the theory developed here to non-literary fiction, such as theatrical, cinematic, and photographic fiction, as well as fictions generated by painting and sculpture. After all, one would be hard-pressed to find an analogue of the narrative informant, who mediates access to the fictional world, in such fictions.[1] The second theme stated above, however, may offer some solace. By treating storytelling as a species of theatrical speech, we can embed literary fiction within a broader theatrical model of fictionality. In a theatrical production, there are a number of conventions operative according to which objects of various kinds – props – count as objects of various other kinds, and actions of various kinds, in which actors engage, count as actions of various other kinds. These conventions generate a class of theatrical truths to which audience members have unmediated (perceptual) access. If, for example, an actor flaps her arms in a certain way and there is in effect a convention according to which such behaviour counts as flying, then it is theatrically true that the character she is portraying is flying; and a member of the audience can observe that the character is flying by observing the actor flap her arms, while being cognizant of said conventions. Insofar as there are conventions operative according to which certain actions count as the performance of illocutionary actions of various kinds, then there may also be a second class of theatrical truths to which audience members have only mediated access. If, for example, an actor portraying a reliable character does something which counts as asserting that the king has been murdered, then it will be theatrically true that this crime has occurred; but an audience member's access to this truth is mediated by the testimony of the character. Theatrical truth can be viewed as the union of these classes of mediated and unmediated truths.

On this picture, literary fiction is just a special case of theatrical fiction wherein the mediated truths are dominant. Moreover, works of photographic and cinematic fiction can be incorporated into the theatrical model by treating them as theatrical performances to which the audience's perceptual access is manipulated and controlled in various ways. Finally, painting and sculpture can be incorporated into this framework by treating their objects as theatrical props. In effect, such fictions can be viewed as theatrical productions with props but not actors. This is, of course, the barest of sketches of a general theory of fictionality, but it reveals a promising line of future research.

Notes

INTRODUCTION

1 Capote, 1966.

2 One might argue, however, that the products of composition are sometimes computer files and even "memory files" which, strictly speaking, are not texts at all. Even if this is right, such files need to be converted into texts in order to be appreciated as fiction.

3 One can, of course, both compose oral texts and engage in storytelling performances via the deployment of written texts. Such means of composition and storytelling are, however, comparatively rare.

4 See, e.g., Searle, 1975; Lewis, 1978; and Currie, 1990.

5 I am not making a historical claim about the origins of fiction here, or claiming that theatrical fiction is, in some sense, more fundamental or pure than other forms of fiction. I only mean to suggest that a theatrical model unifies the various forms in a way that illuminates important similarities and differences between them.

6 Some photographic or cinematic works might be best treated as props and some sculptural or painted works might be best treated as performances to which perceptual access is manipulated and controlled.

7 The terminology comes from Currie, 1990.

8 The distinction between works and texts will be developed in chapter 3.

9 Chandler, 1992, 41.

10 Pratchett, 1997, 41–2.

11 Balzac, 1951.

12 O'Brian, 1997.

13 McMurtry, 1988.

14 Tolkien, 1956, and Rowling, 2004.

15 This will be taken up in more detail in chapter 6.

16   But see Saltz, 1991.

17   Searle, 1975.

18   Currie, 1990.

19   Cappelen and Lepore, 2005. It is worth noting that Cappelen and Lepore's view is not uncontroversial (see, e.g., Travis, 2006) and I do not mean to endorse it. Rather, my position is that *if* Cappelen and Lepore are correct and semantic content is largely context-insensitive, *then* not only is semantic content uninteresting but my own view should be taken as an account of context-sensitive illocutionary content – what is asserted, commanded, etc., by means of an utterance – rather than semantic content. In effect, I accept that the conversationally salient content of an utterance – the content we care about – is context-sensitive, but am neutral about whether this salient content is semantic, illocutionary, or what have you.

20   Currie, 1990.

21   Lewis, 1978.

22   Searle, 1975.

23   Currie, 1990.

24   Byrne, 1993.

25   Hardy, 1886.

26   Taylor, 2000.

27   See, e.g., Thomasson, 1998, and Parsons, 1980.

28   See, e.g., Woods and Alward, 2004.

29   Burroughs, 1967.

30   See, e.g., Alward, 2009a.

31   The "serious"/"non-serious" terminology comes from Searle, 1975.

32   See, e.g., Levinson, 1996b.

33   See, e.g., Parsons, 1980; Thomasson, 1998; Van Ingwagen, 2001, among many others.

34   Parsons, 1980.

35   Thomasson, 1998 and Van Ingwagen, 2001.

36   I do, from time to time, frame my views in terms of (possible and fictional) worlds. As I use it, however, this is merely a bookkeeping idiom without ontological import. And to the extent that I treat such worlds as truth-makers for modal and/or fictional claims, I would insist on an ersatz account of them.

37   Everett, 2005.

CHAPTER ONE

1   Byrne, 1993.

2   Searle, 1975.

3   Searle, 1975; Currie, 1990.

4   There can, of course, be improvised performances in which acts of composition and storytelling coincide.

5   See Searle, 1969.

6   The language must, of course, be one in which she is competent and in which she intends to be speaking. Otherwise, what she has produced are coincidentally meaningful noises or inscriptions.

7   The sense of meaning at issue is that of Kaplan's, 1980, character.

8   One might, of course, argue that by uttering this sentence, a speaker thereby asserts that the proposition that the toilet seat is up could be the content of a number of different illocutionary acts.

9   See Grice, 1957, for a more elaborate account of the intentions involved in illocutionary action.

10   But see Saltz, 1991.

11   Searle, 1975, and Lewis, 1978.

12   Currie, 1990, and Byrne, 1993.

13   Hoffman, 2004, Niniluoto, 1985, and Grant, 2001.

14   Beardsley, 1981, 2004.

15   Searle, 1975, 325.

16   Lewis, 1978, 40. Please note: Lewis, 1978, 39, explicitly equivocates between the compositional activities of authors and the activities of storytellers.

17   Searle, 1975, 327. Searle does not take the satisfaction of this condition to be sufficient for engaging in pretense, requiring additionally at least that the agent intend to do so. The psychological component of pretense will be discussed in more detail below.

18   Searle, 1975, 327.

19   Ibid., 324–5.

20   Lewis, 1978, 39. Presumably Lewis would have to require that the author send the manuscript to his publisher *with the intention of invoking the relevant conventions.*

21   Brown and Steinmann, 1978.

22   In addition, Pavel, 1981, 171–2, has argued that, contra Searle, there simply is not a sharp distinction between serious action and pretense. And Walton, 1990, 81–2, while (apparently) conceding the cogency of this distinction, has argued that Searle's analysis of pretense is askew. After all, one can intentionally and non-deceptively play a harpsichord as if one were playing a piano without thereby pretending to play the piano.

23   Currie, 1990, 17–18.

24   Walton, 1990, 82.

25   One might argue, of course, that if an author records a text by writing it out in longhand, pretending to assert the sentences she inscribes would yield a more authentic script. Even if this is correct, it is, I take it, a marginal case.

26 In my view, by generating and invoking local conventions, one can pretend to do almost anything by means of doing almost anything. This will be discussed in more detail in chapter 6.

27 Following Searle, 1975, 327, I am assuming that pretense must be intentional.

28 The kind of case I have in mind is one in which a friend jokingly suggests that a work of fiction is true, rather than a case of deception wherein an author tries to pass off fiction as fact.

29 Of course, in improvised storytelling one engages in both activities simultaneously.

30 Ibid., 328.

31 Ibid., 329.

32 Ibid., 330.

33 Ibid.

34 Ibid., 329.

35 Ibid., 330.

36 Ibid.

37 Ibid., 329.

38 Ibid., 329–30.

39 Margolis, 1983.

40 Miller, 1992, 3.

41 Martinich, 2001, 107. It is worth noting that, strictly speaking, Martinich does not follow Searle and defend the view that authors engage in assertive pretense. Instead they perform genuine assertions (and other illocutionary acts) while suspending the Supermaxim of Quality (which requires that one not perform a speech act unless all conditions for its non-defective performance are satisfied).

42 Lewis, 1978.

43 See, e.g., Parsons, 1980.

44 One might also worry that only appreciators attending storyteller performances would be in a position to refer to the fictional existents storytellers create. Such a worry might be alleviated, however, by adapting Kripke's, 1980, causal-historical theory of referring to allow pretended reference to play a role analogous to that of initial baptisms. I expect, however, that Searle would disapprove of any such manoeuvre. See Searle, 1983, 231–61.

45 Currie, 1990.

46 Ibid., 31. Currie goes on to present a number of revisions to this account in order to make it more general.

47 Currie, 1990.

48 Byrne, 1993.

49 Searle, 1975, 324.

50 Currie, 1985, 385.

51 Currie, 1990, 14.

52 Ibid., 15.

53 Ibid.

54 Hoffman, 2004.

55 Strictly speaking, the conclusion that can be drawn here is that *if* authors express fictive illocutions by means of their compositional utterances *then* either these utterances do not *literally* express fictive illocutions *or* their non-compositional utterances do not *literally* express non-fictive illocutions. The latter disjunct is, I take it, prima facie implausible.

56 Hoffman, 2004, 525.

57 Niniluoto, 1985, 220.

58 Grant, 2001, 400.

59 Hoffman, 2004.

60 Currie, 1990, 39.

61 Ibid., 49.

62 Walton, 1990, 87.

63 One advantage of the pretense view is that in order to address such worries, its proponents need only claim that authors can pretend to perform all the familiar kinds of illocutionary acts we perform in ordinary speech.

64 Of course, in some instances the request might be made tacitly.

65 Beardsley, 1981, 2004.

66 Beardsley, 2004, 190.

67 Of course, one can commit oneself to believing something without actually believing it. This would be a case of insincere assertion.

68 Beardsley, 2004, 190.

69 One difference is that quoted dialogue putatively represents a particular illocutionary action – of the subject to whom the quote is attributed – whereas in representational saying there is indefinite reference: in the same sense that "a man" does not pick out a particular man, representational saying does not pick out a particular illocutionary act. At times, however, Beardsley seems to suggest that fictional texts should be understood to occur within tacit quotation marks and as tacit direct discourse attributions to fictional narrators: "When Tolstoy writes that Vronsky put up the roof of the carriage, he is producing text that could be used in describing an event. But since the name 'Vronsky' does not refer to any actual person, no illocutionary act of describing occurs; it is only represented – as the fictional act of a fictional narrator" (Beardsley, 1981, 301).

70 Beardsley, 2004, 191.

71 Ibid.

72 Ibid., 193.

73 I do not mean to suggest that I endorse Beardsley's account of the interpretation of fictional texts, only that his approach to the analysis of compositional speech acts is promising.

74 I would argue that storytellers also refrain from illocutionary commitment when making their storytelling speech acts. This will be addressed more fully in chapter 6.

75 Beardsley's view seems to imply, however, that the sentence produced – or any sentence produced by any means or for any purpose – would still represent a speech act. I take it this suffices to undermine any temptation to take fictional works to be those whose constituent texts represent illocutionary actions.

76 Walton, 1990, 78.

CHAPTER TWO

1 Of course, what is at issue here is the nature of this "concern," "focus," or "attention."

2 This formulation draws on that of Levinson, 1997, 23.

3 See, e.g., McCormick, 1985; Lamarque, 1981; and Novitz, 1991.

4 See, e.g., Currie, 1990; Walton, 1990.

5 See, e.g., Radford, 1975; Schaper, 1978. My "predicational" belief is equivalent to Schaper's "second-order" belief.

6 See, e.g., Walton, 1990, and Currie, 1990, among others.

7 This is hardly surprising. A doxastic fictional-world account would take engaged readers to be seriously deluded – believing (or half believing or what have you) that they inhabit a fictional world they believe (or half believe) exists. And, arguably, an imaginative actual-world account would abandon the view that engagement is an attitude toward fictional characters and events without gaining extra purchase on the paradox of fiction.

8 Tolkien, 1956.

9 Pratchett, 2008.

10 Walton, 1990, at least in some moods, is an exception. This issue will be taken up more fully below.

11 *De re* imagining is arguably required of the sorts of fictionalizing attitudes discussed above.

12 In some moods, I am inclined to claim that *de se* imagining undermines proper appreciation of literary fiction. This is because I am tempted to view it as a kind of daydreaming that distracts an appreciator from the fictional story.

13 Radford, 1975.

14 Schaper, 1978.

15 This is the same distinction as Schaper's, 1978, distinction between first-order and second-order beliefs. But since Schaper takes existential beliefs to be first-order and predicational beliefs to be second-order, rather than the more natural alternative, I have decided to adopt a neutral (and, I hope, less confusing) terminology.

16 Tolkien, 1937.

17 Radford, 1975, 1977.

18 Radford, 1975, 78.

19 Radford, 1977, 208.

20 As it stands, however, this yields no inconsistency in the case of emotional reactions prompted by the (fictional) plights of immigrant objects – actual entities that play a dual role as inhabitants of fictional worlds. A similar inconsistency may arise at the level of predicational beliefs, however, at least for those who have sufficiently rich beliefs about the actual plights of fictional immigrants.

21 Radford might, however, claim that *appropriate* reader engagement requires that one not believe in the existence of fictional entities and, hence, that to respond emotionally to fiction is an inappropriate misuse of a fictional work. But such an emotionally detached account of reader engagement seems to rob fiction of much of its value.

22 I am, of course, taking disbelief in some proposition, p, as the belief in negation of p, as opposed to either (i) a failure to believe that p or (ii) as a *sui generis* attitude, distinct from belief, toward p.

23 Schaper, 1978, 34–5.

24 Ibid., 34.

25 Ibid., 38–9.

26 Unless, of course, the character is a fictional immigrant.

27 Of course, this account of entailment cannot be usefully applied to inconsistent fictions. This complication will be ignored for present purposes.

28 Ibid., 42.

29 Ibid., 41.

30 Ibid.

31 Rosebury, 1979, 125–6. Rosebury argues that our habit of speaking of "the monster I dreamed of" rather than "the monster-ness of my dream experience" obscures this fact.

32 Shaper is not confused about this point. She thinks that in the case of fiction the emotional response can be grounded in the underlying structure of existential and predicational beliefs.

33 A more orthodox Fregean alternative would be to take the contents of attitudes toward non-existents to be general propositions which lack denotations as opposed to incomplete singular propositions.

34 For present purposes, I remain neutral as to whether this discovery renders the mark's prior belief false or truth-valueless. Please note: were the mark to discover instead that, although the grifter had a child, it was entirely healthy, his psychology would presumably undergo a similar alteration. This would be more analogous to an emotional reaction to the plight of an immigrant object – an actual entity that is at the same time a character in a work of fiction – than to the central cases that concern us here.

35 McCormick, 1985, 378.

36 Lamarque, 1981, 293.

37 Novitz, 1990, 127.

38 Weston, 1975, 85–6.

39 Skulsky, 1980, 11.

40 Lamarque, 1981, 302.

41 The narrative informant just is the fictional narrator if there is one. Otherwise she is a non-actual teller who describes the goings on in a fictional world she does not inhabit. This figure will be discussed in more detail in chapter 4.

42 See Walton, 1990, and Currie, 1990, among (many) others.

43 Moreover, not any old game will do. It must be an authorized game, that is, a game in which it is the function of the work to serve as a prop, where "[a] thing may be said to have the function of serving a certain purpose, regardless of the intentions of its maker, if things of that *kind* are typically or normally meant by their makers to serve that purpose" (Walton, 1990, 52).

44 See, e.g., Walton, 1990, 213 ff.

45 Matravers, 1997.

46 I do not mean to suggest that the contents of *de se* imaginative states are propositions to the effect that certain images are the contents of the subject's experiential states. Rather, the images in question are the contents of the subject's states of imagining *de se* experiencing something.

47 The issue of unreliable narrators will be addressed below.

48 Walton, 1978a.

49 On Walton's, 1978a, view, actually being in a quasi-emotional state that has been brought on by imagining that someone is in emotion-appropriate plights makes it fictional that one is in the corresponding genuine emotional state.

50 See, e.g., Currie, 1997; Feagin, 1997; and Walton, 1997.

51 Walton, 1978a. His case of Charles and the slime is a paradigmatic example.

52 Walton, 1990, 243 ff.

53 Matravers, 1997, 84.

54 Ibid., 81. Matravers, 1997, 82, goes on to argue that, even as an account of visual depictions, the perceptual model runs afoul of appreciator phenomenology. He says, "[on] a very simple level, if we are to imagine Mrs. Yeobright bitten by a

snake, what are we to make of those parts of our experience that tell us we are in a comfortable seat in an air-conditioned row?"

55 Boulle, 1963.

56 See Matravers, 1997, 83. Of course, readers of fact can sometimes intervene by changing their physical locations. The point is simply that when moved by something we read about, we are not normally in any position to do anything about it, at least during the process of reading itself.

57 Walton, 1990, 194.

58 Matravers, 1997, 83.

59 This manoeuvre, of course, makes any account of readers' inability to intervene unnecessary.

60 Walton, 1990, 400.

61 According to Walton, 1990, 52, "[a] thing may be said to have the function of serving a certain purpose, regardless of the intentions of its maker, if things of that *kind* are typically or normally meant by their makers to serve that purpose."

62 Walton, 1990, 402–4. Walton goes on to suggest that the speaker who produces the sentence about fiction, in a way that is not in the "spirit of pretense," does not display an example of the requisite type but goes through the motions of so doing.

63 Walton, 1990, 403.

64 An earlier version of this critical point occurs in Woods and Alward, 2004, 269.

65 Walton, however, denies that this is even a possibility: "I am inclined to think that imagining is *essentially* self-referential in a certain way ... the minimal self-imagining that seems to accompany all imagining is that of being aware of whatever else it is that one imagines." (Walton, 1990, 28–9) In my view, Walton is just wrong on this point: it is possible for someone to imagine *of* what she reads or observes *that* it is thus and so without imagining reading, observing, or being otherwise aware of it. Theatrical audiences are, in my view, a paradigmatic example.

66 Being in a state of quasi- or off-line pity or fear does not even count as imagining pitying or fearing for someone if, as the imaginative trans-world view has it, appreciators refrain from *de se* imagining.

67 Currie, 1997, 65.

68 Snow, 1976.

69 Currie, 1997, 64.

70 By a trivial account I mean one to the effect that reader/listeners are invited to imagine being the kind of person who would react the way they do to the text. Such a view would offer no explanation of reader/listeners' responses to fictional works.

71 Hardy, 1886.

72 Thackeray, 1856.

73 This view is developed in more detail in Alward, 2006.

CHAPTER THREE

1   In chapter 6, I argue that storytelling consists of illocutionary pretense. See, also, Alward, 2009b.

2   See, e.g., Levinson, 1990b, and Kivy, 1993, for more on the creation/discovery dispute as it applies to musical works.

3   This may sound vaguely reminiscent of Levinson's, 1990b indicated-type analysis of musical works. In what follows, such appearances will prove to be deceptive.

4   There is, of course, no reason why something other than aural or inscriptional sequences could not serve as words. In order for an entity of a certain sort to play the relevant kind of communicative role in a linguistic community, it needs only to be repeatable, and efficiently and reliably "readable" and "writable" by the members of the relevant community. As a result, not only could communicative roles be occupied by different sound or inscription sequences than their actual occupants – convention being arbitrary as it is – different sorts of entities altogether could occupy those roles. In a community whose members had a more discriminating sense of smell than ours, and who had more control over the odours they emitted, complex odours could serve as words.

5   This is not to say that accidentally formed tokens could not be used in communication. But in so doing, the user would be thereby transforming non-words into words.

6   Kaplan, 1990. In addition, word-occurrences of the same orthographic or phonographic type can be occurrences of distinct words: consider spoken occurrences of "hear" and "here," for example.

7   Kaplan, 1990.

8   Ibid., 105.

9   Alward, 2005. See also Cappelen, 1999, 97.

10   Alward, 2005.

11   The notion of appropriate unity is intended to rule out sequences of words uttered/inscribed by distinct agents in spatio-temporally non-contiguous contexts. Paradigmatic instances include spatially contiguous sequences of written words on a page of paper and temporally contiguous sequences of spoken words, produced by a single agent.

12   For more on texts, see Gracia, 1996.

13   Howell, 2002, 70. The conclusion Howell draws, however, is that fictional works do not fall into a fixed ontological kind.

14   Consider, for example, Joseph Grand's (fictional) work of written fiction which, when we first encounter it, consists of the following text: "One fine morning in the month of May an elegant young horsewoman might have been seen riding a handsome sorrel mare along the flowery avenues of the Bois de Boulogne"

(Camus, 1966, 96). It subsequently consists of "One fine morning in May a slim young horsewoman might have been seen riding a handsome sorrel mare along the flowery avenues of the Bois de Boulogne" (Camus, 1996, 123) and then finally, "One fine morning in May a slim young horsewoman might have been seen riding a glossy sorrel mare along the flower-strewn avenues of the Bois de Boulogne" (Camus, 1996, 125). In each case, we have the same work but a different text.

15 Of course, one might argue that a single word can have occurrences in distinct languages, especially given the account of words on offer here. Even if this is right, it is highly unlikely to be true of most or even many words in any given translation of a work, especially since translation is largely guided by the goal of meaning preservation and not word preservation.

16 Of course, the finished version might not be the product of a linear sequence of "improving" word-sculpture occurrences. It might, for example, be the product of merging two distinct drafts.

17 If Gettings (manuscript) is correct and words spoken in one's sleep can count as an occurrence of a work, then a weaker (than intention) psychological relation may suffice.

18 Goodman, 1968.

19 This will be developed in section 3.3 and chapter 4.

20 See, e.g., Lewis, 1975.

21 This will be developed in section 3.4.

22 Of course, one or more of the conversational participants might remember some of what was said.

23 I am assuming that the composed sentences are designed to achieve a particular illocutionary purpose in a specific conversational context.

24 This is not the trivial point that what proposition is expressed by a sentence containing indexicals depends on features of the context of utterance including the speaker.

25 A similar anomaly might occur if a love note were orally deployed by an author whose feelings for her desired lover had (temporarily, let's say) lapsed. Such an author might nonetheless recite a love note she wrote before her feelings changed, perhaps in the expectation that her feelings would be rekindled down the road.

26 Currie, 1990 and Walton, 1990.

27 Currie, 1990 and Lewis, 1978.

28 The status of works whose authors' design-intentions are unsuccessful will be addressed in section 3.4.

29 Wilder, 1988, 72.

30 Ibid., 74.

31 Currie, 1990, and Searle, 1975.

32 Walton, 1990.

33 Wilder, 1988.

34 Walton, 1990, 72.

35 Ibid., 52.

36 Of course, content properties are themselves relational.

37 The theory on offer here is formally similar to Levinson's, 1990a, historical definition of art.

38 Donnellan, 1966.

39 Strictly speaking, an author could have such an intention if the practice once but no longer existed. She could not, however, so intend if the practice had never existed.

40 This could be made explicit by adopting a subscripting convention: a work, w, might be fictional$_{2009}$ but not fictional$_{2050}$.

41 Frey, 2004.

42 Of course, a work originally intended to be read as non-fiction might be subsequently re-released by the author, or someone with proprietary rights over it, as a work of fiction. This new intention – that it be read as fiction – can in my view transform it into a work of fiction. Please note: this, of course, entails that a single work can be fictional at one point in its history and non-fictional at another.

43 If someone insisted that a naturally occurring phenomenon could literally be a fictional work, I could adopt the view that the person (or persons) who introduced it to the reading (or listening) public with the intention that it be read or listened to as fiction thereby artifactualizes the phenomenon and, hence, counts as an author of fiction.

CHAPTER FOUR

1 One could, of course, listen to a fictional story as a report and vice versa.

2 Grice, 1975.

3 Presumably the mechanism here is that the supposition that Jones was involved is required to reconcile the informant's assertion with Grice's maxim of relevance.

4 The point is not that such information could not be gleaned from a meteorological report, but rather that we would not want to include it among the revelations attributed to the report itself.

5 And since reliability does not entail infallibility, even reliable informants can produce inaccurate reports.

6 An illocutionary pretense analysis of the speech acts storytellers actually perform is defended in chapter 6.

7 It is worth noting that although naturally occurring phenomena, such as noises produced by the wind, are not, strictly speaking, fictions, they can nevertheless be listened to as fiction. This involves imagining *de re* of a phenomenon that it is report and, hence, the product of an informant, without imagining *de re* of anyone or anything in particular that it is said informant.

8 Given that fictional texts normally contain a number of fictional and hence empty names, the *de dicto* imaginings cannot be understood to consist in imagining propositions expressed by the sentences that constitute such texts, even in cases in which the narrative informant is reliable. This issue will be addressed in chapter 5.

9 It is worth noting that imagining *de re* of what one reads/listens to that it is the report of a narrative informant does not require that one imagine *de re* anything of the narrative informant. Moreover, since the view on offer requires of engaged reader/listeners only that they imagine the text to be the product of a narrative informant rather than believing this to be the case, there is no sense in which it is committed to the existence of such tellers.

10 The fact that engaged readers imagine *de re* of the words they read that they are written (or anything at all) does not entail that the words themselves occur in the story.

11 Similarly, it can be part of an oral story that the words one listens to are written and not spoken. In such cases, a reader does not (or at least should not) imagine *de re* of the sentences she hears that they are illocutionary actions.

12 There could, of course, be a story in which the words one reads are spoken but not used in the performance of illocutionary acts. Cases of this kind will be discussed below.

13 Nor does imagining *de re* of the words one listens to that they are written require imagining *de se* reading them.

14 My inclination is to be permissive here – readers may but need not imagine of authors of fiction that they are authors of non-fictional reports. In my view, nothing is gained, but little harm comes from some such imaginative exercises.

15 Kania, 2005, 50.

16 Kania, 2005.

17 Ibid., 47. Please note: "literary narratives," as Kania uses the expression, are a subclass of fictional narratives.

18 Some of the material in the section appeared previously in Alward, 2007.

19 Kania, 2005, 48.

20 Ibid., 49.

21 Tellers here include both speakers and writers.

22 Kania, 2005, 49. Kania, 2005, 52–3, does hint at a third category – non-actual but non-fictional tellers – in his discussion of hypothetical intentionalism.

23 Given that real persons can occur as characters in fictional stories, a real person
    can be a fictional teller. What is essential, however, is that her speech act occurs
    in the fictional world and not the actual world.
24 Searle, 1975, 320 ff.
25 Storytelling will be discussed in chapter 6.
26 See Kania, 2005, 52.
27 See, e.g., Levinson, 1996b. This category is the primary stalking horse of Stecker,
    1987.
28 Kania, 2005, 50–1.
29 Ibid., 50.
30 After all, if it is not assumed that fact-telling narrators need to occupy the worlds
    they describe in order to have beliefs, write reports, or make assertions about
    them, then there is no reason to assume that such narrators need to occupy the
    actual world to communicate their beliefs to readers.
31 Of course, a naive backwoodsman might, upon occasion, give a fact-telling per-
    formance of a fictional story. This is, presumably, a relatively rare occurrence.
32 The propositions expressed by sentences containing fictional names will be
    addressed in chapter 5.
33 In cases of narrative unreliability, not all of the propositions expressed or
    implied by the sentences which occur in the work are included among the fic-
    tional truths. Nevertheless, determining what is true in some such story requires
    first determining what is expressed and implied.
34 The maxim of relation simply requires that one's conversational contributions
    be relevant.
35 Grice, 1975.
36 Byrne, 1993, 32. Byrne's "Author" is an ideal author – a non-actual (and non-
    fictional) fiction-teller – and his "Reader" is an ideally informed reader. Please
    note: the considerations raised here pose a difficulty for the generation of unex-
    pressed propositions by actual authors as well as Byrne's ideal author.
37 Grice, 1975.
38 One might, of course, rejoin that acts of fiction-telling offer information about
    fictional worlds as opposed to the actual world. But fiction-telling involves gen-
    erating fictional worlds – or, perhaps, selecting from among pre-existing worlds
    – rather than describing them.
39 Alternately, Byrne might invoke very general maxims from which both the
    familiar Gricean maxims and the fiction-specific maxims follow.
40 Kania, 2007, 406.
41 Walton, 1990, 145.
42 Ibid., 151.

43 Currie, 1990.
44 Thackeray, 1856.
45 Currie, 1990, 123.
46 Currie, 1995, 20.
47 Booth, 1983, 158–9.
48 Currie, 1995.
49 See section 4.3 above. If one nevertheless insists that there can be tellings lacking intelligent origins, then the same point can be made by appeal to untold fictions.
50 Byrne, 1995, 30.
51 Currie, 1990, 125–6.
52 One might, of course, worry that the notion of someone reporting about a world they do not inhabit brings with it its own incoherence. But this is exactly what actual appreciators of fiction do when they discuss fictional stories with one another.
53 Of course, the fictional author might be embodied in worlds similar to the actual world but disembodied in (more remote) fictional worlds.
54 Disembodied possessing spirits also seem to be ruled out in realistic fictions.
55 With all due apologies to fictional realists.
56 See, e.g., Lewis, 1978; Currie, 1986b, 1990; Byrne, 1993; and Matravers, 1995.
57 Currie, 1990.
58 Byrne, 1993, invites this interpretation.
59 Lewis's, 1978, analysis only roughly fits into this format.
60 Lewis, 1978.
61 Currie, 1986b, 1990.
62 Byrne, 1993.
63 Lewis, 1978.
64 Ibid., 42.
65 Ibid., 45.
66 Ibid., 44.
67 Ibid., 40n7.
68 But see Krasner, 2002, 265.
69 Lewis, 1978, 41. I am assuming here that Lewis is correct about nineteenth-century British undergarment conventions. If he is not, simply replace this example with "Holmes lacked a tail" or something of the kind.
70 Currie, 1986b, 197. Walton, 1990, 148–9, suggests that this sort of fictional "clutter" should simply be ignored.
71 Lewis, 1978, 45.
72 Ibid., 45.
73 Lewis, 1983, 277.

74 Currie, 1990, 69.

75 Ibid., 80. An informed reader is someone who "knows the relevant facts about the community in which the work was written" (1990, 79).

76 Ibid.

77 Currie, 1990, 124.

78 Of course, the fictional author of an inconsistent fiction could not tell it as known fact.

79 Byrne, 1993, 28.

80 Ibid., 31.

81 Ibid., 33.

82 Ibid., 31.

83 It is, of course, theoretically possible that more than one theory will equally (and best) fit the evidence. In such circumstances, what a narrative informant reveals will have to be identified with what is entailed by all such best theories.

84 See Kania, 2005, 52.

CHAPTER FIVE

1 Fictional realists who take fictional names to refer to (actual) abstract entities, as opposed to non-actual concreta, would likely balk here. See, e.g., Thomasson, 1998; van Inwagen, 2001.

2 See, e.g., Lewis, 1978; Currie, 1990.

3 See Kaplan, 1980.

4 See, e.g., Cappelen and Lepore, 2005.

5 Kripke, 1980.

6 Salmon, 1986 and Soames, 1988, among others, have argued for a Millian account of content in a broader range of sentence frames. The view is so-called because it was first defended in Mill, 1874.

7 Some fictional realists take fictional names to refer to actual abstract entities. See, e.g., Thomasson, 1998, van Inwagen, 2001. But since they characteristically distinguish between the properties the abstract referents of fictional names actually have and the properties attributed to them in the stories in which they appear, such theorists should be understood to take fictional names in metafictive sentences to occur within the scopes of fictionality operators.

8 See, e.g., Taylor, 2000.

9 See, e.g., Parsons, 1980.

10 Millians often respond by distinguishing between the Millian proposition literally expressed by a sentence and the descriptivist proposition pragmatically imparted (Salmon, 1986) or pseudo-asserted (Taylor, 2000) by it, and claim that

it is the latter which is capable of truth or falsity. See Alward, 2000, for a critique of such manoeuvres.

11   See Woods and Alward, 2004, for a more complete assessment of Meinongian approaches to fictionality.

12   O'Brian, 1979.

13   Currie, 1990.

14   Lewis, 1978.

15   Please note: if you are worried that "Deep Throat" is not really a proper name, you can further fictionalize the case by supposing that Felt called himself "Fred" rather than "Deep Throat" when acting as Woodward and Bernstein's source.

16   An earlier version of this argument can be found in Alward, 2000.

17   Lewis, 1978, 41.

18   Ibid.

19   Moreover, since proper names are rigid designators, the value of the function which serves as the content of "Captain Broke" is Broke himself at all worlds in which Broke exists; and this function is valueless at worlds in which Broke does not exist.

20   Ramsey, 1978.

21   Currie, 1990, 150.

22   Ibid., 180.

23   See, e.g., Byrne, 1993; Kania, 2005.

24   O'Brian, 1979.

25   O'Brian, 1983.

26   The exceptions, of course, are conceptual relations whose objects are denoted by means of picking out their essential properties.

27   At worlds in which distinct entities fully occupy the same region of space-time, experiential and reputational relations may be instantiated by multiple subject-object pairs.

28   Another issue concerns diachronic identity conditions for cognitive relations. For example, one might wonder what has to be true for my visual relation to my computer screen at t_1 to be the same cognitive relation as my visual relation to the screen at t_2. I do not have a general answer to this issue; questions concerning diachronic identity almost always prove to be quite thorny. Nevertheless, such issues will, I hope, prove to be irrelevant to the account developed here.

29   This picture is, of course, reminiscent of Searle's, 1975, cluster theory of proper names. One central difference worth noting is that, unlike Searle's clusters of descriptions, C-teams are not associated with particular names. Various different referring devices can be used to enter into a conversation and add one's cognitive relations to the corresponding C-team.

30 Kripke, 1980.

31 See Alward, 2009a.

32 Advocates of Davidsonian (Davidson, 1968) or neo-Davidsonian (Cappelen and Lepore, 1997, e.g.) analyses of indirect quotation would presumably balk at the anti-Millian implications on offer here.

33 See, e.g., Salmon, 1986. Salmon's own view is somewhat more nuanced than this.

34 Strictly speaking, only names which occur in complement clauses of act/attitude attributions have collections of cognitive relations as their contents.

35 If a speaker has heard about a character in a work she has not read, her cognitive relation to that character remains reputational; but her relation to the character is mediated both by the report of the narrative informant and the report of the reader from whom she heard about him.

36 See, e.g., Parsons, 1980.

37 Alternatively, we could formulate things in terms of a multiplicity of cognitive states of the reader/listener corresponding to each of the cognitive relations she imagines the narrative informant to stand to the referent of "Stephen Maturin."

38 A Gollum-imagining is to be understood as a type or kind of imagining.

CHAPTER SIX

1 Searle, 1975.

2 Currie, 1990.

3 Saltz, 1991.

4 Walton, 1990.

5 Insofar as propositional content is identified with truth conditions this trivially follows.

6 The exceptions, of course, are unambiguous eternal sentences without any fictional names. Such sentences, I take it, occur relatively rarely in works of fiction.

7 Searle, 1975.

8 Currie, 1990.

9 Saltz, 1991. Strictly speaking, Saltz offers an account of theatrical speech. In my view, however, storytelling is a species of theatrical speech.

10 Gibson, 1984, 47.

11 See, e.g., Grice, 1957 and Searle, 1969, 1983.

12 Searle, 1983, invokes a more nuanced account of the intended effects on listeners. Such subtleties, however, do not concern us here.

13 It is important to note, however, that a speaker who fails to meet this obligation may nevertheless make a genuine illocutionary act, albeit one that is insincere. A speaker fails to satisfy the sincerity-obligation criterion, and hence fails to make

a genuine illocutionary act, only if she is under no obligation to be in an appropriately corresponding mental state.

14 Currie, 1990.

15 Alward, 2009b.

16 Olivier, 1948. For present purposes, the differences between theatrical and filmic acting will not be important.

17 Strictly speaking, kissing Gertrude and kissing Eileen Herlie are distinct action types. Nevertheless, Olivier made it fictionally true that Hamlet kissed *someone* by means of actually kissing *someone*.

18 I have in mind here cases where the action-type is (physically or logically) impossible for anyone to perform or, more specifically, for an actor to perform. I would argue that genuine illocutionary action falls into the latter category.

19 Saltz, 1991.

20 As Saltz, 1991, 39, puts it, "actors can perform real and sincere actions on stage by adopting game intentions that arise if they accept as part of the convention of performance a rule that actors work to achieve the conditions of satisfaction implied by the character's actions."

21 Saltz, 1991, 39.

22 Ibid., 40.

23 I have in mind here events or circumstances which occur during the storytelling performance and which forestall the achievement of the narrator's goals by means of uttering the sentences of the text.

24 For more developed versions of the arguments of this section, see Alward, 2009b.

25 In fact, my view is that the action-type actually performed in pretense is necessarily distinct from the action-type the agent thereby pretends to perform. Someone who is actually washing windows, for example, cannot be pretending to wash windows (although she can pretend to be a window-washer). This issue is orthogonal to our present concern.

26 Searle, 1975, 327. Searle does not take the satisfaction of this condition to be sufficient for engaging in pretense, requiring additionally at least that the agent intend to do so. The psychological component of pretense will be discussed in more detail below.

27 Saltz, 1991, 32.

28 Ibid., 42.

29 Ibid. Strictly speaking, Saltz offers this suggestion as an account of what actors "really do" on stage rather than as a necessary condition of pretense.

30 Arguably, at least, they are inoperative in certain very solemn contexts like funerals or criminal trials. Of course, one could rejoin that they are operative even in these contexts but to invoke them in such contexts would be inappropriate.

31 Following Searle, we might instead take such utterances to be constituents of genuine illocutionary actions. Nothing in what follows will hang on how the verbal behaviour by means of which actors engage in illocutionary pretense is characterized.

32 Searle, 1975, 326.

33 Ibid., 325.

34 Ibid., 326, says, "[what] distinguishes fiction from lies is the existence of a separate set of conventions which enables the author to go through the motions of making statements which he knows to be not true even though he has no intention to deceive."

35 Trollope, 2002.

36 On Walton's, 1990, view, readers engage in assertive pretense when they make extensional metafictive utterances. This will be taken up in section 6.5.

37 A disengaged speaker could, of course, refrain from illocutionary commitment for various reasons.

38 One might argue, however, that revelation reports of this kind provide an apt account not only of truth in fiction but also of truth through fiction. And not only is the latter primarily a matter of the nature of the actual world rather than fictional worlds, it is also a matter with which a disengaged speaker discussing a work of fiction might be concerned. Although the appeal to revelation reports may provide the basis for an account of truth through fiction, there are two things to note for present purposes. First, while it might be actually true that an author – an actual fiction-teller – can reveal something about the actual world by means of her utterances/inscriptions, it cannot be actually true that a narrative informant – a non-actual fact-teller – has done so. And second, whatever their connection to truth through fiction, reports of the revelations of authors are not metafictive utterances, and it is the latter that are our concern here.

39 Walton, 1990, 392.

40 Ibid., 398.

41 Ibid., 394.

42 Ibid., 400ff.

43 Ibid., 394.

44 Grice, 1975.

45 This example comes from Howell, 1979, 151.

46 Rowling, 2004.

47 One might, of course, try to brazen it out by taking God or Mother Nature to occupy this role. I take it that this strategy has little appeal.

48 This account of category (iii) may seem unsatisfactory because it offers no explanation of how fictional works need to be related in order for Sam Spade to

be Philip Marlowe, for example. This issue will be taken up in the discussion of engaged two-worlders below.

49 Walton, 1990, 405–16. Strictly speaking, Walton's view is that a speaker who utters what I have been calling a trans-fictive sentence *may* make an assertion of this form, but she may also make an assertion of some other form and even fail to assert anything at all. Nevertheless, Walton claims that such paraphrases capture a "common background role of unofficial games … [which] gives us the 'smooth and uniform' handling of these and similar statements Howell, 1990, 415, rightly insists on."

50 Walton, 1990, 410.

51 But see Currie, 1990, 171–80.

52 Strictly speaking, since the contents of predicates in the scopes of revelation operators are, on my view, collections of cognitive relations to properties rather than properties themselves, a more complicated analysis along the following lines will have to be given:

$$(\exists P)(\exists Q)(\exists F)(\exists G)(\text{Revealed } (N_A, \text{<a is P>}) \ \& \ \text{Revealed } (N_B, \text{<b is Q>}) \ \&$$
$$\text{FDP} \ \& \ \text{GDQ} \ \& \ \text{PR}^*\text{Q}),$$

where "F" and "G" denote variables ranging over collections of cognitive relations and D is a relation that holds between such collections and individual properties just in case the latter is the relatum of all of the (salient) members of the former. For present purposes, I will ignore this complication.

53 Strictly speaking, the genetic relation in which certain of the revelations of a narrative informant stand to some prior revelations or entity is distinct from the relation in which the writings of an author stand to some prior writings or entity. More on this below.

54 Strictly speaking, we need to deploy two distinct but related G-relations: one in which authorial fictional truths stand and the other in which narrative informant revelations stand. Moreover, the latter G-relation is best understood to be dependent on the former.

55 A distinct and stronger claim is expressed by

Holmes is merely fictional.

On my view, this is elliptical for

Holmes is fictional and Holmes does not exist.

Although giving an account of negative existentials is beyond the scope of my current project, the following analysis fits well with the view presented here:

$$(\exists P)(\exists W)(F_W(\text{<Cteam}^{\text{Holmes}}, \text{P-ness>}) \ \& \ \sim(\exists x)\text{Cteam}^{\text{Holmes}}Dx)$$

The basic idea here is that to say that Holmes is merely fictional is to say that there is some fictional work relative to which the Holmes-collection of cognitive relations is a propositional constituent and that there is no actual entity which is the relatum of all the (salient) members of this collection.

56 Howell, 1979, 155.
57 See, e.g., Currie, 1990. It is worth noting that Currie's, 1990, 171–80, appeal to roles in his account of trans-fictive discourse, because it identifies roles with such complex properties, does not avoid the difficulties Howell raises.
58 Howell, 1979.

CONCLUSION

1 One might, I suppose, invoke a non-actual documentary filmmaker or photographer in an account of cinematic or photographic fiction. But no such manoeuvre is available in the case of theatrical fiction; and, arguably, theatre and film/photography warrant a similar treatment.

Bibliography

Adams, Fred, Gary Fuller, and Robert Stecker. 1997. "The Semantics of Fictional Names." *Pacific Philosophical Quarterly* 78 (1997): 128–48

Alward, Peter. 2000. "Simple and Sophisticated 'Naïve' Semantics." *Dialogue* 39: 101–21

– 2004. "The Spoken Work." *Journal of Aesthetics and Art Criticism* 62: 331–7

– 2005. "Between the Lines of Age: Reflections on the Metaphysics of Words." *Pacific Philosophical Quarterly* 86: 171–86

– 2006. "Leave me out of it: *de re*, but not *de se*, imaginative engagement with fiction." *Journal of Aesthetics and Art Criticism* 64, no. 4: 451–60

– 2007. "For the Ubiquity of Nonactual Fact-Telling Narrators." *Journal of Aesthetics and Art Criticism* 65, no. 4: 401–4

– 2009a. "Cluster Theory: Resurrection." *Dialogue* 48: 269–89

– 2009b. "Onstage Illocution." *Journal of Aesthetics and Art Criticism* 67, no. 3: 321–31

– 2010. "That's the Fictional Truth, Ruth." *Acta Analytica* 25, no. 3: 347–63

Austin, J.L. 1975. *How to Do Things with Words*, 2nd ed. New York: Oxford University Press

– 1979. "Pretending." In *Philosophical Papers*, 3rd ed., edited by J.O. Urmson and G.J. Warnock, 253–71. Oxford: Clarendon Press

Balzac, Honoré de. 1951. *Old Goriot*. Harmondsworth: Penguin Classics

Beardsley, Monroe. 1978. "Aesthetic Intentions and Fictive Illocutions." In Hernadi, *What is Literature?* 161–77

– 1981. "Fiction as Representation." *Synthese* 46: 291–313

– 2004. "Intentions and Interpretations: A Fallacy Revived." In *Aesthetics and the Philosophy of Art: The Analytic Tradition*, edited by Peter Lamarque and Stein Haugom Olsen, 189–99. Oxford: Blackwell Publishing

Booth, Wayne. 1983. *The Rhetoric of Fiction,* 2nd ed. Chicago: University of Chicago Press

Boulle, Pierre. 1963. *La Planète des Singes.* Paris: Pocket Junior

Brown, Jr, Robert L., and Martin Steinmann, Jr. 1978. "Native Readers in Fiction: A Speech-Act and Genre-Rule Approach to Defining Literature." In Hernadi, *What is Literature?* 141–60

Bruin, John. 1999. "An Aristotelian Ontology of the Text." *Symposium* 3: 93–117

Burroughs, Edgar Rice. 1967. *I am a Barbarian.* Tarzana, CA: ERB Inc.

Byrne, Alex. 1993. "Truth in Fiction: The Story Continued." *Australasian Journal of Philosophy* 71: 24–35

Camus, Albert. 1966. *The Plague.* Translated by Stuart Gilbert. New York: Alfred A. Knopf

Capote, Truman. 1966. *In Cold Blood.* New York: Random House

Cappelen, Herman. 1999. "Intentions in Words." *Nous* 33, no. 1: 92–102

Cappelen, Herman and Ernest Lepore. 1997. "Varieties of Quotation." *Mind* 106: 429–50

– 2005. *Insensitive Semantics.* Oxford: Blackwell

Chandler, Raymond. 1992. *Farewell, My Lovely.* New York: Vintage Crime/Black Lizard

Charlton, William. 1984. "Feeling for the Fictitious." *British Journal of Aesthetics* 24: 206–16

Cohen, Philip, ed. 1991. *Devils and Angels: Textual Editing and Literary Theory.* Charlottesville: University of Virginia Press

Currie, Gregory. 1985. "What is Fiction?" *Journal of Aesthetics and Art Criticism* 43: 385–92

– 1986a. "Works of Fiction and Illocutionary Acts." *Philosophy and Literature* 10: 304–8

– 1986b. "Fictional Truth." *Philosophical Studies* 50: 195–212

– 1990. *The Nature of Fiction.* Cambridge: Cambridge University Press

– 1995. "Unreliability Refigured: Narrative in Literature and Film." *Journal of Aesthetics and Art Criticism* 53: 19–29

– 1997. "The Paradox of Caring." In Hjort and Laver, *Emotion and the Arts,* 63–77

– 2001. "Imagination and Make-Believe." In *The Routledge Companion to Aesthetics,* edited by B. Gaut. New York: Routledge, 253–62

Danto, Arthur. 1964. "The Artworld." *Journal of Philosophy* 61: 571–8

Davidson, Donald. 1967. "Truth and Meaning." *Synthese* 17: 304–23

– 1968. "On Saying That." *Synthese* 19: 130–46

Davies, David. 1996. "Fictional Truth and Fictional Authors." *British Journal of Aesthetics* 36: 43–55

Donnellan, Keith. *1966.* "Reference and Definite Descriptions." *Philosophical Review* 75, no. 3: 281–304

Eaton, Marcia. 1969. "Art, Artifacts, and Intentions." *American Philosophical Quarterly* 6: 165–9

– 1979. "Liars, Ranters, and Dramatic Speakers." In *Art and Philosophy: Readings in Aesthetics,* 2nd ed., edited by William Kennick, 356–71. New York: St Martin's Press

– 1982. "A Strange Kind of Sadness." *Journal of Aesthetics and Art Criticism* 41: 51–63

Everett, Anthony. 2005. "Against Fictional Realism." *The Journal of Philosophy* 102: 624–49

Everett, Anthony and Thomas Hofweber, eds. 2000. *Empty Names: Fiction and Puzzles of Non-Existence.* Stanford: CSLI Publications

Faulkner, William. 1929. *The Sound and the Fury.* London: Jonathan Cape and Harrison Smith

Feagin, Susan. 1997. "Imagining Emotions and Appreciating Fictions." In Hjort and Laver, *Emotion and the Arts,* 50–62

Frege, Gottlob. 1997. "On Sense and Reference." In *The Frege Reader,* edited by M. Beaney, 151–71. Oxford: Blackwell

Frey, James. 2004. *A Million Little Pieces.* New York: Random House

Gale, Richard. 1971. "The Fictive Use of Language." *Philosophy* 46: 324–40

Gettings, Michael. Manuscript. "An Ontology of Literary Works"

Gibson, William. 1984. *Neuromancer.* New York: Ace Books

Goldman, Alan. 1993. "Representation and Make-Believe." *Inquiry* 36: 335–50

Goodman, Nelson. 1968. *Languages of Art.* Indianapolis: Bobbs-Merrill

Gordon, Robert M. 1986. "Folk Psychology as Simulation." *Mind and Language* 1: 159–71

Gracia, Jorge. 1996. *Texts: Ontological Status, Identity, Author, Audience.* Albany: SUNY Press.

Grant, Robert. 2001. "Fiction, Meaning, and Utterance." *Inquiry* 44: 389–404

Grice, Paul. 1957. "Meaning." *Philosophical Review* 66: 377–88

– 1975. "Logic and Conversation." In *Syntax and Semantics,* vol. 3, *Speech Acts,* edited by P. Cole and J.L. Morgan, 41–58. New York: Academic Press

Guthrie, Jerry. 1981. "Self-Deception and Emotional Response to Fiction." *Journal of Aesthetics and Art Criticism* 21: 65–74

Hammett, Dashiell. 1992. *The Maltese Falcon.* New York: Vintage Books

Hardy, Thomas. 1886. *The Mayor of Casterbridge.* London: Smith, Elder, and Co.

Hernadi, P., ed. 1978. *What is Literature?* Indiana: Indiana University Press

Hjort, M. and S. Laver, eds. 1997. *Emotion and the Arts.* Oxford: Oxford University Press

Hoffman, Sarah. 2004. "Fiction as Action: Currie and Searle on Speech Act Theory and the Nature of Fiction." *Philosophia* 31: 513–29

Howell, Robert. 1979. "Fictional Objects: How They Are and How They Aren't." *Poetics* 8: 129–77

– 2002. "Ontology and the Nature of the Literary Work." *Journal of Aesthetics and Art Criticism* 60: 67–79

Kania, Andrew. 2005. "Against the Ubiquity of Fictional Narrators." *Journal of Aesthetics and Art Criticism* 63: 47–54

– 2007. "Against Them Too: A Reply to Alward." *Journal of Aesthetics and Art Criticism* 65, no. 4: 404–8

Kaplan, David. 1980. "Demonstratives." In *Themes from Kaplan*, edited by Joseph Almog, John Perry, and Howard Wettstein,481–565. Oxford: Oxford University Press

– 1986. "Opacity." In *The Philosophy of W.V. Quine*, edited by L.E. Hahn and P.A. Schlipp, 229–88. La Salle, IL: Open Court

– 1990. "Words." *Proceedings of the Aristotelian Society: Supplement* 64: 93–119

Kivy, Peter. 1993. "Platonism in Music: Another Kind of Defense". In *The Fine Art of Repetition: Essays in the Philosophy of Music*, 35–74. Cambridge: Cambridge University Press

Krasner, Daniel. 2002. "Semantics and Fiction." *Erkenntnis* 57: 259–75

Kripke, Saul. 1980. *Naming and Necessity*. Cambridge: Harvard University Press

– 1988. "A Puzzle about Belief." In Salmon and Soames, *Propositions and Attitudes*, 102–48

Lamarque, Peter. 1981. "How Can We Fear and Pity Fictions?" *British Journal of Aesthetics* 21: 291–305

Levinson, Jerrold. 1990a. "Defining Art Historically." In *Music, Art, and Metaphysics*, 3–25. Ithaca: Cornell University Press

– 1990b. "What a Musical Work Is." In *Music, Art, and Metaphysics*, 63–88

– 1990c. "Artworks and the Future." In *Music, Art, and Metaphysics*, 179–214

– 1993. "Making Believe." *Dialogue* 32: 359–74

– 1996a. "Film Music and Narrative Agency." In *Post-Theory: Reconstructing Film Studies*, edited by D. Bordwell and N. Carroll. Madison: University of Wisconsin Press, 248–82

– 1996b. "Intention in Interpretation and Literature." In *The Pleasures of Aesthetics: Philosophical Essays*, 175–213. Ithaca, NY: Cornell University Press

– 1997. "Emotion in Response to Art." In Hjort and Laver, *Emotion and the Arts*, 20–34

Lewis, David. 1968. "Counterpart Theory and Quantified Modal Logic." *Journal of Philosophy* 65: 113–26

– 1975. "Languages and Language." In *Mind and Knowledge,* edited by K. Gunderson, 3–35. Minneapolis: University of Minnesota Press

– 1978. "Truth in Fiction." *American Philosophical Quarterly* 15: 37–46

– 1983. "Truth in Fiction." In *Philosophical Papers,* vol. 1, 261–80. New York: Oxford University Press

Margolis, Joseph. 1983. "The Logic and Structure of Fictional Narrative." *Philosophy and Literature* 7: 162–81

Martinich, A.P. 2001. "A Theory of Fiction." *Philosophy and Literature* 25: 96–122

Matravers, Derek. 1995. "Beliefs and Fictional Narrators." *Analysis* 55: 121–2

– 1997. "The Paradox of Fiction." In Hjort and Laver, *Emotion and the Arts,* 78–92

McCormick, Peter. 1985. "Feelings and Fictions." *Journal of Aesthetics and Art Criticism* 43: 375–83

McMurtry, Larry. 1988. *Lonesome Dove.* New York: Pocket Books

Mill, John Stuart. 1874. *A System of Logic.* New York: Harper and Brothers

Miller, Seumas. 1992. "Truth and Reference in Fictional Discourse." *South African Journal of Philosophy* 11: 1–4

Mounce, H.O. 1980. "Art and Real Life." *Philosophy* 55: 183–92

Nehamas, Alexander. 1981. "The Postulated Author: Critical Monism as a Regulative Ideal." *Critical Inquiry* 8: 133–49

– 1987. "Writer, Text, Work, Author." In *Literature and the Question of Philosophy,* edited by A.J. Cascardi, 267–91. Baltimore: Johns Hopkins University Press

Neill, Alex. 1991. "Fear, Fiction, and Make-Believe." *Journal of Aesthetics and Art Criticism* 49: 47–56

Niniluoto, Ilkka. 1985. "Imagination and Fiction." *Journal of Semantics* 4: 209–22

Novitz, David. 1980. "Fiction, Imagination, and Emotion." *Journal of Aesthetics and Art Criticism* 38: 279–88

– 1991. "Critical Discussion: *Mimesis as Make-Believe.*" *Philosophy and Literature* 15: 118–28

O'Brian, Patrick. 1979. *The Fortune of War.* London: Collins

– 1983. *Treason's Harbour.* London: Collins

– 1997. *The Ionian Mission.* London: Collins

Ohmann, Richard. 1971. "Speech Acts and the Definition of Literature." *Philosophy and Rhetoric* 4: 1–19

Olivier, Laurence. 1948. *Hamlet.* Twin City Films

Parsons, Terence. 1980. *Non-Existent Objects.* New Haven: Yale University Press

Paskins, Barrie. 1977. "On Being Moved by Anna Karenina and *Anna Karenina.*" *Philosophy* 52: 344–7

Pavel, Thomas. 1981. "Ontological Issues in Poetics: Speech Acts and Fictional Worlds." *Journal of Aesthetics and Art Criticism* 40: 176–8

Pettersson, Anders. 1984. "The Ontology of Literary Works." *Theoria* 50: 36–51

Pratchett, Terry. 1997. *Hogfather*. United Kingdom: Corgi Books.

– 2008. *Making Money*. United Kingdom: Corgi Books

Radford, Colin. 1975. "How Can We be Moved by the Fate of Anna Karenina? (I)." *Aristotelian Society Supplementary Volume* 49: 67–80

– 1977. "Tears and Fiction: A Reply to Weston." *Philosophy* 52: 208–13

Ramsey, Frank. 1978. "Theories." In *Foundations*, edited by D.H. Mellor, 101–25. London: Routledge and Kegan Paul

Rosebury, B.J. 1979. "Fiction, Emotion, and 'Belief': A Reply to Eva Schaper." *British Journal of Aesthetics* 19: 31–44

Rowling, J.K. 2004. *Harry Potter and the Philosopher's Stone*. Vancouver: Raincoast Books

Salmon, Nathan. 1986. *Frege's Puzzle*. Cambridge: MIT Press

Salmon, N. and S. Soames, eds. 1988. *Propositions and Attitudes* Oxford: Oxford University Press

Saltz, David. 1991. "How to Do Things on Stage." *Journal of Aesthetics and Art Criticism* 49, no. 1: 31–45

Schaper, Eva. 1978. "Fiction and the Suspension of Disbelief." *British Journal of Aesthetics* 18: 31–44

Searle, John. 1958. "Proper Names." *Mind* 67: 166–73

– 1969. *Speech Acts: An Essay in the Philosophy of Language*. Cambridge: Cambridge University Press

– 1975. "The Logical Status of Fictional Discourse." *New Literary History* 6: 319–32

– 1983. *Intentionality*. Cambridge: Cambridge University Press

Skulsky, Harold. 1980. "On Being Moved by Fiction." *Journal of Aesthetics and Art Criticism* 39: 5–14

Snow, C.P. 1976. *The Masters*. London: Macmillan Publishing Company

Soames, Scott. 1988. "Direct Reference, Propositional Attitudes, and Semantic Content." In Salmon and Soames, *Propositions and Attitudes*, 197–239

Stecker, Robert. 1987. "Apparent, Implied, and Postulated Authors." *Philosophy and Literature* 11: 258–71

Taylor, Kenneth. 2000. "Emptiness without Compromise." In Everett and Hofweber, *Empty Names*, 17–36

Thackeray, William Makepeace. 1856. "Memoirs of Barry Lyndon, Esq., Written by Himself." In *Miscellanies*. London: Osgood & Co.

Thomasson, Amie. 1998. *Fiction and Metaphysics*. New York: Cambridge University Press

Tolkien, J.R.R. 1937. *The Hobbit*. London: George Allen & Unwin Ltd.

– 1956. *The Lord of the Rings*. New York: Ballantine

Travis, Charles. 2006. "Insensitive Semantics." *Mind and Language* 21: 39–49

Trollope, Anthony. 2002. *The Last Chronicle of Barset*. London: Penguin Classics

Van Ingwagen, Peter. 2001. "Creatures of Fiction." In *Ontology, Identity, and Modality*, 37–56. New York: Cambridge

Walton, Kendall. 1976. "Points of View in Narrative and Depictive Representation." *Nous* 10: 49–61

– 1978a. "Fearing Fictions." *Journal of Philosophy* 75: 5–26

– 1978b. "How Remote Are Fictional Worlds from the Real World?" *Journal of Aesthetics and Art Criticism* 37: 11–23

– 1979. "Style and the Products and Processes of Art." In *The Concept of Style*, edited by Berel Lang, 72–101. Ithaca, NY: Cornell University Press

– 1990. *Mimesis as Make-Believe*. Cambridge: Harvard University Press

– 1997. "Spelunking, Simulation and Slime." In Hjort and Laver, *Emotion and the Arts*, 37–49

Weston, Michael. 1975. "How Can We Be Moved by the Fate of Anna Karenina? (II)" *Aristotelian Society Supplementary Volume* 49: 81–93

Wilder, Hugh. 1988. "Intentions and the Very Idea of Fiction." *Philosophy and Literature* 12: 70–9

Wolsterstorff, Nicholas. 1980. *Works and Worlds of Art*. Oxford: The Clarendon Press

Woods, John and Peter Alward. 2004. "The Logic of Fiction." In *The Handbook of Philosophical Logic*, 2nd ed., edited by D. Gabbey and F. Guenther, 241–316. Netherlands: Kluwer

Index

act/attitude analysis, 7–9, 100–2,
118–20
author. *See* teller

Beardsley, Monroe, 31–3, 177n69,
178n75
belief, 36, 37–43, 130–1; existential,
37–42, 179n15, 179n32; predicational,
36, 37–42, 178n5, 179n15, 179n20,
179n32
Boulle, Pierre, 52
Brown, Robert, 20
Byrne, Alex, 95–7, 105–7, 186n36,
186n39

Camus, Albert, 182n14
Cappelen, Herman, 6, 174n19
cluster theory, 189n29
cognitive relations, 120, 125–39,
189n28; teams of, 127–39, 168,
189n29, 193n52
composition, 4, 15–33, 69–78, 141–2
content, 6, 115–39, 168, 174n19, 188n6,
189n19 ; illocutionary content, 6,
115, 174n19; semantic content, 6, 116,
174n19; and truth conditions, 6, 56,
110, 190n5

c-team. *See* cognitive relations
Currie, Gregory, 7, 20, 26–31, 50–1,
57–60, 76, 98–100, 104–6, 122–5,
144–5

Davidson, Donald, 190n32
Donnellan, Keith, 79

emotion. *See* fiction and emotion
engagement. *See* fictional engagement
Everett, Anthony, 10–11

fiction and emotion, 34–60, 179n20,
179n21, 179n32, 180n49
fictional author, 98–100, 104–6, 122,
187n53
fictional character, 6–7, 10–11, 23–6
fictional discourse, 5–7, 92, 140–69;
fictive discourse, 5, 141–2; metafictive
discourse, 5, 23–4, 116–20, 151–7;
trans-fictive discourse, 5–6, 66–168
fictional engagement, 9, 34–60, 76,
84–90, 178n7, 179n21
fictional immigrant, 7, 117
fictional name, 6–7, 23–6, 54–6, 115–39,
fictional narrator. *See* teller, fictional
fact-teller

fictional realism, 10–11; abstract existents, 10–11, 188n1, 188n7; concrete
   non-existents, 10, 24, 35, 135, 188n1
fictional truth, 54–6, 100–11
fictional work. *See* fictionality
fictionality, 28–9, 78–81; weak institutional theory of, 79–81
fictionality operator, 8–9, 41–2, 116–20,
   163–9
fiction-centred practice. *See* word-
   sculpture practice
fictive discourse. *See* fictional
   discourse
fictive illocution, 26–31, 74, 106–7,
   144–5, 177n55
Frege, Gottlob, 10, 44, 120, 179n33
Frey, James, 81

game of make-believe. *See*
   make-believe
game model. *See* storytelling
Gettings, Michael, 183n17
Gibson, William, 142
Goodman, Nelson, 68
Grice, Paul, 95–7, 157

Hoffman, Sarah, 27–8
Howell, Robert, 66, 167–9, 182n13
hypothetical author. *See* teller, non-
   actual non-fictional fiction-teller

illocutionary content. *See* content
illocutionary pretense, 6, 18–26, 74,
   148–51, 155–7
illocutionary representation, 31–3,
   177n69
imagination, 36–7, 48–54, 56–60, 76,
   84–90, 137–9, 185n14; *de dicto*, 36,
   49, 84–5, 185n8; *de re*, 36–7, 48–9,

76, 84–90, 178n11, 185n7, 185n9,
   185n10; *de se*, 36–7, 49, 52–4, 80,
   178n12, 180n46
inconsistent fiction, 104, 179n27,
   188n78
intensional context, 116, 151
intentional object, 24, 42–4

Kania, Andrew, 90–7
Kaplan, David, 65–7, 182n6
Kripke, Saul, 176n44

Lamarque, Peter, 45, 46
Lepore, Ernie, 6, 174n19
Lewis, David, 18, 19–20, 102–4, 121–2,
   123–4, 175n20
literary fiction, 3–4; and literature, 4
literature. *See* literary fiction

make-believe, 25, 37, 48–56, 78, 106–7,
   144–5, 155–7
Martinich, A.P., 24, 176n41
Matravers, Derek, 51–3, 180n54
McCormick, Peter, 45
metafictive discourse. *See* fictional
   discourse
Miller, Seumas, 24
mindless fiction, 99–100, 103, 107,
   109
mutual belief principle, 97–8

naive backwoodsman, 39, 52–4
narrative informant, 47, 76–8, 83–111,
   134–9, 159, 180n41, 185n9
narrator. *See* teller
naturally occurring story. *See* text
Novitz, David, 45, 46

Olivier, Laurence, 145, 191n17

paradox of fiction, 34–5, 50–1
Pavel, Thomas, 175n22
possible world, 41, 42, 102–4, 121–2
pragmatic implication, 94–8, 156–7, 188n10
pretense. *See* illocutionary pretense
prop, 25–6, 48–9, 78; reflexive, 48–9

quasi-emotion, 50, 52–4, 180n49

Radford, Colin, 38–9, 179n21
Ramsey, Frank, 122
reality principle, 97
representation. *See* illocutionary representation
revelation, 84–7, 108–11, 160–1, 188n83, 192n38
Rosebury, B.J., 43, 179n31

Saltz, David, 145–8, 149, 191n20, 191n29
Schaper, Eva, 39–43, 178n5, 179n15
Searle, John, 18–26, 26–7, 148–51, 175n17, 189n29, 191n26
semantic content. *See* content
simulation, 50–1
Skulsky, Harold, 46
Snow, C.P., 58
speech act, 6, 9, 15–17; illocutionary act, 16–17, 26–31, 68, 73–4, 142–8, 190n13; perlocutionary act, 17, 28; propositional act, 16; utterance act, 16
Steinmann, Martin, 20
storytelling, 15, 22–3, 25–6, 30, 142–51, 175n4; game model of, 145–8

storytelling narrator. *See* teller, fictional fiction-teller
suspension of disbelief, 39

teller, 9; actual fact-teller, 9, 92, 94; actual fiction-teller, 9, 92; fictional fact-teller, 9, 90–4, 98–100, 102–3, 104–5, 177n69; fictional fiction-teller, 9, 92, 110; non-actual non-fictional fact-teller, 9, 90–8; non-actual non-fictional fiction-teller, 9, 91–2, 185n22
text, 66, 173n2; naturally occurring story, 68–9, 81, 88–9, 184n43, 185n7
Thackeray, William Makepeace, 59
theatrical model, 4
Thomasson, Amie, 188n7
transfictive discourse. *See* fictional discourse
truth conditions. *See* content

unreliable narration, 60, 85–6, 99, 103, 186n33

Walton, Kendall, 20, 32–3, 49–50, 54–6, 78–9, 155–7, 162–3, 175n22, 180n43, 180n49, 181n61, 181n62, 181n65, 193n49
Weston, Michael, 45–6
Wilder, Hugh, 77–8
word, 64–6; common currency conception of, 65–6
word-sculpture, 63–82, 183n16
word-sculpture practice, 69–74; fiction-centred practice, 75–8, 80